MW00637406

Salt *and* Light

Studies in Chinese Christianity

Carol Lee Hamrin, Series Editor

SALT *and* LIGHT

LIVES OF FAITH THAT SHAPED MODERN CHINA

EDITED BY

Carol Lee Hamrin

with Stacey Bieler

☞PICKWICK *Publications* · Eugene, Oregon

SALT AND LIGHT
Lives of Faith that Shaped Modern China

Studies in Chinese Christianity

Copyright © 2009 Wipf and Stock Publishers. All rights reserved. Except for brief quotations in critical publications or reviews, no part of this book may be reproduced in any manner without prior written permission from the publisher. Write: Permissions, Wipf and Stock Publishers, 199 W. 8th Ave., Suite 3, Eugene, OR 97401.

Pickwick Publications
A Division of Wipf and Stock Publishers
199 W. 8th Ave., Suite 3
Eugene, OR 97401

www.wipfandstock.com

ISBN 13: 978-1-55635-984-2

Cataloging-in-Publication data:

Salt and Light.

Salt and light : lives that shaped modern China /.Edited by Carol Lee Hamrin with Stacey Bieler.

Studies in Chinese Christianity

xii + 240 p. ; 23 cm. Includes timeline and photographs.

ISBN 13: 978-1-55635-984-2

1. China—Church history. 2. China—Religion. 3. Christianity—China. 4. Young Men's Christian Association—China—History. I. Hamrin, Carol Lee. II. Bieler, Stacey. III. Title. IV. Series.

BR1288 S15 2009

Manufactured in the U.S.A.

LIST OF NAMES
Variations and Characters for Chapter Subjects

Pinyin (with variations)	Characters
1. Rong Hong (Yung Wing)	容闳
2. Tang Guo'an (Tong Kwoh On), Tang Jiechen (Tong Kai-son)	唐国安 唐介臣
3. Shi Meiyu (Mary Stone)	石美玉
4. Fan Zimei (T. M. Fan, Fan Yi)	范子美 (范祎)
5. Ding Shujing (Ting Shu Ching)	丁淑静
6. Mei Yiqi (Yi Chi Mei)	梅贻绮
7. Lin Qiaozhi (Lim Kah T'i)	林巧稚
8. Wei Zhuomin (Francis Wei)	韦卓民
9. Wu Yifang	吴贻芳
10. Yan Yangchu (Y. C. James Yen)	晏阳初

NOTE ON ROMANIZATION

Chinese names are given with surname first. Along with other Chinese words, names and place names are romanized according to the pinyin system used by the People's Republic of China, including its standard exceptions, such as Tsinghua and Peking universities and "Kuomintang" for the Nationalist Party. Other exceptions include the names of scholars who live in the West and have adopted Western-format names, as well as some names widely known to English readers, such as Sun Yat-sen, Chiang Kai-shek, and Yangtze River. We have maintained variations that occur in references.

CONTENTS

Rong was the first "returned student" from America and founder of the Chinese Educational Mission. He paved the way for the first hundred Chinese to receive a state-sponsored modern education, and as a diplomat helped to stop the international coolie trade.

Tang became the first president of Tsinghua University. With other early diplomats, Tang helped stop the opium trade and revive official U.S.–China educational exchanges after a lapse of three decades.

Shi was among the first Chinese women graduates from a U.S. medical school. On return to China, she founded a hospital and developed the nursing profession.

10 YAN YANGCHU

Reformer with a Heart for the Village 171

by Stacey Bieler

Yan, a Yale graduate who pioneered urban literacy training through the Mass Education Movement, also began a rural reconstruction model program and college.

ACKNOWLEDGMENTS

We are grateful for the excellent research and patient cooperation of our contributors, and for the administrative support provided by the Global China Center, a nonprofit center for research on Chinese culture and society based in Charlottesville, Virginia. We thank the Center's director, advisors, and associates, especially Dr. Li Yading and Dr. Peng Cui'an, for their advice and encouragement for this project. Our gratitude also goes to Bob Hamrin and Tom Bieler for their practical and moral support and editing assistance, and to Tom for technical support for the book illustrations.

June 2008

INTRODUCTION

by Carol Lee Hamrin and Stacey Bieler

Salt and Light reveals the stories of ten outstanding Chinese citizens, all of them Christians, who helped their country make progress from 1850 to 1950 despite economic depression, war, and revolution. These Chinese were pioneers in modern education, medicine, media, diplomacy, public leadership roles for women, civic organizations, and social work.

This is a good time to recover these lost stories, given the renewed development of China's civil society and widespread interest in both earlier waves of global transcultural interactions and the history of world Christianity. This volume goes beyond the history of missions and of church leaders to explore the role of lay Christians in shaping today's China.

These ten stories also highlight an important part of the history of social and cultural relations between China and America, which are often neglected by scholars. Most of these reformers studied in the United States and lived and worked with American colleagues in China's coastal cities. The thick fabric of personal and professional ties brought valuable resources for China's development and created a buffer that helped preserve the cross-cultural relationships despite periodic political and military crises.

Many of those profiled in this book are known in China for their public accomplishments. Yet few people know how their family backgrounds, personal traumas, and faith commitments shaped their characters. While most of them did not know each other personally, they were shaped by similar experiences, and some learned from each other's writings.

The ten men and women served others out of a sense of altruism and of vocation, a "calling" from God, stemming from their Christian convictions. These Chinese were not perfect saints but modeled essential virtues and inspired long-lasting admiration.

Living on the boundaries of East and West, traditional and modern China, these reformers creatively applied their Western knowledge and experience to solve problems facing their nation. They lived out the command of Jesus in his Sermon on the Mount to do good deeds as the salt of the earth and the light of the world. Like salt, they served as a moral preservative in a society under enormous stress from economic dislocation and corrupt power politics, typical of early industrial capitalism worldwide. And like light, they offered hope and truth to others in dark times of despair. Citizens in today's global society can find encouragement in the lives of these builders of civil society and cross-cultural ties in an earlier global era.

A Wave of Globalization

During the decades before 1900, new communication and transportation technologies interconnected the globe in new ways. China was forced by a series of military defeats to open its economy and society to these outside forces and was buffeted by growing international competition for resources that led to rapid territorial expansion by European and Japanese imperialist powers.

Some modernizers in the Qing court after 1850 worked together with coastal business leaders to gain control over some industrial development for the benefit of China. Extended families or clans with networks throughout Guangdong, Fujian, the greater Shanghai region, and Tianjin were already familiar with the outside world due to several generations of treaty port life, Western education, and overseas travel or emigration. They took the lead in helping China regain control over key resources and respect as part of the international community, adapting to modernity by "changing Chinese ways through barbarian ways."[1]

Ironically, the new internationalist concept, of being one country among many in the world, strengthened Chinese national identity. Then, as the Empire of China gave way to the Republic of China in 1911, men and women with a modern education and patriotic loyalty, many of them Christians, became a central element in shaping China's early modern society one hundred years ago.

The "Progressive" Era Touches China

Chinese in the coastal cities, including those profiled in this book, were influenced by international trends that began in Britain and later spread to America. Rural workers migrating to the new industrial centers, and the rapid growth of both the working class and middle class, resulted in social dislocation. The public's concern then spurred moral and social reform movements to address the problems. These efforts gradually formed a new social equilibrium through the renewal of social capital, a society's stock of shared values and habits that promote cooperation and trust. This return to order was illustrated by the decline in the crime rate in Britain beginning in the 1840s and in urban America in the 1870s.[2]

In Britain and America, "Victorianism" was a moral movement that deliberately sought to create new social rules and instill virtues in the urban migrant population. Change agents included public universal education, modern police forces, and religious institutions. The Methodists led the Second Great Awakening that sparked the Sunday School, YMCA, abolitionist, and temperance movements, which quickly transformed society. The rural and urban poor became disciplined workers and responsible citizens. Victorian virtues such as politeness, cleanliness, punctuality, and diligence were among the bourgeois values of middle-class conformity that served the cause of capitalist development and also brought individual well-being and social progress.[3]

Religious leaders and missionary statesmen in England launched the first international social movement, the abolitionist campaign against slavery and the slave trade. After the American Civil War, their experience was transferred to other international movements such as the campaigns against the coolie trade and the opium trade. The Student Volunteer Movement led to the rapid growth of the YMCA and other nondenominational, non-church-based religious organizations.

British reform movements spread quickly to America and grew into a broad international trend centered on the concept that social progress could be made through the exercise of human will, creativity, and technology.[4] The ideal of "progress" and the importance of social activism reflected two strands of thought, one secular and one religious. The concept of life and death competition among nation-states according to the "law" of the survival of the fittest, which marked Social Darwinism, offered a rather stark vision of human perfectibility. It spread fear that China's backwardness might lead to national extinction under colonial rule. The Puritan concept of God as Providence working out his plans for history offered hope that an enlightened, righteous, and hardworking public could serve others and save the nation.

Christian revivals and the resulting social reforms and social services brought a wave of optimism in Britain and America.[5] The Methodist movement inspired believers to pursue holy living, not merely in private piety but also in humanitarian acts of charity and public service. Progressive ideas and social projects contributed to Western confidence. A new boldness in promoting international progress, combined with the new industrial wealth of this global era, boosted the missionary movement.[6] Most missionaries shared a sense of the universality of the church and were optimistic about its potential global impact.[7]

In China, missionaries began to present the case that Christianity could make the country strong and prosperous, gradually adopting the assumptions and language of progress.[8] Foreign Protestants working in China grew from a few dozen in 1840 to thirteen hundred by 1890 and thirty-five hundred in 1905.[9]

Chinese who studied in the United States were influenced by the American experience. When rapid urbanization and industrialization between 1890 and 1929 caused economic dislocation and social tension, a progressive movement responded by giving special attention to the rural and urban poor who suffered the most under unregulated capitalism. Urban missions began to provide services to migrants and immigrants in the big cities. For example, one study found that nearly all emergency food and housing services in San Francisco were being provided before 1925 by Christian agencies such as the Salvation Army.[10]

These models for moral renovation were carried back to China when students returned, and meanwhile, Chinese back home read mission publications and joined missionaries in social services. American-style voluntary associations responded to dislocations in the new industrial economy in Shanghai and other coastal cities in China as well as periodic floods and droughts that devastated areas of the countryside. Hundreds of voluntary associations of all kinds, including religious, professional, and charitable types, could be found in the larger cities. Christian colleges in China and the congregational form of Chinese Protestant churches became places to participate in associational life.

Many urban Chinese came to share an optimistic modernizing agenda, centered on the vision of making China a strong, modern nation-state through renewal of the Chinese people by means of education, citizenship training, and social reform. Many felt that the old traditional Confucian values could not meet the needs of a modernizing China. In the face of rampant corruption, immorality, and huge inequities of wealth, some Chinese were receptive to Christianity as a comprehensive social and moral philosophy that could help renew public morality and build a new and equitable social order.

This optimistic bubble burst due to the chaos under warlord rule in China and the tragedies of the First World War, which greatly undermined confidence in global progress toward a peaceful world civilization. Chinese felt betrayed by Western acquiescence in Japan's ambitions in China. During the May Fourth era after 1919, educated Chinese were more critical in weighing the value of Western ideas, favoring Enlightenment ideals of science and democracy. A nationalistic anti-Christian movement surfaced after 1922, spiking in 1926–27 with the mass exodus of missionaries.

Partly in an effort to distance Christianity from the worst of imperialistic capitalism, the "social gospel" grew strong in YMCA circles in China. The 'Y' leadership began to emphasize the social nature of Christianity and de-emphasize spiritual life. The National Christian Council and the Chinese YMCA, both headquartered in Shanghai, partnered together to sponsor committees and conferences in 1927 and 1931 to research and debate how to use moral principles to help tame capitalism.[11]

Support for a liberal democratic path for China finally collapsed, however, in the crises of political-military competition between Nationalists and Communists and Japanese encroachment after 1931, followed by invasion in 1937 as part of a new world war. The moderate long-term reform agenda of "national renewal" gave way to the urgent, immediate need for political and military mobilization for the sake of "national salvation." Many Chinese Christian leaders who had been internationalists and pacifists joined the nationalist cause.

Most reform efforts dissipated under Japanese occupation of the coast and Chinese evacuation to the interior. The resources of Protestant organizations were absorbed in sustaining themselves as refugees and organizing relief efforts for the dispossessed. After 1941, through the civil war of 1945–49, and on into the 1950s, Chinese Christians were on their own more and more, as missions were closed and transfers of funds ceased.[12]

Lasting Social Impact in China

The seeds of public responsibility and personal character planted in the late nineteenth and early twentieth centuries by China's early professionals, such as those covered in this volume, had major influence in a number of important fields. Their work continues to bear fruit today.

After the spectacular failure of the 1898 Reform, with its ambitious aims to bring about a host of institutional reforms overnight in arenas ranging from education to constitutional politics, educated Chinese began to work on long-term moral and cultural reforms that were needed to support eventual institutional change. Protestants pioneered new forms of social and political activism as they sought gradual and peaceful progress through social work with the poor, social justice legislation, and democratic reform in domestic and international politics, all to mitigate the negative impact of industrialization.

A Foundation of Moral and Scientific Education

Families from one tiny county in Guangdong had the foresight to invest in a modern scientific education for some of their children. Rong

Hong, the first Chinese to graduate from an American institution of higher education, also became a Christian in America. His new faith inspired a vision for a government-sponsored Chinese Educational Mission (CEM) to the United States as a means of gaining both Western expertise and Christian moral culture. Rong assisted a few high court officials in gaining military equipment and diplomatic victories, and then gained their backing in 1871 to implement his dream. But he was ahead of his time; the Mission was aborted after ten years due to the rise of the conservatives in the Chinese government and heightened tension between Americans and Chinese. The 120 students were brought back to China in 1881.

At first, the cosmopolitan English-speaking youth who studied abroad with the CEM struggled to find a place back home in traditional Qing society. Many were distributed among government technical colleges or were hired in low-level official positions in managing state industrial ventures. Some worked for foreign endeavors in the treaty ports. However, after 1895, following China's defeat by a modernized Japanese navy, some leaders called for radical reforms. Former CEM students quickly ascended the official ladder of promotion.

Western education was to replace discredited Confucian social norms. Students who attended mission schools in China and leading liberal arts colleges in America were introduced to Christian moral education and social life. As a result, Chinese Protestant converts played a role in reforming modern urban China well beyond their small percentage of the populace.

The late Qing educational reforms included the abolition of the Confucian basis for the imperial examination system in 1905. In this more supportive environment, Tang Guo'an helped revive Rong Hong's dream and served as the founding president for Tsinghua as a preparatory school for students going to the United States. Tang also supported Christian activities on campus. That tradition of combining a modern scientific education and Christian extracurricular activities produced a number of Tsinghua University graduates who became leaders and educators of China's major schools. Mei Yiqi, a Tsinghua alumni who became its president, preserved China's three key universities during the Japanese occupation.

Modern Professions

In the receptive environment after 1900, educated Protestants were pioneers in urban professions. New channels of social mobility elevated a number of returned CEM students as China's first mining engineers, military professionals, and diplomats. With Rong Hong as a forerunner, Tang Guo'an joined the official diplomatic service to further the goal of Chinese-American educational exchange. In this capacity, he also followed Rong's precedent in turning the tide against a major social evil: Rong, the trade in coolie labor, and Tang, the opium trade.

Shi Meiyu and Lin Qiaozhi applied a strong sense of Christian vocation to medicine. Shi established the first nursing school in China out of a desire to serve rural residents, who had little knowledge of hygiene or access to medical care. Later, her nursing students served the urban poor in Shanghai. Her integrated medical and evangelistic work at the Bethel Mission of Shanghai continues its work today in Hong Kong. Lin's Christian community at the Peking Union Medical College emphasized strong professional ethics. Lin did not sequester herself in the elite hospital environment; she often served women in the poor city neighborhoods nearby and later in the countryside. She still is regarded as a model alumna, and her values still serve as basic principles for doctors, nurses, and students in China's premier medical school and hospital, now part of Tsinghua University.

Public Media and Civic Organizations

In the first decades of the twentieth century, a growing Chinese middle class developed, mainly along the urbanized east coast and major Yangtze River ports. The YMCA based in Shanghai proved to be a central influence that touched most of the people described in this volume in one way or another, fostering commitment to moral and social reform as key to China's survival and renewal in the world of nations.

YMCA editor Fan Zimei was mentored by American missionary and publisher Young J. Allen. They sought to change Chinese social relationships with a fusion of religion, morality, and science. They began with the education of women and children, hoping thus to transform families and ultimately shape the nation.[13] Fan popularized these conceptions as longtime editor of the YMCA journals. The life stories of Fan at the YMCA and Ding Shujing at the YWCA illustrate their focus on character building and development of citizenship, with its natural outgrowth in work among the rural and urban laboring classes.

Fan Zimei strongly believed that the people of any nation had an obligation to assist their rulers in governance by forming community associations and, like others in this volume, worked to build up the autonomy and effectiveness of the Chinese church as a contributing social organization. Tang Guo'an provided leadership in business, academic, religious, and social organizations in Shanghai. He and a close associate started China's first Chinese-run English-language publication in order to give a voice to Chinese opinion in the foreign sector of the city, and they were nearly forced to leave town due to their advocacy of change in the treaty port system.

Women in Public Leadership

The stories of Chinese women who were among the first to gain a modern education show the impact of Christian values on both family and society, not least upon the men who dominated China's patriarchal society. Traditionally, women were constrained to live their whole lives within the extended household, first as daughters and then as wives and mothers. Childbearing and the challenges to health that came with it was the extent of their lives. Education was minimal and traditional in content (music, poetry, etc.), and women's status and influence was weakened by the widespread practices of foot binding, concubinage, and prostitution.

Shi Meiyu and Lin Qiaozhi became pioneers of medicine in China because they had enlightened Christian fathers who were inspired by the examples of women missionaries to prohibit foot binding for their daughters and to support them through years of education. Lin's brother took over the task of supporting her when her father died, and Wu Yifang's uncle fulfilled this function of encouragement and support.

Ding Shujing was a pioneer of public leadership roles for women both in her personal life and in her shaping of the YWCA's principles and activities. Wu Yifang, who lost her whole family in a series of tragedies, found a new extended family on the campus of Jinling College, the first of the Christian colleges that pioneered higher education for women. As part of the first tiny ripple of educated women in China, Wu, Ding, and Shi all felt a special obligation to educate young Chinese women.

Social Work

The Progressive ethos focused on helping those on the margins of society, the poorest of the urban and rural poor, who suffered most from natural disasters and who paid the biggest price for rapid economic change. Most of the Chinese in this volume were active in social service associations. Yan Yangchu was among the first to see the urgency of addressing China's rural problems. He developed a model for combining literacy training, public health, and rural development, which was later copied by other private and government agencies. YWCA and YMCA leaders developed similar holistic approaches to problems of the urban working class.

Building International Bridges

By the early twentieth century, Western foreign policy was beginning to shift from aggressive "high imperialism" toward more reciprocal concepts of internationalism. Some of this came from pressures brought to bear on the British Parliament and the U.S. Congress by more enlightened public opinion, often reflecting missionary influence. Tang Guo'an and other young, Western-educated diplomats had a hand in shaping this change as they worked on U.S.–China cooperation against the opium trade and use of Boxer Indemnity funds for education.

In later decades, Wei Zhuomin and other Chinese Christian leaders helped to spread and develop the theories and practice of mutuality in world church relations. Both Wei and Wu Yifang became active in China's National Christian Council (NCC) and represented the organization at international conventions. Wei's theories contributed to the World Council of Churches' commitment to spreading the understanding of Christianity as nonracial, nonpolitical and nonterritorial in nature. Wu's experience as an unofficial diplomat led to her appointment to the Chinese delegation that signed the UN charter.

The Chinese portrayed in this volume protested the wrongs of imperialism. But at the same time, their cosmopolitan experiences helped them avoid a narrow nationalism that blamed foreigners for all of China's troubles. Their friends, partners, and institutions were two-way conduits of mutual exchange. Organization executives like Shi Meiyu and Yan Yangchu sought to maintain autonomy from foreign religious institutions and the Chinese government alike. Ding Shujing aimed to create in the YWCA a model of world community, bridging nation and class, which would counter the narrow nationalism rampant in Europe and China. Wei Zhuomin also hoped his university would become a model for how people from different cultures and languages could live and work together in harmony.

Salt and Light: Lives of Virtue and Faith

The ten people highlighted in this book helped to shape a new China in a new world community as they lived through challenging times. After the collapse of the traditional order, they joined in the exploration for new ways to create a modern order. They promoted the virtues necessary to bring moral and social renewal to early modern China.

As some of the earliest Chinese to live and study in the West, they were positioned to see both its best and worst aspects while also gaining a more objective perspective on their own culture. Their common conviction was that China must adopt the best of Western science and the Christian religion, not just industrial and military technology, in order to survive and to compete in the international system of nation-states dominated by the Western powers.

The Christian worldview that all humanity is created equal in the eyes of God played an important role in motivating their efforts, whether in diplomacy or in social work with the poor. They found ways to be both truly Christian and truly Chinese. They saw a close match between the Confucian conviction that "rectifying the heart was the basis of a country's greatness" and their Christian convictions. The values common to the liberal arts colleges and youth associations with which these

Chinese were closely allied began with a clean heart and wholesome ("holy") living. Inner integrity, humility, and a high regard for others led to good relationships.

Their faith, a transcendent anchor for their souls, gave them courage to respond to challenges with vigor, hope, and persistence during decade after decade of turmoil and occasional terror. Their faith gave them the insight and courage to make a difference in their chosen professions.

Much of the "salt and light" agenda of the early reformers highlighted in this book—spiritual revival, moral reformation, civic institutional development, charity, and philanthropy—is relevant today. China is immersed in the global transformation based on communications technology and intellectual innovation. The national agenda includes building up the human capital needed to compete in the global economy. The public is worried about corruption and social disorder. Internalized, informal norms become even more important in the shift from an industrial to a postindustrial economy and complex society. Virtues that build and sustain economic assets and renew the social order can be produced by a number of public and private sources working together: public civic education, religious activities of all kinds, professional education and standards, managerial training, and nonprofit associations and standards.[14]

The biographical portraits in this book focus on people who shaped history with their character and their deeds, not just their words. These were practitioners rather than theorists of change. Citizens in today's global society can find encouragement in the lives of these builders of civil society and cross-cultural ties in an earlier global era.

1

RONG HONG

Visionary for a New China

by Stacey Bieler

Rong Hong struggled with many social challenges at Yale College from 1850–1854, as he was the first and only Chinese student and he had a naturally reserved personality. However, people began to take notice when he won the first prize in English composition twice in a row during his sophomore year. Despite the acclaim, he was still distraught over his lack of ability in calculus.[1]

During his junior year, he wrote to American missionary Samuel Wells Williams to share his thoughts about his future profession. "There are so many things, and every one of them is so valuable to a man who intends to benefit his country, that it is extremely trying to know which to choose. I shall not rely upon my own judgment [and] not consult my own inclinations in regard to the choice. I hope God will direct me; with his aid I hope to decide satisfactorily."[2]

In his search, Rong never forgot China's desperate state. Though he did not have many close friends he enjoyed long walks and talks with his classmate, Carroll Cutler, who later became president of Western Reserve College in Cleveland, Ohio. Rong opened up to him and discussed a project that was forming in his mind.

> All through my college course, especially in the closing year, the lamentable condition of China was before my mind constantly and weighed on my spirits. . . . I was determined that the rising generation of China should enjoy the same educational advantages that I had enjoyed; that through western education China might be regenerated, become enlightened and powerful. To accomplish that object became the guiding star of my ambition.[3]

In his class book, his Yale classmates encouraged his vision, expecting him to use the "Power of Knowledge in his hands" to become the "leader of moral reform in China," by emancipating his land from "tyrants' sway and from superstitious chains."[4] Unlike most Chinese, who believed in Chinese cultural superiority, Rong had come to believe that Western literature, science, and religion were necessary to strengthen China.[5] Many people came to the commencement in 1854 at Yale just to see a Chinese student graduate.

After seven years in the United States, during which he became a naturalized American citizen (in 1852), there was little in China to draw Rong back. Though the thought of going back was like exile from the place where his tastes and intellectual and moral affinities now lay, a verse from scripture haunted him and followed him like the voice of God. "If any provide not for his own, and specially for those of his own house, he hath denied the faith, and is worse than an infidel" (1 Tim 5:8). The words "his own" and "his own house" meant to Rong the nation of China. Soon after his graduation he sailed for Hong Kong, a voyage of 151 days. He could barely understand the Chinese pilot who came on board and could not speak any Chinese to him.[6]

Early Opportunities

Rong Hong (also called Yung Wing or Jung Hung) was born November 17, 1828, in a village now part of Zhuhai, only four miles from the Portuguese trading colony of Macao in southern China. Through a neighbor, his father heard of a girls' school in Macao run by Mrs. Gutzlaff, an English missionary who married her husband Charles in 1834. While most Chinese parents were suspicious of Christian missionary schools, Rong's parents saw Western schooling as the way to prepare their second son for a career in diplomacy or commerce. At the age of seven, his father took him to the school in Macao, where he was one of the first boys to join. When Mrs. Gutzlaff took three blind girls to the United States, the school closed and Rong returned home. In 1840 his father died, leaving his mother to care for four children. Rong's English skills got him a job helping a Roman Catholic priest fold papers.

After four months a message came from Dr. Benjamin Hobson, a medical missionary Rong had met at the school. Hobson had been looking for him because Mrs. Gutzlaff had asked the doctor to find and enroll Rong in the new Morrison Education Society School for boys, established in honor of Dr. Robert Morrison, the first Protestant missionary to China from 1807 to1834.[7] In 1841 Rong joined five boys who were older and had a one-year head start, and then he moved with them to Hong Kong the next year, where the school sat on a hill overlooking the harbor.[8]

In 1847 Rong and two other boys were offered an opportunity to study in the United States when the school principal, Rev. Samuel Brown (Yale, 1832), returned home due to ill health. He and the other two boys stayed in the home of Mr. Brown's mother. He attended Monson Academy in Monson, Massachusetts, for two years. During that time he converted to Christianity and became a member of the Monson Congregational Church.[9] Though he was initially supposed to come to the United States for only two years, he decided to stay and go to Yale. The trustees of Monson Academy promised to support him through college if he would promise to go back to China as a missionary. Rong declined because he wanted freedom to do the "greatest good for China," for he believed that "there can be hardly any limit put upon one's ambition to do good, if one is possessed of the Christ-spirit." Around the same time Brown, visiting his sister in Savannah, Georgia, mentioned Rong's plight. Members of the local Ladies' Association agreed to help Rong through college without conditions. He supplemented their aid by working as a librarian for the Brothers in Unity debating society.[10]

After spending eight years in the United States, Rong returned to China in 1855. During a visit with his elderly mother, he tried to explain to her why she should be honored to be the mother of the first Chinese graduate from an American college. Rong was not prepared to take the Confucian examinations required to enter the ranks of officialdom since he had not spoken or read Chinese for several years. He studied the language for six months before working as a businessman and translator.[11] Rong knew that in order to present his vision for educating Chinese in America before the throne, he had to develop connections with high officials willing to use Western education as a way to strengthen China.

In the 1860s, Chinese rulers discussed alternative approaches for strengthening China through introducing Western technology. They could establish modern schools by inviting foreign experts to teach Western languages and technology. They could send delegations on short-term trips to glean information about the West and bring back Western armaments so that the Chinese could learn how to make them. Or students could be sent abroad, who would then return and teach other Chinese the West's secrets of wealth and power.[12]

Many conservative officials opposed the latter educational plan because of the time and money required, and the fear that the Chinese would "lose face" for admitting their need to learn from other countries. Most scholars were also against sending students abroad because the whole concept emphasized technology, rather than the traditional value of right behavior, as the means to ensure national protection and prosperity. But Viceroy Zeng Guofan, the most influential official at that time, and Li Hongzhang, his protégé, advocated sending students abroad as part of the Self-Strengthening Movement. Li argued that overseas study was the quickest, most effective way to acquire Western secrets.[13]

In the midst of the suppression of the Taiping Rebellion by Viceroy Zeng in 1863, Rong became a member of his personal group of talented men after he had made friends with a Chinese astronomer who was an officer in Zeng's group. After some time, Zeng met with Rong at his camp along the Yangtze River. When Rong was ushered into Zeng's presence, he was given a long, intense, piercing gaze such as Rong had never felt before.[14] Apparently satisfied, Zeng sent Rong back to the United States to order machinery to equip an arsenal in Shanghai.

Upon completion of that mission in 1865, Zeng sent a memorial (official document) to the court, asking that Rong be given an official rank in the bureaucratic hierarchy. When Rong received the fifth civil rank (out of nine), his reputation was raised in the eyes of Chinese officials who had previously regarded him more as a foreigner than as a Chinese.[15]

Rong's next opportunity for visibility came in 1870 when Zeng called on him to serve as an interpreter during negotiations with France after rumors stirred peasants to kill ten nuns and two priests who were taking in orphans in Tianjin. The four commissioners who worked with Rong during the settlement learned of his educational plan and submitted to the court a memorial he had drafted.[16]

Zeng and Li successfully used Rong's proposal to implement the overseas study plan that had been thwarted by conservatives in the court for seven years. The Chinese officials chose to send students to the United States for several reasons. First, they believed that a U.S. education was more practical than a European one. Second, Rong had firsthand knowledge of the American educational system that could help smooth the way for the young boys. Finally, China and the United States had signed a treaty in 1868 that allowed mutual rights of attendance at any public schools, including U.S. military academies.[17]

In 1871 the throne finally approved the Chinese Educational Mission (CEM) to the United States. The court's plan was to send thirty boys each year to the United States for four years (1872–75). They would graduate from American high schools and colleges and return to China in 1887 to serve during the prime of their lives. When Rong heard that the program would be established, he could neither eat nor sleep for two days. "He walked on air and worshipped God. It was sixteen years after his return to China that God had granted his prayer."[18]

Leader of the Chinese Education Mission

Though the court had high hopes for the plan, few candidates from the Shanghai area presented themselves. Parents were reluctant to let their young sons, between the ages of ten and fifteen, go to a strange country for fifteen years. So Rong went instead to the region around his home in southern China to recruit students from families who had more overseas contacts and experience. Even then, he convinced the parents only by promising them that their sons would receive official ranks and jobs within the Chinese government upon return.

The court established a preparatory school in Shanghai, which still emphasized Chinese classics rather than English or science. In the summer of 1872 the first thirty students, 90 percent of them from the southern province of Guangdong, sailed for the United States. Viceroy Zeng, the architect and proponent of the overseas study plan, died before the first group of students departed, but his successor, Viceroy Li, who had now become the most powerful official, continued to champion the project.[19]

Rong went ahead of the other co-commissioner, the Chinese teachers, and the students in order to establish the Mission in the United States. After consulting with Noah Porter, president of Yale, Rong worked with the Connecticut Board of Education to request American families to open their homes to two or three students. Up and down the Connecticut Valley, doctors, teachers, and ministers in each town promptly and overwhelmingly responded with room enough for 244 students. Prince Kung, Regent of the Chinese Empire, wrote a note of appreciation that "such acts of kindness tend to strengthen and make lasting the sympathy and friendship now so happily existing between your country and mine."[20] Both countries embarked on the educational adventure with high hopes.

Rong set up the Mission's headquarters in Springfield, Massachusetts, where the students would live during the summers in order to study Chinese and assemble at periodic intervals to fulfill their Confucian duties of hearing the "Sacred Book of Imperial Edicts" and of honoring the Emperor by bowing toward the direction of his palace in Beijing. After renting a building for two years, Rong was authorized to erect one in Hartford, Connecticut. His purpose for advocating a permanent headquarters was to root the Mission in the United States as deeply as possible, so as not to give the Chinese government any chance of rescinding it. The boys later nicknamed the building the "Hell House" because it was there they studied Chinese during the holidays and received reprimands for inappropriate behavior.[21]

After taking a train from San Francisco to Hartford, the first thirty students were greeted by their American families. The welcoming hugs and kisses at the train station were an embarrassment to at least one, who had not been kissed since he was an infant. They had much to adapt to in their new surroundings with their Connecticut families. The Puritan Yankees were proud of their historical sites, including the oldest preserved school building in the nation (1778) and the third oldest university, Yale (1701). Connecticut was also experiencing a manufac-

turing boom in hats, typewriters, electrical supplies, textiles, and ammunition, with the gross product more than doubling between 1870
and 1900.

Chinese students who were advanced in English were sent to
school, while the others were given private language lessons at home.
Language acquisition was accelerated in at least one home by not allowing the students to eat if they could not remember the name of the food.
The widow of Professor David Bartlett, Fannie, and her three daughters
hosted four of the boys. (In 1910 two of the daughters spent a year in
China, hosted by one of the former students, Liang Dunyan, who had
become an official.)[22]

Diplomatic Ventures

Rong returned to China in 1873 in order to introduce the Gatling gun
to his patrons, being "anxious that China should have the latest modern
guns as well as the latest modern educated men."[23] While Rong was in
Tianjin, Viceroy Li asked him to attend a meeting with the Peruvian
commissioner, who was hoping to make a treaty with China in order
to import contract "coolie" labor from China. After the commissioner
gave a rosy picture of coolie life in Peru, Rong told how he had seen
kidnapped people tied to each other by their queues in Macao and had
read how they were forced to sign labor contracts for work in Cuba or
Peru that essentially made them slaves for life. He told how the crossing of the Pacific was so horrible that either the coolies would commit
suicide by jumping into the ocean or join in mutiny and then drift helplessly in the ocean. Rong told the Peruvian commissioner not to expect
his help in this "diabolical business" and bade him good morning.

After Viceroy Li heard about the conversation, he sent Rong back
to Hartford to prepare to go to Peru while Chen Lanpin, his fellow educational commissioner, was sent to see firsthand the conditions in Cuba.
Rev. Joseph Twichell, pastor of Asylum Hill (Congregational) Church
in Hartford, and Dr. E. W. Kellogg accompanied Rong to Peru for the
three-month investigation. Rong's report included two dozen photographs taken clandestinely that told "a tale of cruelty and inhumanity
perpetrated by the owners of haciendas, which would be beyond cavil

and dispute."[24] When the Peruvian commissioner came for another meeting in Tianjin to discuss the treaty, the photographs were used as final evidence, and China no longer allowed coolies to go to Peru or Cuba.[25] Chen and Rong were then appointed jointly as the first Chinese ministers to the United States, Spain, and Peru in December 1875. Rong wanted to focus on the CEM, so he requested to stay in Hartford. Rong thus became associate minister, with Chen as chief minister in Washington, D.C.

After Rong returned to Connecticut, he married Mary L. Kellogg, the daughter of a prominent local doctor in a Hartford suburb and the sister of E. W. Kellogg. Rev. Twichell performed the ceremony and later reflected in his diary,

> The engagement was entered into about a year ago. Miss K. was teacher (at her home) of two of the pupils of the Mission. The match was a good deal commented on. Some people feel doubtfully about it; some disapprove of it utterly; some (like me) gloried in it. I have felt from the outset that in case it should not injure Wing [Rong Hong] in China or hamper him in his life work in any way, it was to be altogether rejoiced in. My wife and I often used (before this union was contemplated) to suggest the thought of marriage to Wing as we sat at our fireside, and to his reply that there was no Chinese whom he would marry and no American lady who would marry him, we have many a time replied that as for the latter point he had no proof of it, and that we didn't believe he judged rightly upon it.[26]

The couple named their first son Morrison, after missionary Robert Morrison, and their second son Bartlett, after David and Fannie Bartlett and family who had been supportive of the CEM.[27]

Cultural Tensions

Though the CEM students quickly changed from long Chinese gowns to American trousers and coats, their American schoolmates could not resist teasing them about their queues, long single braids down their backs, which the Manchu rulers made the Chinese wear as a symbol of their subservience. Some wore their "pigtails" inside their clothes, while others circled and pinned them to the top of their heads. The boys excelled at baseball, figure skating, and football. They also enjoyed the pleasure of American girls' company, much to the consternation of the American boys. Though the families took the students to church, they did not pressure them to believe in Christianity, because they knew that the court would not approve. Still, many attended church and Sunday school, and some became Christians. The boys' genius for adaptation led Louise Bartlett, an "American sister," to describe them as "favorites with their schoolmates and delight[s to] their teachers."[28]

When Rong's nephew, Rong Kui (Yung Kwai), became a Christian and cut off his queue, he was ordered back to China. The CEM students, staff, and host families all feared there would be drastic, even fatal, consequences. Since he had passed the entrance examination to enter Harvard, Rong Hong secretly gave Rev. Twichell money to help Rong Kui stay in the United States and finish his education. In 1884 Rong Kui was appointed secretary in the Chinese Legation in Washington, where he served for fifty years.[29]

Those students who graduated from high school began attending Yale, Harvard, Amherst, Brown, MIT, and Rensselaer Polytechnic Institute. Most were just beginning to enter colleges and technical schools when their high hopes were shattered in 1881.[30]

Rong's successive co-commissioners had sent negative reports to the court about the students' adaptive behavior. After Qin Lanpin, an older scholar known for his devotion to Chinese learning, returned to China, Wu Zideng, who was even more conservative, replaced him in 1878. Rong described Wu as measuring things and his pupils only by Chinese standards. "He must have felt that his own immaculate Chinese training had been contaminated by coming in contact with Occidental schooling which he looked upon with evident repugnance."[31] When Wu called the students to Washington to receive Confucian instruction, he scolded them for not kneeling down to him and accused them of forgetting their ancestors and showing no respect to their elders.

Wu was especially upset that some of the students had become Christians and had organized "The Chinese Christian Home Mission" in order to bring Christ to their native land. In the winter of 1877–78 five students told the pastor and professor Rev. A. R. Merriam they desired to publicly profess their faith in Christ. Rong advised against the proposed action but encouraged the students to meet and study the Bible. After the boys started meeting on Sundays the group grew in number. That fall they organized the society and wrote a constitution. When Commissioner Wu found out, he sent word quickly to China.[32]

In secret letters, Wu denounced the students for becoming denationalized and recommended that the court recall them without delay and strictly watch them after their return. Wu regarded the Mission's liberal education as "subversive of the principles and theories of Chinese culture."[33] Viceroy Li Hongzhang wrote to Rong to tell him of Wu's reports, warning him to stop overemphasizing Western studies. Rong tried to refute the reports, but the damage had been done.[34]

The high cost of running the Mission, $1,200 per student per year, had always been a source of conflict. China was struggling financially after suppressing the Taiping Rebellion (1850–65) and fighting wars with Western countries.

Mistreatment of Chinese laborers in the western part of the United States further dampened the Chinese court's interest in continuing the Mission. Exaggerated stories of "barbaric" Chinese customs circulated there, further intensifying racial bigotry. As China's associate minister, Rong visited Washington and wrote letters of complaint to the U.S. government about the maltreatment of Chinese and about the pending law restricting Chinese immigration. He was confounded as to why U.S. Congressmen, "eminent public men," would debate on the Senate floor using the same offensive language as common people in the western United States. (The debate in Congress ultimately led to the adoption of the Chinese Exclusion Act of 1882.)[35] Though the Burlingame Treaty provided for the reciprocal right of American and Chinese students to enter the government schools of either nation, Viceroy Li was disappointed when he was informed that it would require a special act of Congress for foreigners to enter West Point or Annapolis (quite unlikely at that stage).[36]

Despite these tensions, the Mission continued for two more years, partly due to the informal diplomacy performed by former President Ulysses S. Grant toward the end of his round-the-world tour in 1879, when he met with Viceroy Li, the most powerful official in China. Though the two toasted each other as "soldier and statesman," neither had the power to sustain the dream.[37]

Closure of the Chinese Education Mission

The conservatives in the court, who had always criticized the CEM, grew in power and hoped to disgrace Li by closing the Mission. When Li withdrew support from the Mission in the face of growing opposition, it was doomed.[38]

When the court recalled the Mission in 1881, Yale President Porter drew up a petition, telling how the students were progressing in their studies and about their success as unofficial ambassadors for China and expressing disappointment that China had changed its mind. It was signed by a group of prominent men, including Laurenus Seelye, president of Smith College, Rev. Joseph Twichell, pastor of the church in Hartford that many of the students attended, and author Samuel Clemens (Mark Twain), a friend of Twichell's. Twichell wrote to the U.S. Minister in Beijing, James Angell, asking him to put the petition into Viceroy Li's hand and request that Li not abandon the Mission. Former President Grant also wrote his own letter to Viceroy Li, arguing that recalling the Mission would be a mistake.[39]

1-1 Rev. Joseph Twichell and Rong Hong in Connecticut, 1881

Although the letters averted the closure of the Mission for several months, on June 8, 1881, the Chinese government ordered the Mission to be abolished and the teachers and students to return to China as soon as possible.[40] In August 1881 nearly all of the students (100 of 120) sailed back to China. Over 60 percent of them had only just begun their education in colleges or technical schools. Only two had completed their bachelor's degrees. Three had died in the United States. A few others had been sent home earlier for insubordination, for acquiring debts, or for cutting off their queues. Ten students who refused to return to China became engineers, worked in banks, or served as interpreters in the Chinese embassy.[41]

The students were coldly received in Shanghai. After disembarking from the ship, they had to walk, carrying their own luggage, "an almost inexcusable act of debasing oneself in the eyes of the so-called Chinese gentleman," while being mocked for their ill-fitted clothing by Shanghai's stylish dandies. After the initial roll call they were escorted by a detachment of Chinese marines to a building that one student described as worse than a "Turkish prison." Another student recalled their return: "All the muck and ruck of lies, falsehood and calumny were raked over and dished out to the public, and we were considered and looked upon as denationalized beings and treated as such."[42]

What crimes had the students committed? First, Rong and the students from southern China were never completely trusted by the conservative Northern court. Moreover, the students had lived in the "contaminated" West and did not behave like proper Chinese gentlemen. Chinese officials saw these attributes as "crimes" against the state, since they did not believe that the students could be *both* Chinese patriots and promoters of American science and culture. The students' worst "crime" was the potential threat they and their dangerous ideas posed to the existing power structure. By keeping the students at lower ranks, court scholars hoped to lessen the students' influence, thus preventing the revelation of their own inadequacies.[43]

The boys waited in Shanghai for Rong's return from Beijing, where he was making official calls and pleading their cause. They hoped to be liberated from "such outrageous treatment by our government," but some began to doubt his power to influence the leaders. In a letter to Mrs. Bartlett, Wong Kaijia wrote, "We are like the shoots of young trees transplanted from the rich soil and luxurient [sic] climate to the arid desert of ignorance and superstition. We are not flourishing but withering away slowly though perceptibly." Newspapers commented on the students' fate. While one called them "mixed-up people" (*zaren*), another said that the best thing to do for the students would be to send them abroad again since China was not ready for them.[44]

Rong also went to Tianjin to see Viceroy Li, who asked him why he had allowed the forced return of the students. Rong replied, "If I had stood out alone against carrying out the imperial mandate, would not I have been regarded as a rebel, guilty of treason and lose my head for it?" Li said he wished that the students had been allowed to continue their studies, to which Rong replied, "How was I supposed to know your mind at long distance?"[45]

Rong's month-long advocacy failed, but Viceroy Li took action to rescue many students from obscurity. Realizing their potential, he distributed them as students among the technical colleges in Tianjin, such as the Telegraph School or the Naval College and Torpedo School, and sent others to supervise the coal mines north of the city. Gradually other progressive viceroys and governors hired the young men to "manage" relations with foreigners or to assist in industrial, mining, railroad, and telegraph ventures.

Wong Kaijia, who became a translator in the office of Shanghai's city magistrate at the salary of an ordinary office clerk, wrote another letter to Mrs. Bartlett describing the students' fate. "The rest of the boys are distributed in various places to finish their education not according to their predilections nor to the course they had been pursuing in America, but more in accordance with the wishes of the Chinese Officials whose ignorance and stupidity render them unfit to judge in such matters."[46]

The Mission students' allegiance to China can be partially judged by their technical achievements, which strengthened China despite officials' resistance. Although given low-level positions, surprisingly few of the students left government service for jobs as clerks in foreign firms in coastal cities. After China's disastrous loss to Japan in 1895, some of the court leaders deemed the Self-Strengthening Movement a failure and called for radical reforms. Some of the Mission students then were promoted from their low positions to direct state railway and mining ventures and advanced more rapidly up the ladder of the official bureaucracy.

The students, who were known for their ability to get things done, helped place new technology in Chinese hands. They were the first Chinese to have the following modern careers:

> Thirteen of them served in the diplomatic service of China; six spent most of their lives in connection with the great Kailan [Kaiping] coal mining administration; fourteen of them were either chief engineers or served in managerial capacities on China's newly constructed railroads; seventeen were naval officers, seven of whom were killed in action and two of whom became admirals in the Imperial Navy; fifteen were identified with the Government Telegraph administration; four practiced medicine; three were connected with China's new educational institutions.[47]

Some historians have focused on the top ranks achieved by a few of the students. "Any class at Yale or Harvard would be filled with pride if it could point to so many distinguished men among its members." Others have claimed that the collective effort of the Mission students was the chief instrument in "initiating the modernization movement in China." By using this group of Chinese, China did not have to give all of their new technologies to foreign concessions.[48] Most of the Mission students chose the obscurity of retirement rather than join in the political scuffle after the Qing Dynasty collapsed in 1911.

Reformer Turned Revolutionary

During his year and a half in China, Rong displayed continuing concern for his country by writing a plan to suppress the Indian opium trade in China and extinguish poppy cultivation in China and India. Though the plan was submitted to the Chinese government, the president of the foreign affairs office responded that the plan could not be entertained because they did not have suitable men to tackle the problem.[49]

In 1883 Rong returned to the United States to care for his wife, who had been anxious for his life when the CEM was recalled. After his return, she gradually recovered strength and they were able to take trips together to Atlanta, Georgia, one winter and to the Adirondacks another year. In the winter of 1885, her health began to decline again.

After she died in May 1886, Rong found that raising his two sons helped console him in the loss of both his life's ambition and his wife. In his autobiography he wrote:

> Her death made a great void in my after-life, which was irreparable, but she did not leave me hopelessly deserted and alone; she left me two sons who are constant reminders of her beautiful life and character. They have proved to be my greatest comfort and solace in my declining years. They are most faithful, thoughtful and affectionate sons, and I am proud of their manly and earnest Christian characters. My gratitude to God for blessing me with two such sons will forever rise to heaven, an endless incense.[50]

In 1895, when Rong was again recalled to China, Rev. Twichell and his wife took in his younger son, Bartlett, until he finished high school. Writing later in his autobiography, Rong was thankful for the Twichell's hospitality.

> This is only a single instance illustrative of the large-hearted and broad spirit which has endeared [Rev. and Mrs. Twichell] to their people both in the Asylum Hill church and outside of it. I was deeply affected by this act of self-denial and magnanimity in my behalf as well as in the behalf of my son Bartlett. . . . Knowing that my sons would be well cared for, and leaving the development of their characters to an all-wise and ever-ruling Providence, as well as to their innate qualities, I embarked for China.[51]

This time in China, Rong was to be part of Viceroy Zhang Zhidong's group of men. After a thirteen-year absence, Rong had to buy a complete set of official robes before going to Zhang's headquarters in Nanjing. After the first interview, however, Viceroy Zhang was not interested, so Rong left to try his hand at business in Shanghai. There, Rong's projects for establishing a national bank and for building a railroad between two major ports failed, the first due to internal corruption and the second due to international tensions over the German monopoly of railroads in Shandong province.[52]

Rong then joined Kang Youwei, Sun Yat-sen, and others in encouraging the young emperor, Guang Xu, to instigate a comprehensive program of radical reforms during the summer of 1898. When the Empress Dowager Cixi brought the "Hundred Days of Reform" to an abrupt halt,

Rong fled for his life to the international settlement in Shanghai and then on to Hong Kong, after being named one of the most wanted men in the country.[53]

1-2 Rong Hong (second from right) with Chinese officials, c. 1900

Since his U.S. citizenship had been annulled in 1898 as part of the Chinese Exclusion Act, he was a man without a country. Despite the explicit rules for barring Chinese at ports, however, the elderly Yale graduate, dressed in European clothes, slipped by the inspector at the gangplank in San Francisco in June 1902 and arrived in New Haven in time to see his younger son graduate from Yale.[54] Morrison Brown Yung [Rong] had graduated four years earlier from Yale's Sheffield Scientific School. Both sons settled in China and married Chinese women. Morrison Brown died in Beijing in 1934 and Bartlett Golden lived in Shanghai until 1942.[55]

Rong Hong went into semiretirement in Hartford. He found that he was not always welcomed by other guests in boardinghouses, who did not want to eat with a Chinese. Rong could not keep his mind off China. Liang Qichao, a fellow exile following the 1898 reform, visited Rong in 1903 during a tour of the United States and wrote these words in his diary: "He was 76 years old and as vigorous as ever. Beside his concern for his country he had no other thoughts or business. I called on him for two hours, and he taught me and encouraged me a great deal about the future of our country. His political ideas were very logical and reasonable and commanded my respect."[56]

Rong lived long enough to meet students who began to come in 1909 on the new Sino-American educational plan. In August 1910, he encouraged the next generation of students at the annual conference of the Chinese Students' Alliance in Hartford, Connecticut, to "aim to make China the leading factor in shaping the destiny of the world."[57]

Rong died on April 22, 1912, in Hartford, having spent almost half his life in the United States. His old friend, Rev. Twichell, conducted the funeral at the Asylum Hill Congregational Church and the burial at the Cedar Hill Cemetery in Hartford.

The Chinese students who came to the United States after 1909 praised Rong as an "Educator, Reformer, Statesman, Patriot." As they reflected on the needs of China, they asked,

> In this time of times, when the clash of political and commercial interests among races and nations comes to the forefront of our present day problems, who but men of his loyalty and firmness, of his prophetic insight and high idealism, of his patience and courage to bring possibilities into realities, who but such men can shoulder the responsibilities of peace and reconstruction?[58]

2

TANG GUO'AN

Pioneering China's Rights Recovery Movement

by Carol Lee Hamrin

In mid-February 1909, the American University Club of Shanghai hosted its annual banquet. Chinese diplomat Tang Guo'an joined Rev. Charles Brent, American Bishop of the Philippines, on the platform as a special guest speaker. According to one participant, "All the speakers struck an exceedingly high plane and attempted no jokes or funny stories—an unusual compliment to their audience." In the banquet hall of the New Palace Hotel were eighty-five guests, including Chinese and American leaders of the Young Men's Christian Association (YMCA) and a correspondent from the *New York Herald*.[1]

Both Tang and Brent were taking time out from their busy schedules during the month-long session of the first International Opium Commission, cosponsored by China and the United States. The representatives of thirteen countries were meeting in Shanghai to discuss how to stop the opium trade. Bishop Brent, who had convinced President Theodore Roosevelt to sponsor this initiative, presided over the conference as the prime mover for the U.S. side, and Tang gave the main report and responses for China, as one of three official commissioners. The YMCA in Shanghai, with which Tang was closely associated as former treasurer and board member, played a vigorous role in closing opium shops in the city.[2]

One member of the audience, Shanghai's YMCA General Secretary William Lockwood, referred to Tang as "a man of deep conviction and an orator of ability." He recalled Tang's work during the Opium Commission conference:

> His eloquent and impassioned appeal to the Powers to assist China in her time of need, delivered in perfect English and republished and extensively circulated throughout England and Europe, probably did more to arouse the government of England to favorable action in limiting the importation of opium into China than any other deliverance on the subject.[3]

Eight months later, on October 12, Tang was elsewhere in Shanghai at the Imperial Maritime Customs Wharf boarding a steamer, the S.S. China, bound for San Francisco. On behalf of China's Foreign Office, Tang was accompanying forty-seven students traveling to the United States for higher education, the first group to be sent by the Chinese government in nearly thirty years. The YMCA groups provided support for this new endeavor too, including travel tips in Shanghai and a welcome at the entry port of San Francisco.

During the three-week crossing of the Pacific, according to one of the students aboard, "Tang enjoyed talking informally and most entertainingly for hours about his experiences in America" as a student in the 1870s. "When telling about his college days at Yale, he said, 'When you boys study in America, you want to get into the swing of the American college life.' He gave an extemporaneous speech on American education before a large gathering of foreign passengers."[4]

Finding His Way

Tang Guoan (also known as Tong Kai-son) was born in October 1858 in the Tang clan's ancestral village in Guangdong Province near Macao and was raised in a Christian family.[5] His kinsmen had been among the early students of the nearby Morrison Educational Society's School. So it was natural that another early student, Rong Hong, recruited Tang, along with a number of his relatives and neighbor boys, for study in the United States with the Chinese Educational Mission (CEM). Tang joined the second contingent, sent in 1873.[6]

During his eight years in the United States, Tang developed a well-rounded set of academic, social, and spiritual interests. His host family in Connecticut provided initial home schooling. He completed public high school in Northampton, Massachusetts, at the head of his class of 1879, and then attended college preparatory school at Phillips Exeter Academy.[7]

When the Chinese government's supervisor for the CEM required the students to worship Confucius and stop attending church services, Tang and two dozen other CEM students founded the Revive China Christian Society to strengthen their faith. They helped to hide two students who had chosen public baptism, to prevent their forced return to China. The students promised to help each other after returning home, and in later years held reunions in China. Tang served as Secretary, marking the start of a lifelong commitment to voluntary youth associations. This experience also gave birth to his conviction that moral reform, not just science and literature, was central to China's future progress.[8]

Tang entered Yale College in 1880 and in his first year won a prize in Latin composition and met the requirements for recruitment into the Delta Kappa Epsilon society, "in equal proportions the gentleman, the scholar and the jolly good fellow."[9] But his promising time at Yale came to an abrupt halt after only one year. By 1881, growing concern in the Qing imperial court about the cultural impact of American education joined with anger over anti-Chinese riots and legislation in the United States. All the CEM students were recalled to China many years before the planned completion of the exchange program, the last to be sponsored by the two governments for nearly thirty years.

On return to China, Tang and the other students were not given the high-level state positions that had been promised, but instead were given clerical posts and suffered from political suspicion as potential "traitors," as well as social ostracism for no longer being "pure Chinese." They in turn were shocked and offended by the widespread corruption and abuse of power in late Imperial China.[10] Tang, like the others, struggled to find a place in society. He served as an English interpreter and secretary for several foreign companies and U.S. consulates.[11]

Since Tang's father was a poor village farmer who died while Guo'an was in the United States, Tang had sent back part of his allowance to help support the family. His mother died a few years after his return. Family records emphasize his generosity. In 1884, Tang married a young woman from Hong Kong. They had no children but adopted a nephew Tang Yiguo (or Baoxin) and maintained close relationships of mutual support with other extended family members over the years.[12]

One Step Ahead: The Tang Family Network

In his early thirties, Tang Guo'an finally began to gain stable employment within the Tang family's circles of influence. His first permanent position, from 1890 to 1898, was as English secretary and assistant to the director of the Kaiping Mining and Engineering Company at Tangshan near Tianjin.[13] The company was one of many pioneering joint state-private enterprises sponsored by Viceroy Li Hongzhang, the eminent Qing modernizer. Li had recruited K. S. Tang (Tang Jingxing) to manage both Kaiping and the China Merchant Steamship Company of Shanghai.[14] K. S. and his successor, both of whom Tang Guo'an served as assistant, greatly developed North China's shipping and rail distribution, extending the mine's railway to Tianjin and then to Beijing, forming the core of what became the Imperial Railway. Sometime in 1899, Guo'an moved to Liaoning as resident manager of the Chinese Imperial Railway Administration.

K. S. Tang also headed the family clan, which had long experience in overseas trade and had come to exert great economic and political influence in coastal China during the late Qing and early Republican years. After the death of K. S., Tang Guo'an's cousin Tang Shaoyi, also a CEM student, appeared to take on the role of the family head, at least regarding their North China business. Shaoyi found favor in the imperial court as an aide to Yuan Shikai, who later would become the first President of the Republic of China and would appoint Tang Shaoyi its first Premier.[15] There was not a close personal relationship between these two Tang kinsmen, but considerable circumstantial evidence links their career paths. That they had a cordial relationship is hinted at in a brief reference to a 1903 incident, when Guo'an escorted a friend and houseguest from his home in Hong Kong to the clan hometown in Zhuhai near Macau, where they visited Shaoyi and other notables.[16]

Tang Guo'an took refuge in South China sometime in 1900 while the Boxer War was disrupting North China. He found work in business in Hong Kong, probably through contacts of his and his wife's families. Around 1901, he helped the new China YMCA national director, Fletcher Brockman, launch the Hong Kong Chinese YMCA, serving as the first chairman of the board.

At one early board meeting, when they faced a huge budget, an empty treasury, and almost no other resources, Tang told Brockman, "You tell us to have faith; you deal in faith. But we are businessmen; we have to pay our debts in dollars. If you could turn your faith into dollars, it would be alright." According to a later recounting, Brockman promised to work with them until all the funds for the whole year were raised, and when the board was called together again, Brockman was able to report that each pledge of a "dollar of faith" had been turned into two dollars of Hong Kong currency. "From that time these men began to grow in faith, and then other national and local boards began learning the same lesson." Tang likely carried this experience into his work as a member of the Shanghai, Beijing, and national YMCA boards in later years.[17]

Life in Shanghai Reform Circles

From 1903 to 1907, Tang lived in Shanghai, where he served first as chief auditor for the Canton–Hankow Railroad and then worked again for the Imperial Railway Administration.[18] He also took leadership in voluntary civic associations, which were proliferating in Shanghai. He served as treasurer and board member, as well as an author and editor for the Shanghai YMCA, attending nearly all their meetings during these five years. In the spring of 1907, he addressed the fifth national convention and was elected a national board member. His great interest extended to YMCA athletic meets. One student recalled later, "Though not an athlete himself, often times he would take pains to explain and to show to the youngsters how to run and how to jump."[19]

These were years when a new spirit of patriotism was in the air following the humiliation and shock of the occupation of Beijing by the allied Western powers after their suppression of the Boxers. National flags and songs were created, and foreign goods were boycotted in retaliation for offenses such as the military fortification of foreign legations and American and Australian legislation excluding Chinese immigrants. Patriotic fervor fueled calls for urgent political change to "save China" from extinction as a culture, race, and nation. The Qing court responded with a program of gradual national reforms in education and governance. The Confucian examination system was abolished and plans were made for a modern education system. In 1905, an imperial commission traveled to Japan, the United States, and Europe to research a plan to introduce constitutional government to China over the following ten years. In 1908, the first provincial assemblies were created and elections held.

Although Tang Guoʾan identified himself primarily as a businessman and raised funds for various civic organizations, he began to gain a national reputation as a writer and speaker, actively promoting moral and social reforms. Tang worked on a number of these initiatives with W. W. Yan (Yan Huiqing), a younger Yale graduate who had returned in 1900 to teach at St. John's College. Both families had considerable influence in Shanghai, the Tangs in business and the Yans in cultural circles. Tang's kinsman, another CEM student, was general manager of Jardine, Matheson & Company. Yan's father, Rev. Y. K. Yan (Yan Yongjing), had been the first principal and then professor of St. John's for a decade.

Rev. Yan was noted for an independent spirit that had a strong influence on the two younger men. One of the earliest Chinese to study overseas, Rev. Yan was able to deal with foreigners as equals. He admonished missionaries to be more humble and adopt a Chinese mode of life. In 1894 he had traveled throughout the United Kingdom to lobby against the opium trade, and he later organized and funded a garden for the Chinese populace of Shanghai after they were banned from those in the British settlement area.[20]

Tang was active in the network of Americans and returned Chinese students from the United States who formed part of Shanghai's cosmopolitan social elite. He joined the Anti-Foot-Binding Society. Tang was elected president of the city's branch of the Yale Alumni Association and became an honorary fellow of the American University Club. When T. H. Lee (Li Denghui), also from Yale, founded the World Chinese Students Federation, based in the city, Tang served on its board and wrote articles for its journal. Li later became dean of students at

2-1 Tang Guo'an in Shanghai, 1905

Fudan College and played a major role in mobilizing students to boycott American goods during the 1905 protests over U.S. laws restricting Chinese immigrant labor.[21]

One article Tang wrote for the Federation's journal was widely reprinted in foreign magazines and books. "An Appeal to China's Foreign-Educated Men" began with a long list of offenses by the Western Powers, including the opium trade and territories seized from China. In his view, they were making a profit from enormous indemnities and seemed to make a new sport of oppressing the weak and subverting principles of truth and justice. Many highly nationalistic articles of the day dwelled on such outrages, but Tang went on to state that "it is in the nature of man to seek to take advantage of the weak," and that

> were the positions reversed, China might accord even worse treatment to foreign nations. It behooves us, then, not to entertain unworthy thoughts of hatred and resentment, which will be of no avail, but to concentrate all our energies to the setting of our political and economic systems in order.

Tang concluded his journal article by challenging China's foreign-educated citizens, whose experience and ideas would help them better grasp the dire situation, to seek and find remedies for it.

Tang's gracious attitude toward China's oppressors echoed an earlier sermon he gave at the YMCA, in which he said there were many good reasons to "love the enemy," as taught in the Bible.

> The Lord sends rain on the righteous and the unrighteous. We will be called the children of God if we do this also. And the advantages of loving the enemy are great, better than treating them with hostility. If the enemy accepts our love, then both the one who loves and the one who is loved will have a chance to grow up in Christ. . . . When people encourage each other to do this, then not only will we have more virtue and be more gentle, but the manners of society will also improve.[22]

Tang and W. W. Yan teamed up as partners for a debate in November 1903 against two Westerners as part of a regular series of exchanges between the foreign and Chinese YMCA clubs. They argued that to open up the whole of China on the same basis as the existing treaty ports, essentially colonies under control of the Western Powers, would be detrimental to China. Though they were implying that full sovereign rights should be returned to China, they won over the debate's judge, a prominent local British barrister.[23]

In 1904, Tang and Yan, with a few others, were asked to write for the English section of a new YMCA national bilingual newspaper. The titles of some of Tang's articles, which were among the readers' favorites, revealed ideas close to his heart: "Reasons Why Chinese Patriots Should Become Christians," "The Happiness of Christians," "Chinese Christians Should Take the Responsibility to Reform Society."[24]

The two authors were then invited to launch an English-language section of the new *Nanfang bao* (South China Daily) in order to use Chinese public opinion to influence foreign actions in China at a time of growing tension. Through their efforts, the two gained national fame. Theirs was the "earliest attempt made by our people to defend our rights and interests by means of a newspaper of our own published in a foreign language, and though short-lived [1906–07], it set a good standard for our successors."[25] The one-page section merely contained a short editorial with a few news items, yet it had considerable influence among the English-reading public. Foreign newspapers and books began to include sections on Chinese opinion.

The two men took turns writing the editorials and were almost kicked out of the international concession for their bold advocacy.

When many expressed worry about Tang's safety, he ignored the danger of retaliation, gaining even more respect and fame in the foreign community. "Both of them could express impartial opinions with beautiful language. . . . Tang always had an upright heart, longing for righteousness in society and condemning every injustice, speaking up in public without fear."[26]

It was evident in Tang's writings that he thought moral reform was central to China's future prospects. In one article written for the YMCA journal and later quoted in the foreign press, he wrote,

> The present degradation [of China] is due not so much to the system of education and traditional and military ideas or non-development of manufacturing . . . but to the lack of moral force in the Chinese character, both as individuals and as a nation. Moral force must be regenerated and then when it permeates the Chinese national and individual character, national permanence and greatness will be assured.[27]

Faith Community

Tang Guo'an wrote a number of journal articles in 1905 that gave a constructive critique of the Christian mission establishment in China. These essays revealed a personal commitment to the Christian faith and showed how that faith fueled his strong sense of moral and social justice.

Early in the year, Tang wrote an article that spelled out the difficulties of Chinese Christian leaders for the *Chinese Recorder*, a leading missionary journal. It was clear that these were heartfelt matters to him, due to his close and admiring relationships with a number of these leaders, including senior pastors in Hong Kong, Canton, and Shanghai. Noting their contributions to China, from literary achievements to charity work to opposing foot binding and the opium trade, he had special praise for Rev. Yan, a personal model and mentor. He listed the three great characteristics of Yan's life as self-sacrifice, bravery, and faith.

Tang stressed the serious challenges on several fronts: First, in social and political relations, the Chinese pastor could never have the confidence of the officials or a voice in the communal government of his village or clan. Second, in relations among Chinese colleagues, mutual feelings of jealousy led them to disparage and undermine each other. Finally, even worse were the relations between Chinese pastors and foreign colleagues, who often treated their assistants more like servants and inferiors than co-workers. In Tang's observation, Chinese church workers, with meager salaries and delayed promotions, constantly had a life-and-death struggle in efforts to maintain a family.[28]

In the last five issues of the 1905 edition of *The Missionary Review of the World*, published in New York, Tang addressed more broadly the topic of the obstacles to Christian missions in China, reassuring his international readers that his attitude was one of speaking without reserve but in a spirit of charity. He wrote as an insider, expressing hope that his views would spur change so that the kingdom of God would grow in China.[29]

Quickly setting aside any discussion of "the thousand and one things which might be set down to the credit" of the missionaries, for most of whom he had a very high regard, Tang set out to explain the problems. His list of circumstantial external barriers to the Christian Gospel, over which the missions had little control, included the all-pervading influence of Confucianism, the antagonism of the educated elite, the poverty and ignorance of the people, the lowly social position of native converts, poor facilities for travel and communication, and government opposition to progressive reforms.

His list of obstacles internal to the mission community, which he thought they could and must change, included the following:

1. THE MIXED RELIGIOUS-POLITICAL CHARACTER OF CHRISTIAN PROPAGATION. Tang listed this as first in importance. Due to the unequal treaties, toleration of Christianity had been imposed on China and supported by force, so the government and people alike naturally saw religion as serving the goals of politics. As in ancient Rome, the Chinese imperial government always had "looked askance at all associations not recognized by and subordinate to the public law." He faulted missionaries for encouraging Chinese converts to ignore or disobey their own officials.

2. AN "ACTIVE COMBATIVE" SPIRIT OF MISSIONARIES IN DEALING WITH CHINESE CULTURE. Tang urged missionaries to adopt instead a spirit

of patience and forbearance, especially regarding veneration of ancestors. "It is not the duty of Protestant missions to propagate prescribed forms of theology, dogmatic sentiments, modes of worship, church government or customs, but rather to spread the Gospel of Jesus and implant the new life of fellowship with God in Christ."

3. UNPRINCIPLED CONDUCT OF SO-CALLED CHRISTIAN NATIONS IN POLITICAL AND DIPLOMATIC RELATIONS. Tang exclaimed that "the long series of unjust treaties . . . rob[bery] of valuable portions of China's domains, as well as dictation of the polic[ies] of internal administration . . . the presence of foreign troops in the capital . . . would shame the followers of any pagan religion." He highlighted opium trafficking as one of the chief injustices, with the opium habit so universal in some provinces of China that "people will tell the inquirer that 'eleven out of every ten' are opium smokers. . . . What is the loss of a few million pounds of revenue when compared with the fate of millions of China's sons and daughters, whose non-acceptance of Christianity deprives them of happiness in this life and salvation in the life to come?"

4. THE MISTAKES OF THE MISSIONARY SOCIETIES. On this topic, Tang Guo'an used his own knowledge of the Christian faith and community in China to criticize denominationalism, the poor selection, education, and preparation of missionaries, and the poor quality of Christian literature. He expressed longing for a Bible that would be "nothing short of a real masterpiece of Chinese literature."

Tang Guo'an concluded his essays by challenging the missionaries first of all to voluntarily give up all their special treaty privileges and place all Christian establishments throughout the provinces under official supervision. This should be accompanied by total separation of the missions from all political interests, and support only by nonofficial representation of mission interests.

Secondly, he urged them to expand Christian schools, especially for women, to circulate high-class Christian literature more widely, and to launch a major effort to train young Chinese Christian leaders, pastors, teachers, and writers. In this way, he was hopeful that "the next ten years will see greater results than all the previous years together . . . knowing that the light cannot be forever excluded."

The "Young China" Movement to Recover Sovereign Rights

In 1907, Tang Guo'an made a major shift of career to government diplomacy. He left for Beijing to join the Foreign Office, along with a number of other former CEM students recruited to help bring about the reform goals that they had been promoting, centered on the recovery of China's full sovereignty by rescinding those special rights ceded under duress to foreign powers. The Foreign Office had been created to satisfy the Western demand in the Boxer Protocol of 1901 for better communication at a higher level in the Chinese government.[30] Yuan Shikai, later to become the first President of the Republic of China, was in charge of foreign affairs (and much else) for this last decade of the empire, either as supervisor or as actual president of the Foreign Office (1907–09). Yuan wanted to recover Tibet and Mongolia, counter Japanese encroachment in Manchuria, and prevent any further partition of China, which seemed imminent. So he filled the office with Western- and Japanese-educated men with the knowledge, skills, and personal ties overseas to counter foreign aggression in more sophisticated and effective ways. Yuan had a "hands-on" style of management and often met with his "brain trust" to get input for decisions, working closely with his subordinates and thus earning their loyalty.[31]

Yuan's long-time aide Tang Shaoyi, Guo'an's more politically minded kinsman, helped recruit other foreign-educated Chinese with practical experience in modern industry, including Guo'an, Liang Dunyan, and Yan Huiqing. (Liang and Yan later would serve as ministers of foreign affairs.) These diplomats became known in the foreign community as members of a well-educated "young China" political group, whose attitude and work style contrasted starkly and favorably with the aging and reactionary political elite in Beijing. The Foreign Office launched a more assertive diplomacy intended to cut through the bureaucratic morass at home and counter more effectively the foreigners who were aggressively seizing territory and demanding Qing concessions of control over key developing industries, especially the mines and railways.[32]

At first, Tang Guo'an coordinated oversight of the Jing–Feng Railway linking Beijing to Fengtian (now Shenyang) and served as English interpreter and secretary for Yuan Shikai and for high-level missions by Manchu princes. Tang also took on an additional job as English tutor for Yuan's family, needing to supplement his low salary. The combination of poor pay and exorbitant expenses required to meet the official court dress code was a challenge, as was the stifling, bureaucratic atmosphere in Beijing, with officials fixated on minute distinctions of rank and status.[33]

When Tang served as interpreter for Yuan Shikai's first official foreign interview in June 1908, the New York Times reporter recognized Tang. In his report he mentioned, "The last time I had seen Mr. [Tang] he was dressed in European clothing and was editing the South China Daily Journal [sic]. . . . When I spoke of his change in appearance, he laughingly said, 'Ah, yes: Peking is not Shanghai, you know. They are more conservative up here.'"[34]

A major goal of the new diplomacy was to obtain U.S. support as an ally to counter the power of Europe, Russia, and Japan, since the United States was seen as more willing to treat China as an equal and to develop mutually beneficial relations. Yuan's New York Times interview launched a major campaign to align U.S. and Chinese interests against the danger of partitioning China. He claimed America had always been China's friend in deed as well as word, and he praised the U.S.-trained officials around him as superior to those who had studied in Europe or Japan. Yuan stressed that the new spirit of patriotism was not intended to be antiforeign and expressed admiration for U.S. institutions and for both outgoing President Roosevelt and presidential candidate William Howard Taft, who had visited China the previous year. Yuan claimed that Taft's speech in Shanghai had impressed the Chinese with his knowledge and positive attitude toward China.

Yuan concluded the interview by extending a welcome to the U.S. Pacific fleet, soon to make its first official visit to China. Pointedly, he said, "You know, China has been visited by many foreign squadrons, friendly and otherwise, but never before has even a friendly fleet considered our wishes in the matter, or waited to be invited. . . . It will be considered by Chinese as a turning point in the foreign relations of our country."[35] Tang Guo'an served as interpreter and advisor for the imperial delegation that hosted the U.S. fleet's visit to Xiamen in late 1908.

Soon, Tang Guo'an was spending his time working on two major initiatives of Yuan Shikai and Tang Shaoyi: 1) to work with the United States on a basis of equality and mutual benefit to speed up international cooperation in stopping the opium trade, and 2) to resume bilateral sponsorship for educating Chinese students in the United States after a three-decade hiatus. Both initiatives were belated fulfillment of much earlier goals of the visionary Rong Hong.[36]

A Year of Breakthroughs: 1909

Throughout February 1909, Tang Guo'an played a very important role as a commissioner and spokesman for the Chinese delegation to the first International Opium Conference at Shanghai. This was the first international forum in which China was positioned as an equal participant and signing power in dealings that greatly affected its future. Tang's detailed report, in impeccable English, on China's rapid progress in eradicating domestic opium sale and use served to put pressure on Western Powers to do the same, beginning in the treaty ports they controlled in China. In the report, Tang highlighted the economic, social, and moral burden of opium use in China.[37]

Tang gave an impassioned speech at the close of the proceedings, in which he pressed for even wider foreign understanding and greater support for the anti-opium movement. Tang highlighted the full importance of the opium issue: it was the first question that had aroused the whole of the Chinese people to joint action, and the conference's principle of reciprocity and mutual accountability foreshadowed the enjoyment by China of a "new relationship of friendship and understanding with the rest of the world."[38] Tang offered China's official gratitude to those non-Chinese, including Christian parliamentarians in Britain such as Lord Shaftesbury and missionary statesmen such as J. Hudson Taylor and Benjamin Broomhall of the China Inland Mission (CIM), for all they had done for the cause.

For over three decades, Taylor had mobilized other missionaries in India and China to lobby Parliament, testify before the British Royal Opium Commission, and campaign at church and mission conferences around the world to build public opinion against the opium trade, demanding legislation to ban it. Christian leaders also communicated to Qing officials the idea of a gradual ten-year plan of mutual Chinese and British steps to solve the problem.[39]

Broomhall, head of the CIM in London, was also an executive of the Society for the Suppression of the Opium Trade. He used their media outlets to shame society into opposition to what he depicted as a sinful trade that endangered the souls of every citizen of the British nation. It was Broomhall who had invited Rev. Yan of Shanghai on a speaking tour of Great Britain in 1894, when his testimony regarding the destruction of Chinese families by opium made a deep impression on more than one hundred audiences in fifty-two cities. Yan also had testified before the Royal Commission. The mission community increasingly had used customs statistics and testimony by medical missionaries in China to counter the conventional wisdom of the day that opium was useful as medicine and its side effects were not that harmful.

Tang Guo'an effectively used moral argumentation to appeal to the Shanghai conference delegates in 1909. He asked them to remember the higher moral law transcending culture and politics, citing both Confucius and Christ on the Golden Rule. His speech inspired strong conference resolutions urging immediate action in the foreign concessions and foreign territories to match China's effort. Tang's deep conviction and eloquence led to the translation of his speech into multiple languages, with wide circulation and public support for his views in Europe, especially in Britain. This helped arouse the British government to real action in implementing limits it had pledged earlier. His speech became known as "the first shot . . . which China fired in her proclamation to the world of her determined intention to eradicate the opium curse."[40] The strong Chinese government actions and diplomacy of 1906–09 thus restarted the anti-opium movement after a decade of delay for "study" by the Royal Opium Commission. Two years later, the news of a long-delayed Sino-British agreement would reach Broomhall on his deathbed and gladden his final moments.[41]

Later in 1909, Tang turned his full attention to the field of education, on assignment to the new Office for Study in the United States, set up jointly under the foreign affairs and education ministries to resume state-sponsored American education for Chinese students. The program was supported by reparation funds paid by the Qing court to the United States in excess of actual claims for American losses during the Boxer Uprising. Again, China missionaries had paved the way, first lobbying against the large amounts demanded by the 1901 Protocol, and thereafter advocating the return of any excess, which turned out to be

$11 million. The U.S. decision to return excess funds was openly aimed at building goodwill for the United States in China, but it also served China's long-term modernization program and shamed other countries into doing the same.[42]

Bilateral agreement in 1908 established a long-term plan for 1909 to 1940, the year marking the end of the Boxer Protocol payments. China would send one hundred students each year for the first five years and fewer thereafter. Tang was heavily involved in the planning and negotiation of the program during 1907–08 and was one of three officials in charge of selecting Chinese students to send to the United States. In December 1909, he accompanied the first group of forty-seven boys to America, effectively realizing the dream he had shared so long with Rong Hong, the CEM's founder, and fellow students. After twenty-eight years, Tang was able to revisit the familiar places and close friends of his youth.[43]

2-2 Tang Guo'an (seated, right) and two other officials with the first Boxer Indemnity students, 1909

When Tang returned from escorting the first group of students, he was accorded the official degree of fifth rank. He also accompanied the second group of students in 1910, staying on for awhile to work out housing arrangements. In January 1911, he spoke in New York City at the annual reunion dinner for the Yale Class of 1884, the first he had been able to attend. "He entertained us by recalling many incidents which were still fresh in his mind. . . . He created much amusement by telling how . . . he had carried that [class] song back to China and sang it there to the great mystification of all who heard him." He parried close questioning by those interested in hearing about the new regime in China. Participants recalled his "graceful speech and winning smile."[44]

Dedication and Exhaustion

For the next several years, Tang Guo'an was busy alternating attention to his major duties in both opium eradication and founding a new school. The Imperial Tsinghua Academy was set up as a state preparatory school for the China-U.S. exchange program, opening in April 1909 with 468 students. In August, Tang became assistant director with full-time primary executive responsibility. To reach the new campus required either a three-hour carriage ride or a donkey ride that cut across fields outside the city gate to reach the ruins of the former imperial palace grounds. Rising from those ashes, Tsinghua was to become one of China's most beautiful campuses.[45]

Controversies raged over criteria for student recruitment and the curriculum. The Ministry of Education favored only select mature students already well versed in a Chinese classical education. Foreign Minister Liang Dunyan, a close friend of Tang Guo'an since they were CEM students together, disagreed. He worried they would be like earlier students sent to Japan, who studied mainly political science and law and returned as revolutionaries or politicians anxious to rise in the bureaucracy. Instead, Liang and his foreign ministry colleagues favored sending thousands of younger boys from the provinces to receive a modern education in scientific and technical subjects that could develop the economy and thoroughly reform China. The compromise solution, which required students to be fluent in Chinese and focus on a modern scientific education, remained elitist and modest in scale by necessity, due to a scarcity of qualified students. Nevertheless, early leaders continued to build up Tsinghua, and its graduates were to serve China well in the decades to follow.[46]

In the midst of launching a new institution in a contentious political environment, Tang traveled to Europe and the United States, both to explore ideas for the school and to represent China at the December 1911–January 1912 session of the Opium Commission at The Hague. This session produced the first international regulation of the narcotics trade: the International Opium Convention. In 1911, the British Parliament had finally committed to ending the global trade. Tragically, the negotiation of the rules for actual implementation formally ended only after an arduous four-year process and another four-year hiatus during World War I.[47]

After Tang's return to Beijing in 1912, he was immersed in the pressing needs of Tsinghua, which had closed for half a year due to the Republican revolution of October 1911. A financial and personnel crisis ensued when the desperate Qing court used the school's Boxer funds in a vain attempt to suppress revolutionaries, and senior school leaders were suddenly appointed as high-level officials in the new Republic. But Tang chose to stay out of government and prepared to reconstitute and rename Tsinghua College for its reopening in May 1912. It now had greater internal autonomy, under the foreign ministry's general supervision in close coordination with the U.S. embassy. Tang Guoʾan became the founding president and was to leave a strong personal imprint on the college with the help of his capable appointees, Zhou Yichun as vice president in charge of academic affairs and Tang's nephew Tang Menlun (Tang Yi) in charge of administrative affairs.

Although Tsinghua was a secular state institution with an emphasis on science and technology in the curriculum, Tang set a high moral tone for the students. The largely Christian staff and faculty stressed the importance of personal discipline to "cultivate the whole human character" as the beginning of true talent.[48] Following the American model of schools like Yale or St. John's, campus activities were designed to create a moral community. There were speech and debating clubs, student newspapers, evangelistic summer conferences, and campus Bible studies. Tsinghua had the largest (half the students) and most active campus group in the Beijing city YMCA network. As a national board member, Tang addressed the YMCA's sixth national convention in December 1912 and often gave personal talks to the young members. In the spring of 1913, five Tsinghua students traveled to Manila as part of China's team participating in the first Eastern Olympics, a forerunner of the modern Asian Games.[49]

During late 1912 and early 1913, President Tang recruited high-quality faculty among returned students and made a series of critical decisions for the college regarding organization, channels for sustained funding, and building expansion. He knew that his time on earth was short—his heart disease was steadily worsening. Finally, he resigned the presidency and recommended Vice President Zhou as his successor, just one day before he died of heart failure on August 22, 1913.

Tang Guo'an's Legacy

While Tang Guo'an did not live to see the results of his hard work, he and Zhou, who supervised the campus building program planned by Tang, established a strong base for what has become one of China's world-class universities. He was loved and respected by teachers and students alike because he was open-minded and open-hearted, refusing to put on bureaucratic airs. Chen Heqin, a member of Tsinghua's first graduating class and later a famous educator, recalled, "As a Christian, he was very sincere with people, enthusiastic about the work, and regarded students as brothers and colleagues as friends. . . . We all felt grief as if we had lost a beloved mother."[50] One of the students in the United States who had traveled by ship to America with Tang in 1909 eulogized him as "exemplary in a very high degree" and as one who had "won admiration from both his fellow countrymen and foreign residents in China. . . . As a companion, Mr. [Tang] was most congenial. His cheerful and pleasant ways would impress anyone that met him. He would talk informally with all friends, and yet maintain his dignity. . . . He worked unselfishly and gathered around him a host of admirers. . . . China has lost one of its best citizens."[51]

Tang's personal legacy at Tsinghua also lasted far into the future. So many other family members served the university that the "Four Generation Tsinghua Family" became famous. In the first generation,

Tang Guo'an's nephew Tang Menlun joined the university staff in 1909. He in turn brought in the next generation, his nephew Tang Guanfang, to serve in the library in 1921. The third generation had two members: Guanfang's daughter Tang Shaozhen, who worked in the library after 1947, and his son Tang Shaoming, who graduated from Tsinghua and served on the faculty for eight years. (Tang Shaoming, now retired from the National Library of China, where he served as Deputy Executive Director for six years, has researched the life of Tang Guo'an.) Finally, Tang Shaozhen's daughter-in-law, Wang Qiping, currently is on the staff of the university library.[52]

Tang Guo'an also left a larger national legacy. Working with like-minded foreign-educated students sprinkled through the various modern professions just then developing in late Qing China, he helped build both the practical and the moral bases for later modernization programs during the Republic and the People's Republic. The continuity of reform ideas and efforts provided a hidden current of progress beneath the surface waves of political turbulence. Motivated by love of Christ, family, and country, Tang's part in the development of railways and shipping, the ending of the opium trade, the recovery of China's sovereign rights, and the founding of modern education constitutes a major contribution.

Tang's death from heart disease when he was only in his midfifties came as a shock for many who had known him before his Tsinghua days and who also had great respect and deep affection for him. Kuang Fuzhuo (Fong Foo Sec), a fellow Cantonese and chairman of the board of the Shanghai YMCA, recalled how Tang had "worked hard to find many ways to help me and our association" ten years earlier. The two men had stayed up talking late into the night just before Tang left Shanghai for his new career in Beijing, and Kuang had been in the audience when Tang returned and spoke during the opium trade conference in 1909. "Mr. Tang was a Christian with exemplary behavior and very deep academic accomplishments. He worked in various professional fields toward reforming society, and also had a very warm heart." At a time of great difficulties facing the nation, he did a lot to achieve "his aspiration to change the country and reform the society. His death is a great loss to his country."[53]

SHI MEIYU

An "Army of Women" in Medicine

by Connie Shemo

In the late 1870s, Shi Zeyu (Shi Tseh-yu), the first Chinese Methodist pastor in the treaty port city of Jiujiang, in Jiangxi Province, went to Gertrude Howe, an American missionary, with a highly unusual request: to prepare his daughter for medical school. Howe and the Shi family, by all accounts, had an extremely close relationship. Shi had begun his association with the American Methodist Episcopal community as a Chinese teacher for the missionaries, having come from a Chinese gentry family that had lost its property in the course of the Taiping Rebellion. He converted to Christianity and became a pastor, and his wife opened up a mission day school for Chinese girls.

When Howe first came to Jiujiang in 1869 as one of the first missionaries for the newly created Woman's Foreign Mission Society (WFMS), she appears to have quickly developed strong ties with the Shi family. Howe would often recall that she had been the first person to hold the Shi's first daughter, Meiyu, in her arms after the child's birth in 1872. Howe adopted an infant Chinese daughter, Kang Cheng (or Ida Kahn), at about the same time as Meiyu was born, and the two girls would later describe themselves as companions from babyhood.

Entering an Unmarked Pathway

Both girls were unusual (for the early 1870s) in that their feet were left unbound. The Shi family told Howe on Meiyu's birth that they would not bind their daughter's feet, but Howe had still been extremely surprised when they had in fact refused to put the bindings on, despite great pressure from their extended family.[1]

Yet even this surprise was nothing compared to Howe's amazement at Shi's later request, when Meiyu was seven or eight. He asked her to provide Meiyu with the training necessary to enter an American medical school, in order that she might return to China to begin medical work for Chinese women. He shared the concern of his extended family that, with unbound feet, Meiyu would not be able to marry well. In fact, by the time Meiyu was an adult in the 1890s, unbound feet would be more common in progressive families, and she would in fact receive many proposals from men who were considered to be the best "catches": Chinese men who studied in universities abroad. Yet in the 1870s, it was not clear that this would be the case, so Shi came up with the plan of having his daughter enter into medical work, like an American woman medical missionary whom he had known in Jiujiang.

After some initial hesitation, Howe agreed, and the following year she began to provide special classes for eight-year-old Shi Meiyu, her own adopted daughter Kang Aide, and three Chinese boys. She taught them English and various sciences such as physics and chemistry with the goal of preparing the students for entry into an American medical school. This decision sent shock waves through the Methodist Episcopal missionary community in Jiujiang. Although twenty years down the road, by the late 1890s, mission schools teaching Chinese girls these kinds of subjects would become common, in the 1870s offering this kind of education was a radical innovation.

In making this request of Howe, Shi in effect was pushing the missionaries of the Methodist Episcopal Board to recognize the ability of Chinese girls to receive the training that would enable them to take over the work of American women missionaries rather than remain the assistants of missionaries. Even when teaching English and Western science to Chinese girls later became accepted in mission education, very few missionaries deliberately trained either Chinese boys or girls to take over mission work. The official policy of the Methodist Episcopal Church, like most Protestant missions, was that Chinese Christians would eventually take over the mission institutions. They tended, however, to view this day as occurring in a distant, indeterminable future. In asking Howe to prepare his daughter to run a mission hospital of her own, Shi Zeyu was, in essence, insisting that the Methodist missionaries begin working towards Chinese control immediately.

Shi Meiyu, who would become known in the United States and among American missionaries as Mary Stone, would grow up to be one of very few Chinese Christians—either male or female—to become a regularly appointed missionary of any Protestant mission board. She also was unusual in running her own mission hospital from 1896 onwards. For the most part, Chinese remained subordinate to the American missionaries who ran and controlled the finances of mission institutions until after 1927. At that time, the new Nationalist government required that Chinese be heads of mission hospitals and schools.[2]

Like her father, Shi Meiyu combined a passionate Christian evangelism with an equally vigorous Chinese nationalism. Her commitment to world evangelization led her to continue to work as a WFMS missionary in the face of much more financially remunerative offers to run government hospitals and schools. At the same time, in her writing and the way she ran her mission hospital, she continually emphasized the importance of fostering Chinese control in mission institutions.

Howe faced what Shi Meiyu would later describe as "ostracism from close circles" for her willingness to provide the classes that Pastor Shi had requested, as well as for her adoption of Kang and three other Chinese girls.[3] Yet the WFMS had funded the medical education in the United States of two other Chinese girls: Jin Yumei (King Yamei), a missionary couple's adopted daughter who spent the majority of her youth in the United States and Japan and graduated from the Women's Medical College of the New York Infirmary in 1885, and Xu Jinhong (Hu King-eng), a Chinese pastor's daughter who was born in Fuzhou and graduated from the Women's Medical College of Pennsylvania in 1894. Both of these girls, like Kang and Shi, had grown up close to missionary communities. Xu's father, like Shi Meiyu's, had come from a gentry background, which seems to have given both families important status in the missionary community.[4]

While the Methodist Episcopal Board did not institute programs to train Chinese to take over mission institutions, the perception that Chinese women needed Western medical care but would not see Western male doctors opened a space for both American and Chinese women physicians to practice in China. Prominent converts such as Xu and Shi could therefore influence the WFMS to fund more advanced medical education for their daughters in the United States.

Howe accompanied her daughter Kang Aide and Shi Meiyu to the University of Michigan in 1892. While not a great deal is recorded from their time in the medical school, all accounts stress Kang's and Shi's academic success at the school. They wore Western-style clothes while in the United States, so as not to attract attention, but at the graduation ceremony they wore traditional Chinese dresses, celebrating their Chinese identity at the same time that they were recognized for their academic achievement.[5]

3-1 Shi Meiyu as a young physician

Pioneers of Modern Medicine

Upon their return to China, Shi and Kang enjoyed much more rapid acceptance by the Chinese community than the American missionaries in Jiujiang had expected. The day of their return, they were asked to help with a difficult delivery and, happily for their career prospects, saved the lives of both mother and child. The issue of Chinese control soon came to the forefront. Missionaries, even Howe, had expected Shi and Kang to work in a large mission hospital run by an American medical missionary, not believing that they would have the medical authority in the community to begin their own practice. However, the two insisted on opening their own dispensary.[6] While Shi's father had stretched the missionary view of the possibilities for education of Chinese women, Shi and Kang made sure that, from the beginning of their practice, missionaries recognized their ability to run a medical practice themselves, even though they had to begin on a small scale.

Their confidence in themselves was soon to prove well-founded. Their practice expanded at a rapid rate. In 1897, they saw over two thousand patients, while the next year, in 1898, that number had more than doubled to over five thousand. As their patients increased, they opened a small nursing school to train Chinese girls as assistants. By 1900, with funds from Dr. I. N. Danforth, a physician whom Shi had met during her study in the United States, Shi and Kang had built a small hospital. A memorial for Danforth's wife, the Elizabeth Skelton Danforth Hospital opened with both missionary support and an enthusiastic response from the local gentry, who lent their official approval by making speeches at the opening celebration.[7]

Indeed, Chinese nationalist reformers not only in Jiangxi Province but nationwide became enthusiastic about Shi and Kang's medical practice. Viceroy Zhang Zhidong, a highly influential modernizer, asked Kang and Shi to lead a girls' school he wished to open. While Kang and Shi ultimately decided to stay with their medical practice instead, the attention of such a prominent Chinese official increased their standing among the local gentry. Of perhaps even more importance was an 1897 essay written by the famous reformer and journalist Liang Qichao about Kang, in which he also mentioned Shi. Liang praised both women for their project of "saving" (*qing ming*) Chinese women and "transforming their lives" (*zhuan huan*). Liang reflected his secular views when he not only ignored Shi and Kang's Christian affiliation but even described Gertrude Howe as a "traveler" rather than a missionary.[8] Yet Liang, like many Chinese reformers in Jiujiang, could make common cause with Kang and Shi in their efforts to improve the health of Chinese women, as they shared a conviction that the strength of China depended on healthy and educated Chinese women.

The Boxer Uprising caused a temporary setback in Shi and Kang's medical work. While the anti-Christian violence took place mainly in northern rather than central China, Shi Meiyu's father, evangelizing in an unspecified area, was killed during this time. She would later describe him as a "martyr" of the Boxer Uprising.[9] Kang and Shi ceased their medical work and accompanied American missionaries to Japan, taking the nurses with them. Their newly built hospital was untouched by violence and ready to open on their return in 1901. Shi Meiyu continued to enjoy the companionship and support of her mother, who acted as a "Bible Woman" (often a retiree or a widow like Shi's mother), who explained Christian literature to patients and their families in the hospital.

In the aftermath of the Boxer Uprising, and with the new hospital, Shi and Kang's practice continued to expand. In 1902 they treated over seven thousand patients. This very expansion, however, was to cause Shi a serious dilemma. In 1903, Kang Aide received an invitation from some gentry in Nanchang, the capital of Jiangxi Province, to begin medical work in that city. Excited by the prospect of opening a self-supporting medical outreach in the wealthy city, Kang accepted and departed along with Gertrude Howe. Shi was left to manage a rapidly growing medical practice by herself. In 1903, Danforth Hospital treated over ten thousand patients. Worried that Shi Meiyu would suffer nervous exhaustion, Dr. Danforth proposed sending over an American nurse to assist her.

Shi politely declined her American benefactor's offer. She was determined that medical work remain completely in the hands of Chinese women, both to demonstrate to foreigners the capacity of Chinese women to engage in medicine without foreign assistance and to prove to Chinese women themselves that they were "able to do things of which they have never dreamed."[10] She therefore continued to run the school with only the nurses whom she trained herself, even though this meant a sometimes overwhelming amount of work for her.

While Shi Meiyu insisted on Chinese control of her hospital, she was soon to form a lifelong partnership with an American woman missionary, Jennie Hughes. Originally assigned to Nanchang, Hughes left the city for Jiujiang due to a 1905 uprising. While this was originally supposed to be a temporary move, Hughes remained in Jiujiang to live with Shi Meiyu, sharing all the expenses of her home.[11] Hughes ran the Knowles Bible School, a school for training Bible Women. Shi's nursing school and this Bible school would later become intertwined.

Shi and Hughes would form a family unit, with Shi adopting four Chinese boys, including her nephew, known in missionary sources as Luther Stone, the son of her deceased brother. Other children lived with them for periods of time without being adopted.[12] The respective roles played by Shi and Hughes in the household have been the subject of speculation. Because Shi Meiyu was relatively soft-spoken and easygoing, while Hughes seems to have had a more immediately forceful temperament, some missionaries viewed Hughes as "dominating" Shi Meiyu. From interviews with people who lived with them as children, it would appear that Hughes did most of the disciplining and had more interaction with the children. However, Shi may have exercised ultimate control; she was described as a "brake" on Hughes.[13] Others recall Shi going upstairs to write letters to supporters while Hughes handled the needs of the children and the household. They formed a partnership that defied traditional expectations but worked for them both.

In 1906, Shi Meiyu became incapacitated with appendicitis, which was exacerbated by overwork. The WFMS arranged for her transport, along with Hughes as a caretaker, to the United States for surgery. After her convalescence, Shi turned the trip into an excellent fundraising opportunity. She spoke before hundreds of audiences and was by all accounts a moving and inspiring speaker. Essays that Shi wrote for her audience of American mission supporters give a hint of her style. She could employ soaring rhetoric, as when she described her nurses as "workers filled with faith and love for the Master, who will make this self-denying work their life work, who will ask for no reward or encouragement, only the daily smile of the Lord and Master, and who will go through thick and thin, pain and suffering, only to accrue glory to the Lord." But she also wove in humor, as when she referred to her nurses having to care not only for several babies at once but also "several crotchety old women besides," or when she exclaimed, "Is it not worse than pulling teeth out of a person to get money out of some people's pockets?"[14]

Balancing Autonomy and Dependency

Upon her 1909 return to China, Shi had the funds to expand her hospital, build a new home for herself and Hughes that was considered more in line with her standing as a leader in the mission community, and build a home for her nurses, increasing the comfort of these workers so essential to the success of her hospital.[15]

By this time, according to missionary sources, Shi Meiyu had received offers from the Chinese government to run a government hospital, at three times the salary she was receiving as a missionary for the

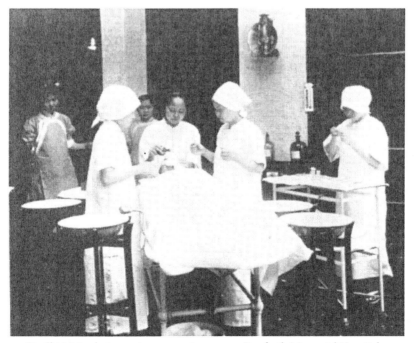

3-2 Dr. Shi Meiyu between two nurses in surgery, Danforth Memorial Hospital, Jiujiang, Jiangxi, c. 1909

Methodist Episcopal Board. She declined these offers due to her commitment to running a specifically Christian medical institution and her wish to continue her affiliation with the WFMS. Because she chose to run a mission hospital rather than a government hospital, however, the hospital was largely dependent on foreign funds. So on the one hand, Shi Meiyu was one of the earliest and most active advocates for Chinese Christians working to financially support the Chinese church. American missionaries referred to the Jiujiang churches as leaders in self-support, and this was largely because of Shi's influence. Yet on the other hand, for major projects such as expanding her hospital, Shi needed the funds of Americans interested in foreign missions.

This would seem to be at odds with her insistence on Chinese control. Yet while American money funded much of Shi's medical work, she emphasized in her mission reports that her work was run exclusively by Chinese women and also suggested that the most important element in the success of any mission work were devoted workers, rather than funds. In a 1913 article she acknowledged that money and equipment were important, but concluded that attracting and retaining skilled people to do the work was by far the most crucial element in the effectiveness of any mission institution. Shi used her own nurses as a primary example.[16] While mission literature by American missionaries often portrayed Chinese as reliant on American help and guidance, Shi's writing focused rather on the skills and effectiveness of her Chinese nurses, subtly making the point that money and equipment would be worth nothing without committed Chinese workers.

Acceptance and Expansion

Shi's medical practice continued to grow after her return in 1909, but expanded at a much sharper rate after the 1911 Revolution. With the establishment of the Republic of China, Western medicine (and education) became broadly accepted in urban areas. At the same time, Chinese Christians in general experienced greater societal acceptance. Both these factors may have contributed to the increased demands for the services of Shi and her nurses. By 1912, the number of patients seen rose quickly to over fifteen thousand, and by 1915, Shi and her nurses saw close to twenty-five thousand.

While Western medicine had become predominant in urban areas, many people in rural areas did not have access to this kind of medical care. Traditional Chinese folk healers could often provide effective medical care, but in many rural areas of China there was a high infant mortality rate. In response to what she viewed as the needs of rural China, Shi began a program of sending out "nurse evangelists" to the countryside. While the Rockefeller Foundation had become involved in spreading Western medicine in China in 1914, their focus was on producing a cadre of elite physicians, most of whom would serve in urban areas.[17] Shi Meiyu, on the other hand, began a program of sending nurses out to areas with no access to Western medicine to perform simple but sometimes lifesaving surgeries, dispense medicine, give vaccinations, and help with difficult deliveries.

While the period immediately following the 1911 Revolution was a time of great growth, Shi also faced difficult challenges. One was the issue of her own health: the strain of running her rapidly growing medical practice caused her to experience three breakdowns of her health during this period, which all required a period of bed rest. The second issue was the introduction of "scientific medicine." Increasingly, even in the mission field in China, good training for nurses included more scientific subjects, such as physics and chemistry. Running a dispensary, hospital, and a nursing school at the same time, Shi lacked the time to provide that kind of training. To keep her training up-to-date, Shi needed more help.

She found this help in one of her nurses, Lillian Wu. The Knowles Bible School, run by Hughes, began to offer physics and chemistry (quite unusual for a Bible school), and Shi had Wu attend the school. This training prepared Wu for one of the Rockefeller nursing scholarships to begin study in 1916 at the nursing school of The Johns Hopkins University in Baltimore. At the same time, Shi Meiyu arranged to do some postgraduate work at The Johns Hopkins School of Medicine, which her younger sister Phoebe was also attending. The plan upon return was for Lillian to run the nursing school at Danforth while Phoebe and Shi Meiyu worked together to run the hospital and dispensary.[18]

Breaking Ties

This plan was never fully implemented. Phoebe and Lillian did return to run Danforth in 1919, while Shi Meiyu and Jennie Hughes were still in the United States attending a Methodist conference. The event proved to be a major turning point for them. Owing to disagreements with the WFMS board, Shi Meiyu and Jennie Hughes resigned from the WFMS at this time. Neither side was willing to forthrightly discuss the exact nature of these disagreements, but surviving letters between Hughes and the WFMS indicate that the immediate issue was Hughes's refusal to sign a statement saying that she would let the WFMS decide the curriculum of the Knowles School. The demand undoubtedly stemmed from WFMS discomfort over including the study of chemistry and physics in a school for Bible Women, subjects that were usually reserved for missionary high schools. After Hughes resigned, Shi Meiyu did so as well, citing how "intertwined" their work had become.[19] It is not surprising that Shi Meiyu would find the WFMS determination to set the curriculum at Knowles disturbing, given how important the training in science had been to some of Shi's nurses, most notably Lillian Wu.

Other issues that came out later included the rejection by Shi and Hughes of what they interpreted as the "modernist" theology of the Methodist Episcopal Board. In the 1920s, a split occurred between "modernism" and "fundamentalism" in churches worldwide, which proved to be a huge setback for much missionary work in China. Another source of disagreement was how the funds raised by Shi and Hughes should be spent. Shi particularly was a compelling fundraiser, and Hughes later indicated that the WFMS had diverted some of the funds raised by Shi for her work to other WFMS projects.[20]

Regardless of the reasons, it was a bitter break that essentially gutted Danforth Hospital in Jiujiang, as most of the nursing students followed Shi Meiyu when she left. Yet the institution did remain in Chinese hands, run by a Chinese woman who had just graduated from Shi's alma mater, the University of Michigan, with a medical degree.[21]

Bethel Mission

Shi and Hughes moved to Shanghai, where they opened the Bethel Mission in 1920. In spite of the trauma and difficulties of leaving the medical institution she had built up over twenty-five years, the opening of Bethel presented Shi Meiyu with new opportunities to pursue broader interests and goals. The new mission consisted of a Bible school led by Hughes and a hospital and nursing school led by Shi.

The Bible school became well known for the "Bethel Bands," small groups that traveled around China evangelizing (including evangelizing foreigners.) In the modernist/fundamentalist feud that was polarizing the mission community in China, Bethel came down firmly on the fundamentalist side, emphasizing personal, often emotional, conversion experiences and rejecting any kind of cultural relativism.

Bethel literature, largely written by Hughes but clearly influenced by Shi, emphasized fostering Chinese Christian leadership for church and society. This had been an important theme in all of Shi's life and work, reflected not only in the way she ran her nursing school, but also in her many other activities. She was the founding president of the Chinese Woman's Christian Temperance Association and a cofounder of the Chinese Missionary Society, a group that aimed to send Chinese missionaries to parts of China rarely visited by Western missionaries, such as the southwestern frontier. Bethel, as a nondenominational institution not under the control of a foreign mission board, gave her new scope to pursue her goal of developing a church led by Chinese.[22]

The hospital began simply, but Shi continually raised funds for improvement, a high point being when she received a gift of an X-ray machine in the early 1930s. The nursing school reflected Shi's commitment to both medicine and Christian missions, as all the nurses attended mandatory Bible classes. The goal was to expand the training of nurse-evangelists that had begun at Danforth, with nurses going out into rural areas where no Western medical care was currently available and becoming primary health care providers. Shi's vision for her nurses reflected the fusion of her nationalism and evangelism: the nurses would strengthen China by ministering to the health of the rural populations, while at the same time acting as evangelists. It is difficult to estimate how many of her students embraced Shi Meiyu's entire vision.

However, her school grew rapidly: by 1928 she had 137 students, while by the 1930s over 200 nursing students enrolled in the school.[23]

In 1928 Bethel faced a challenge to this fusion of nationalism and evangelism. The new Nationalist (Kuomintang) government mandated that all mission schools have a Chinese head and make religious instruction optional rather than mandatory. For Shi's nursing school, the first requirement obviously posed no problem, but regarding the second, Bethel leaders decided to continue to require religious instruction for nursing students, even though this meant sacrificing the benefits of government registration. Bethel's official publication explained that since the Chinese government could now establish its own educational institutions without foreign help, the only rationale for a mission school was to incorporate Christianity into its curriculum. It is perhaps a mark of Shi Meiyu's popularity that Soong Mei-ling, Chiang Kai-shek's wife, still wrote an official statement praising Bethel.[24] While it is uncertain how this decision not to register may have affected enrollment, the student body continued to grow into the 1930s.

Later Years and Legacy

In 1937, while Shi Meiyu and Jennie Hughes were on a fundraising trip overseas, Bethel Mission was destroyed in the Japanese attacks on east China. Shi and Hughes then settled in the United States, where they lived for the rest of their lives. Shi Meiyu focused on evangelical work during this last phase of her life, opening new Bethel Missions, devoted to producing evangelists, in both Pasadena, California, and in Hong Kong. (These are still in existence today.) Hughes helped to promote these missions until her death in 1951. Shi Meiyu died within two years, in 1953.

Shi Meiyu's legacy is wide-ranging. As one of the first Chinese women physicians trained in the West, she served as an inspiration to other Chinese women to enter the medical field. (In the early-to-mid-twentieth century, the profession of physician in China in fact had more female representation than in the United States.) She was one of the earliest physicians in China to develop a plan to reach rural areas with some of the benefits of modern medical care. To people today, she may seem to embody contradictions: devoted to Chinese control yet extensively fundraising in the United States, committed to incorporating the latest medical developments but also embracing Christian fundamentalism rather than modernism, supportive of Chinese nationalism yet refusing to register her nursing school with the new Chinese government in order to maintain mandatory religious instruction. To Shi Meiyu herself, however, her goals were consistent: to establish a vibrant Christian church in China that would be controlled by Chinese Christians but also to work in partnership as part of a broader international Christian community.

FAN ZIMEI

Between Tradition and Modernity

by Fuk-Tsang Ying

In November 1939, an obituary was issued by the executive board of China's Young Men's Christian Association (YMCA), expressing deep grief in remembrance of a long-time staff member:

> Mr. Fan Zimei, a scholar with profuse knowledge, joined the publications department of the YMCA in 1911. He has been the chief editor of two monthly magazines, namely *Jinbu* [Progress] and *Qingnian Jinbu* [Association Progress]. With his profound writing ability, he educated and inspired youth according to our "four-fold program" (body, mind, spirit, social relations), so that our campaign could enjoy swift development through the expression of words. In 1935, at the age of 70, having served our organization for twenty-five years, Mr. Fan retired and led a life of seclusion into his eighties. He suddenly passed away on 10th September this year, and words can hardly express our grief. Mr. Fan was industrious in his studies, and he was particularly interested in classical works. In his early years, he was so hard-working at school that he became famous in the academic field. In middle age, he received the Gospel and became a Christian, and he kept the Christian teaching in his heart, remaining devoted into old age. Such virtue deserves to be an example for

youth. We would like to dedicate these few words to acknowledge Mr. Fan's moral conduct.[1]

The important moments in the life of Fan Zimei (1866–1939) illustrate how a pioneering Christian journalist navigated the changing political tides between two centuries and shaped the interaction between Eastern and Western civilizations. Fan's mental outlook passed from "old, traditional knowledge" to "new knowledge" and then to a Christian belief that also reflected Confucianism. His intellectual and psychological experiences reveal how much an individual's beliefs and thoughts can change in an era of tremendous social change.

The Young Scholar

Fan Zimei (also known as T. M. Fan, Fan Bihui, or Fan Yi) was born in Suzhou in a traditional family of Confucian scholars and officials.[2] At the age of five, he and his father migrated to Shanghai, where they lived with Zimei's uncle's family. Highly intelligent from childhood, within a few years he became familiar with the Chinese classics under the tutelage of his uncle. He passed the first level of the imperial examinations at the very early age of thirteen, earning a reputation as a "young *xiucai*" [holder of an elementary academic degree who had no right to minor official appointment] and attained the *juren* degree (with the right to minor official appointment) in 1893 at the age of twenty-eight. By that time, he had extensively studied the Neo-Confucian philosophy of the Song and Ming dynasties. Thus Chinese traditional knowledge was deeply imprinted in his mind.

Concerned with practical and technological issues, however, Fan also read a lot of translated works from the West, published by the school attached to the Jiangnan Arsenal in Shanghai. Although he lived in an era when success in society was possible only through the imperial examinations, Fan himself despised people who learned only the stereotyped writings necessary for passing the exams. When he was unable to pass the final level of examinations, he decided to discontinue this pursuit and instead to serve as a teacher in Suzhou.

At the age of twenty, Fan married a Miss Zhang in Suzhou. Later, they had two sons, Fan Zhiqiu and Fan Jinhuai.

From Confucianism to Christianity

The tides of radical reform surged dramatically after China's defeat in the 1895 Sino-Japanese War. The shock of military defeat by a quickly modernized Japan, traditionally a subordinate neighbor, disclosed the impotence of the imperial order, and Confucian tradition was challenged. Sharing widespread patriotic concern for saving the country, Fan was greatly affected, and he was disturbed when the traditionalists at court were unable to respond to the urgent needs of the era. At the age of thirty, he switched his loyalty to the reformers' camp led by the young emperor, which urged a full-scale restructuring of the empire along the lines of Japan's new constitutional monarchy.

After the Empress Dowager abruptly terminated the Hundred Days' Reform in September 1898, Fan again experienced a great change, this time more in his action than in his thinking. Formerly a passive observer of events, he returned to Shanghai, the center of reform thinking, and threw himself into public activism. The mass media became an important platform to promote his reform ideas. He took up the posts of reporter and editor in various local newspapers. In the process, Fan developed skills and experience in journalism and broadened his vision to foreign affairs.

Support from the imperial court for the antiforeign Boxer Uprising, followed by military humiliation at the hands of the allied Western powers, was yet another great blow to Fan's hopes for progress. Afterward, he was very disheartened with state affairs.

In 1901, Fan met Young J. Allen (1836–1907), a Southern Methodist missionary in Shanghai. Allen had founded the missionary journal *Jiaohui xinbao* (Church News) in 1868, which was renamed *Wanguo gongbao* (Globe magazine) in 1874 and was the main outlet for the Society for the Diffusion of Christian and General Knowledge among the Chinese (SDK). Allen and the magazine, along with Timothy Richard, another prominent British missionary and the secretary of SDK, had exercised great influence on the Hundred Days' Reform.[3] The journal continued to be quite popular, providing interested Chinese with ideas on Western political systems, science, commerce, education, and Christianity.[4]

Through his acquaintance with Allen, Fan started to appreciate more than just Western technology, expanding his interest to Western institutions and then Western religion. Fan said,

> Mr. Young J. Allen studied European and American religions, academics, politics and cultures and he has changed my thoughts enormously. I have always considered what we used to study as mechanical—the study of Song learning is decadent, while that of Han learning is fragmented. Now Mr. Allen opens my eyes towards the world, inspires me with the profundity of nature and fills me with the spirit of equality, freedom and fraternity. The Western civilization is truly admirable, and I am lucky to have met this wonderful man.[5]

In 1902, Fan and his whole family (mother, wife, and two sons) were baptized. He became the editor of *Globe* magazine, as well as one of Allen's most important Chinese associates in his later years.

Fan turned to Christianity partly due to his strong desire to find an effective response to the cultural and institutional crisis in China. Before the Sino-Japanese War in 1895, he had been deeply affected by traditional thought, even while he was not satisfied with the imperial examination system and had become inclined toward practical knowledge. At that time, the "West" he admired was Western technology, which would not directly affect his belief in Chinese tradition. After 1895, however, Fan experienced intellectual chaos and psychological stress; he started to seek a totally new order and a new way for China. At that time he showed his discontent with the traditions and classics, and his adoration of Western culture. Through reform, he believed a new political and social order could be established.

Upon the failure of the Hundred Days' Reform and the tragic outbreak of the Boxer Uprising, Fan totally rejected all tradition, as he believed that would be the only way for China to gain wealth and power. As he tried to find a new way to strengthen and modernize China, he discerned a causal relationship between Western institutions and Western religion (Christianity). Fan believed that Christianity would be the only salvation for "himself and four hundred million fellow citizens."[6] In other words, Fan's ultimate concern was how to save the country, and this was the main reason for his shift from Confucianism to Christianity. What Fan faced was not just a crisis of political order, but a far deeper crisis—a crisis of fundamental orientation.[7]

Counterposing Christian and Confucian Civilizations

The crisis at the turn of the century delegitimized the previous paradigm and opened up possibilities for new conceptions. However, for Fan the question remained, why should Christianity, but not other thoughts or faiths, become the new paradigm? Why should Christianity be the only faith, rather than just one of many frameworks for reference?

Fan considered the causal relationship between Christianity and the West's prosperity and strength. Fan thought that Western religion was the critical prerequisite for modernization (which included the arts, technology, and political systems):

> Why has the West become wealthy and powerful? It is because of its politics and knowledge. The strength in politics lies in the constitution, and the strength in knowledge lies in the technology. This is true, and I am aware of the origin of such strengths. The origin is in the Christian true civilization. . . . Jesus Christ is the true civilization.[8]

In Fan's mind, China failed in all its previous reforms because all of them were "hypocritical but not practical," and none of them recognized that the genuine root of Western civilization was Christianity.[9]

In asserting that Christianity was the essence and root of Western civilization, Fan also placed Confucianism in a contradictory position, calling it a "false civilization." The process of pursuing the "true civilization" was at the same time a matter of eradicating "false civilization." The negative influence of Confucianism had turned China into a despotic state with a despotic family system. The backwardness of China, with its inequality and slavery, was deeply rooted in Confucianism.[10]

Fan observed that the failures of Chinese reform movements were due to the lack of "true civilization" and the obstruction by "false civilization." Thus, the growth of China depended on the acceptance of "true civilization" and the realization that all Western knowledge and institutions were rooted in Christianity. Purging the old Confucian tradition was necessary for China to leave behind its poverty and weakness.

In the eyes of Fan Zimei, Christianity was the key to China's wealth and power, and traditions were of no use. No matter whether on a transcendental or empirical level, forfeiting the Confucian traditions and turning to Jesus Christ would be the only way out for the Chinese.

Between Old and New

At the age of forty, Fan began to work toward his goal of national wealth and power guided by new principles. There were considerable differences between Fan's work in his earlier days and his work now at *Globe* magazine. During the Hundred Days' Reform, the Western knowledge Fan Zimei promoted for China was mainly Western institutions. After the reform failed, however, Fan came to believe that wealth and power depend on the level of enlightenment of a country, which in turn requires the popularization of knowledge. He believed that popular literacy and freedom were the soul of any effort to set up constitutional government.[11]

Fan's endeavor reflected the increasing emphasis in the early twentieth century of Chinese intellectuals on the work of "enlightenment" and "civilization."[12] Scholars thought China's progress would require the functional equivalent of the Western Enlightenment. The uniqueness of Fan was his affirmation of the role of religion in the process of enlightenment. He believed that opening the hearts and minds of the ignorant must be started from the "inside" working to the "outside," from the heart and mind to social behavior. Only by relying on the root of Christian civilization could China's enlightenment then be successful.[13]

Though Fan Zimei broke from Chinese tradition and turned toward Christian civilization, all his works and concerns in the previous thirty years were not completely abandoned. Fan pursued his continuing commitment to Chinese wealth and power through his new adopted path, navigating his way between old and new. Fan pursued his goal in two practical channels: mass media and popular education.

The news media served as Fan Zimei's medium of enlightenment. First, when he joined *Globe* magazine, he pointed out that printed newspapers and periodicals were the "public textbooks of society," which allowed everyone from every social group to learn. Also, Fan claimed that publications had an important interlocking relationship with the wealth and power of a country.[14]

Thus, after 1905, Fan Zimei started the *General Knowledge News* to share information about history, geography, mathematics, science, and English with Confucian scholars, who now were unable to enter the new modern schools once the imperial examination system was abolished.[15]

Fan realized, however, that whether the news media could achieve these goals depended on the popularization of education. So he also started the Zhenhua ("save China") School to promote popular education among the illiterate. Fan inherited the Confucian idea that habit was essential to the building of personality. Timothy Richard recommended a young beggar fourteen years old to enroll in this school. Unfortunately, this boy was eventually expelled after two years of learning because of his deep-rooted bad habits. Even then, Fan affirmed the significance of youth education.[16]

Fan also taught in the McTyeire School for Girls of Shanghai for ten years. The school was started by Young J. Allen in 1892. Its educational goal was to give girls the capacity to understand both Chinese and American cultural traditions and to learn how to serve in both societies.[17] Allen's book *Woman in All Lands* was an important work advocating the equality of women in status and rights.

Fan's close relationship with Allen undoubtedly opened his eyes on the issue of women's rights and he became a pioneer in female education among the Chinese Christian community. Fan believed that the weakness of China was partly rooted in the custom of suppressing women:

> Now there are 400 million people in China, and 200 million are women leading a quiet and isolated life, having no education, no knowledge and no experience. . . . Alas! How petty our nation's status seems if we disregard half of the people in the whole country! It is impossible to ask for any revival in culture, improvement in customs, progress of society or even sustainability of the country.[18]

To Fan, female education was a key part of enlightenment that could break down the barriers and suppression facing women in the Chinese traditional order and eventually bring China wealth and power. He believed wholeheartedly that rescuing people was the first step in reviving the whole country (through national acceptance of "true civilization"), and freedom of women would be the key to the salvation of people.[19]

Actually, the elaboration of Fan on the relationship between the true (Christian) civilization and wealth and power of a country had great similarities to the Statecraft (*jingshi*) school in Confucianism.

In a moment of national crisis, Fan showed his strong hatred of Neo-Confucianism (Song learning) and the philological studies of the classical texts (Han learning). However, the Confucian conception of statecraft that emphasized practicality (*zhiyong*) was still an important core value that dominated Fan's thinking. It led him not only to discard the impractical Han and Song schools of thought but also led him to discover the practical value of Christian civilization in reviving the culture and country.

Moreover, though Fan Zimei had turned from Confucianism to Christianity, he retained the Confucian ideal of "inner sagehood, outer king" (*neisheng waiwang*), because it was similar to Christian philosophy. The difference was in the content. Inner sagehood traditionally referred to Confucian ethical self-cultivation, whereas Fan reinterpreted it as Christian civilization. To a certain extent, even while Fan, as a Christian torchbearer, had consciously abandoned his old paradigm and claimed to have broken with Confucianism, the statecraft idea of Confucianism was still affecting him. In reality, he was a Chinese Christian caught between old and new.

Saving the Country through Character Building

With the 1911 Revolution, the imperial Qing dynasty was replaced by the Republic of China. To Fan Zimei personally, the year 1911 was also a major turning point in his career. At the invitation of American YMCA Secretary Fletcher S. Brockman, head of the national YMCA in China, Fan joined its publications department as editor in chief of *Jinbu* (Progress), which in March 1917 merged with *Qingnian* (China's Young Men) to form the *Qingnian jinbu* (Association Progress). Fan Zimei continued to serve as editor in chief until the periodical ceased publication in 1932. Fan retired in 1935 at the age of seventy.

Ten years at the Christian Literature Society for China and *Globe* magazine had been the first phase of Fan Zimei's career in journalism, and ten more at the YMCA and *Association Progress* were to be the last phase. In those two decades, Fan steadily broadened his horizon in exploring paths for China to gain prosperity and strength, yet his major concern remained unchanged.

The YMCA leadership attributed all problems in China during that era to the weakness of human character and ethics, and believed that "Christianized character" (*jiduhua renge*) was the ultimate way to solve the problems. Fan Zimei not only wholeheartedly agreed but also experienced deeper self-reflection when he first heard the YMCA's slogan, "saving the country through character building" (*renge jiuguo*).

Fan realized that, in a society composed of the total sum of different individuals, how individuals think and act would have great influence on society.[20] Although the imperial monarchy had been overthrown and replaced by the Republic, the Chinese were still struggling to construct a democratic state. China had a republic in form, but no real democracy: "Oh! Even eight years after the establishment of the Republic of China, the people's ideas still have not changed. How can they understand the principles of "democracy" and "republic," so as to realize a real Republic of China?"[21]

In order to abolish corrupt thoughts and get rid of the root mentality of "slave citizens," Fan urged society to improve "citizen standards" through the cultivation of ethics, knowledge, and physical constitution. He believed that the task of the YMCA was to help China educate citizens with higher standards in terms of spirit (*de*), mind (*zhi*), body (*ti*), and social relations (*qun*). In Fan's eyes, this fundamental task of the YMCA movement reflected the sacrificial spirit of Jesus Christ.[22] In the first issue of *Association Progress*, Fan expressed his expectation for both the journal and the YMCA:

> *Association Progress* is actually the progress of the YMCA in full form. The YMCA has been established in China for twenty-two years. In my previous arguments, I asserted that government was the mechanism above the nation, while association was the mechanism below it. Even if the politics of the government is thorough and well constructed, its power may not reach everything, for example, the human mind and customs, which cannot be effectively influenced without good associations as the mechanism below. The *weakness* of our country today is not only the responsibility of the government, but also the result of the people's reluctance to establish proper association. Isolated government is the result of scattered community and the people's unwillingness to assist the rulers, and those who can work out something are rare. Alas! This is why the YMCA wishes to

come out and to take up the task for the time being when no one is yet willing to do the job.[23]

Fan's reflections on "character salvation" basically stemmed from the core values of the YMCA movement, one of which was citizen education. However, Fan addressed this within the traditional statecraft framework of "inner sagehood, outer king." Christianized character replaced moral perfection as the prerequisite for nation building and social reconstruction.

The Forming of a "New Society"

Based on the foundation of Christianized character, Fan believed, a new society along the lines of the Christian ideal of the "Kingdom of God" should then be constructed.[24] However, given that actual societies comprised complex systems and organizations, how could an individual actually participate in creating the new society?

Fan emphasized that in the forming of a new society, people should address every kind of issue, whether related to family, marriage, sex and children, labor conditions, or international relations and war.[25] Fan produced special issues of the magazine to arouse the Christian community to acknowledge the significance of these matters. Fan did not reduce these issues to purely moral problems, but instead admitted that each issue had its unique nature and structure.

One of the most important issues that Fan discussed frequently was the labor question. Facing the serious disputes between labor and capitalists in the 1920s, he tried to hold a balanced view. On the one hand, he criticized the exploitative acts of the capitalists, while on the other, he opposed the riotous behavior of the workers. He advocated cooperation between the two. Moreover, he showed his concern over the illiteracy of the uneducated workers and advocated a re-education plan for them.[26]

Cooperation in the international family was another issue that Fan discussed often. Although China suffered under the unequal treaties and was not treated as an equal by the Western powers, Fan still upheld the Confucian ideal of "grand unity" (*da tong*). He believed that the peaceful nature of Chinese civilization harnessed to the tolerant nature of Christian civilization could make a contribution to the contemporary world.[27] In 1928 he stated that "from now on in China any political movement, irrespective of its party affiliations, will probably find it necessary, in order to succeed, to be founded on the principle of *da tong*. This, too, will be the solution of all international difficulties."[28]

Rejuvenation of National Essence and Indigenization of Christianity

In the late Qing period, Fan Zimei had strongly opposed Confucianism, discarding it as a false civilization and the major obstacle to the progress of China. However, Fan's intellectual ideas changed in the 1920s. He became actively involved in an intellectual movement for the rejuvenation of national culture, with a clear distinction drawn between "national essences"(*guo cui*) and "national diseases"(*guo gu*).[29]

Why did Fan change his mind and again affirm some of the traditional values of Confucianism? The main reason was his change of attitude toward Western civilization. As stated above, Fan Zimei's conversion to Christianity was the result of his intellectual and religious response to the cultural and national crisis when China faced the West. His Christian identity reflected a practical orientation based on the fact that Western/Christian civilization had proven its superiority to Confucianism. However, the savagery of World War I in Europe revealed the substantial weaknesses and deficiencies of Western civilization. Fan, together with many other Chinese intellectuals, was disillusioned with the so-called superiority of the West.

Furthermore, the Paris settlement and the Treaty of Versailles, which left Shandong under Japanese control, outraged the Chinese people and exposed the total self-interest of the Western powers. After the May Fourth Movement burst out in protest against the betrayal of China's sovereign rights, Fan wrote, "The preservation of national essence is the preservation of a country's spiritual lifeline. The preservation of national essence will do no harm to the progress of the country, and the preservation is by no means a total rejection of the espousal of other cultures."[30]

Fan criticized the mission schools in China for emphasizing the study of English and neglecting the study of Chinese.[31] In order to re-think the values of Chinese civilization, in 1923 Fan began preparations for an "Institute of National Learning." What he meant by "national learning" (*guoxue*) was the treasures of Chinese heritage that were being summarily rejected in the process of Westernization.[32] In January 1924, Fan announced the institute's establishment as the "Society of Chinese Learning" (*Zhongguo wenhua xuehui*), for which the *Association Progress* then became an important intellectual platform. Fan explained in an editorial that the journal would change its old policy of emphasizing the introduction of Western civilization by placing equal emphasis on studying Chinese values and culture, in order to synthesize the two.[33]

Fan's idea of rejuvenation of national essence not only reflected his reaffirmation of the valuable heritage of traditional culture but also revealed his effort to distinguish between Western civilization and Christianity. Thereafter, the relationship between Christianity and tra-ditional Chinese culture became a key issue for investigation.

The Anti-Christian Movement of 1922 convinced Fan of the ur-gency of reforming church structure and advancing doctrine, which would constitute the basic elements of an indigenous Christian church. The rejuvenation of national essence was thereby integrated with Fan's thinking about the indigenization of Christianity. In 1929, he published *Wo de xin Yesu guan* (My concept of belief in Jesus), which emphasized a "Sinicized Jesus" (*Zhongguohua Yesu*). "If Christ cannot be Sinicized, China cannot be Christianized," he concluded.[34]

Fan's effort to construct an indigenous Confucian Christianity was affirmed by some western missionaries at the time. In 1928, David W. Lyon, in the *Chinese Recorder*, cited Fan's viewpoint that the followers of Jesus in China can "take the underlying conceptions of Heaven and the Ruler Above, which the Chinese have, and enrich them until they stand for the Christian concept of a Heavenly Father, who cherishes a loving concern in the highest welfare of all His creatures."[35]

By the late 1920s, Fan had changed his view on the relationship be-tween Christianity and Chinese culture. He no longer portrayed them as mutually exclusive, but instead emphasized mutual complementa-rity and coordination between the two as the essence of indigenized Christianity.

The Way to China's Modernization

The life of Fan Zimei showed his ultimate concern for the pursuit of prosperity, strength, and modernity in China. In the late nineteenth century, Fan came to know and approve of Western civilization and even viewed the West as equal to modernity. His embrace of modernity had inevitably led him to criticize tradition, and even totally reject its value. In the meantime, in his exploration of the West as a model for China, Fan had discovered the relationship between the West and Christianity, and thus considered the Christian West to be the perfect paradigm. By embracing such a paradigm, Fan had broken his ties to tradition, joined forces with proponents of Christian values, and tried to bring China to modernity through enlightenment.

But as it turned out, the traditions Fan had rejected were only the outdated Han and Song learning. The practical school of Confucianism and its statecraft ideal were still hidden in his thinking and became a leading element of his Christian faith.

The experience of World War I stimulated Fan to rethink the values of East and West. He started to question the "myth of the perfect West," and his "perfect paradigm" collapsed. He rethought his assumption that Western civilization could be identified with Christian civilization in a direct cause-and-effect relationship. At that time, Christianity remained his framework of reference to criticize, diagnose, and reform China's current situation, but tradition was becoming another useful paradigm to criticize or check and balance the West. Living between the two paradigms, Fan on the one hand reaffirmed the contribution of Christianity for enlightenment and "saving the country through character building," while on the other hand, he returned to Chinese tradition by promoting rejuvenation of national essence as a supplement for Christianity and the resulting indigenous Christianity as the path to world unity.

Fan Zimei's Retirement, Death, and Ongoing Legacy

In 1935, Fan retired from the YMCA at the age of seventy. In order to acknowledge Fan Zimei's contribution, a ceremonial farewell dinner was held by the YMCA board. The climax of the dinner was the

4-1 Fan Zimei

presentation of a special testimonial to Fan. It was a silver bowl en-
graved with the words "Famous Mountain, Great Task" (*mingshan
weiye*), which symbolized a high commendation of the achievements of
Fan in climbing the "mountain" of China's deep cultural crisis.

Fan's life in retirement was full of unrest. Manchuria had already
been occupied by Japanese troops, and the Nationalist government
was on the verge of war with Japan. After the outbreak of war in 1937,
Japanese troops rapidly occupied Shanghai. China was in a struggle for
national survival.

The burden of national crisis seemed too heavy for a seventy-year-
old man. Fan experienced deep grief over China's national tragedy. In
September 1939, Fan died in Shanghai at the age of seventy-three.

The life of Fan Zimei unfolded at the turn of the century when
coastal China was on the boundaries between East and West, old and
new, and the Qing empire gave way to the Republic of China. This was a

time of cultural clashes, interaction, and mutual influence. His choices regarding Chinese tradition and Christianity, and his changing views of both, reflected his life effort to integrate East and West. At a time of grave national danger, Fan Zimei the intellectual showed his concern for the country and its people and optimistically sought to implement his own way to achieve the country's prosperity and strength. His career and ambition are best described as "Confucian Christian."

Did Fan's life make a difference in China? His dreams for nation building based on the dual heritage of Chinese tradition and Christian civilization was an unaccomplished task. Moreover, his lifelong intellectual quest for an integration of East and West was a long and difficult pilgrimage. In 1927, Fan made a self-examination at the age of sixty-one: "I am old, but I feel that there are so many missions unaccomplished that I have not given up on enlightening the world. I do hope that today's youth can earnestly seize the day to strive for progress."[36]

The construction of a modernized China and an autonomous indigenous church were the lifelong goals and visions of Fan. However, neither China nor the Chinese church, still under mission control, could achieve these goals by the time Fan left this world in 1939. How deeply does Fan's unaccomplished mission echo in the hearts of young Chinese and Christians today?

5

DING SHUJING
The YWCA Pathway for China's "New Women"

by Elizabeth A. Littell-Lamb

"I as a Chinese woman must do it."

With these words thirty-three-year-old Ding Shujing accepted a challenging invitation to become the Young Women's Christian Association's (YWCA) associate national general secretary in 1923.[1] Ding spoke with conviction, but also with hesitation, since she had initially declined the promotion, her third in as many years. She probably was feeling pressured by national general secretary Rosalee Venable, who was determined to have Ding succeed her. But in the end, Ding recognized the need for Chinese women to step forward and embrace public service: "I have no right to keep refusing to take these positions of responsibility when you have asked these same things of the foreign secretaries in China, and I as a Chinese woman must do it."[2]

Ding did not serve as associate national general secretary for long. The following year, the YWCA sent her to America for advanced training, and before that training was even completed, Venable resigned to clear a path for the YWCA to be led by one of China's outstanding "new women." Ding made that pathway her own through her broad religious tolerance, her confidence in the collective power of women, and her commitment to building a world community. These characteristics defined a life that bridged traditional and modern China, and one that endured revolution, renaissance, and war.

The Pathway to Womanhood, 1890–1916

Ding Shujing (1890–1936) was born in February 1890 in Linqing in western Shandong Province.[3] Her family welcomed the birth of the first girl in several generations. She had at least one brother, probably older, as he predeceased her. Her parents, who had been devout Buddhists, converted to Christianity when Ding was ten or twelve. Why they did so is not known, although ensuring an education for their children provides one possible motive. Ding attended mission schools, first in Dezhou and later in Tongzhou.

Ding's spiritual journey began when she was a child. As she recounted to a colleague years later, one night when she was around six years old she awoke to see her mother kneeling in prayer before a small Buddhist altar, lamenting her inability to go on a pilgrimage. Ding recalled that as she watched her mother's face in the candlelight, she experienced "a feeling of awe and worship, and a sense of inner life" that she never lost.[4] That moment was the genesis of her broad religious tolerance, grounded in a "sense of inner life" centered on faith in Christ but transcending religious boundaries. As incumbent YWCA national general secretary three decades later, Ding would insist that Western secretaries sent to China have a deep-rooted Christian faith but also appreciate the truth in other religions.[5]

Ding's open-mindedness enabled her to relate the fundamental truths found in the Confucian tradition to Christianity and the modern world. In a YWCA brochure published shortly after she assumed office, Ding quoted Confucius: "When the Great Way prevails, the world belongs to all. Men of great virtue and talent are elected who will cultivate mutual trust and promote universal understanding. Thus, men do not regard as their parents only their own parents, nor treat as their children only their own children."[6] She then commented,

The Confucian saying above means that when "the Great Will," that is the will of God, is carried out, the world will belong to all of us, with no dividing lines between us, and we will enjoy a "world state" in peace. The Young Women's Christian Association of China sends greetings to the other national Associations, with this message of our ancient leader which we find fulfilled in Ephesians 2:14 ["He is our bond of peace; he has made the nations one, breaking down the wall that was a barrier between us"]. For if we have the love of Christ, Confucius' prophecy will really be possible.[7]

Ding's faith in Christ centered her and she urged others to search for their own "sense of inner life" through him:

Our first and most important emphasis shall be to study again into the message of Christ for our own lives and to deepen our fellowship with Him and with each other—all in order that we may show forth the power of Christ through our organization.[8]

Ding's words illustrate how her love of Christ influenced her leadership philosophy, particularly her belief in the mission of the YWCA as a community of women who shared religious values and a commitment to world peace.

The decisions she made to pursue higher education and then a career shaped how Ding lived her faith. It is quite possible that the example of her mission schoolteachers inspired her to continue her education and pursue a career in lieu of marriage. By the turn of the century, there was a sharp increase in the number of young single women with professional training entering the mission field.[9] These college-educated women had more in common with Progressive-era reformers than earlier evangelicals. Intentionally or not, they showed impressionable Chinese girls that it was possible to remain single, live independently, and still be fulfilled as a woman. Ding's next step was certainly unusual for a Chinese woman in 1907: she enrolled in North China Union College in Beijing, which was the first Christian college for women in China, sponsored by a union of several denominations.

The college had opened its doors in 1905 amid tremendous challenge and change in Chinese society. It was a tumultuous time for a girl to grow to womanhood. The college's newness, limited resources, and very small cadre of teachers and students limited Ding's education to some extent, yet she was among the first women to graduate from an institution of higher learning in China. Upon her graduation in 1911, she and her classmates joined the ranks of those returning from study abroad, a tiny and elite group of women with modern educations.

Soon after her graduation, China underwent a momentous historical change. On October 10 a minor revolutionary plot in Wuchang provided the spark that finally toppled the Qing court and, with it, two millennia of imperial rule. For women, however, the world remained largely unchanged. The constitutional assembly denied women suffrage and the government school system continued to promote Confucian ideals of womanhood. Marriage rather than career remained women's primary social goal.

Ding, however, never married. It is not known whether her parents had arranged a marriage at some point, although it would have been unusual for them not to have. Since most college-educated women married college-educated men, her options would have narrowed considerably when she graduated. Once she went to work for the Beijing YWCA in 1916, she would have been in a position to meet single YMCA secretaries interested in marrying an educated Christian woman. Yet Westernized Chinese men often sought traditional wives, and Ding was anything but traditional. Perhaps Ding never met a man she considered suitable, or maybe the attractions of a career outweighed the social advantages of marriage. Or, like women in both China and the West, she chose not to marry simply because she now had that choice.

After graduation, Ding taught briefly at a mission school in Shandong. Then in 1914 she accepted a position at the Bridgeman Academy, the middle school associated with her alma mater, North China Union College. When the Academy board appointed her to replace a dismissed foreign teacher, a member of the college's board and longtime China missionary protested vehemently to the college president Luella Minor, claiming the foreign teacher's dismissal was unwarranted and Ding unqualified.[10] Five months later, Ding left the Academy to embark on her life's pathway by joining the staff of the newly organized Beijing city YWCA.[11]

In 1916 the YWCA movement in China was less than two decades old and was growing very slowly.[12] From the time World YWCA general secretary Clarissa Spencer toured China in 1907, the Chinese YWCA considered itself part of the worldwide YWCA movement. World policy insisted that member associations be led by their own nationals. During her tour, Spencer emphasized that "we must make our work as Chinese as possible . . . bringing Chinese women onto the committees as fast as they are ready for the work, calling Chinese secretaries as we can find the suitable women."[13]

This policy shaped the early history of the Chinese YWCA and, at the same time, defined its greatest dilemma: finding suitable Chinese women willing and able to lead lives of public service as lay volunteers or as trained professionals. Occasionally, the Western leadership pressed Chinese women to accept roles for which these women felt unprepared.[14] However, by 1920 the YWCA national committee and many city association boards were led by Chinese lay volunteers, many of whom were prominent civic leaders in their communities. The earliest Chinese secretaries came from the few educated women who chose to work full-time. They learned YWCA techniques by working side-by-side with foreign secretaries. Those with recognizable ability and commitment to the YWCA moved rapidly into leadership positions. Frequently, however, they relented to family pressure to marry and left. Only a few remained committed full-time to the YWCA's pathway for China's "new women." Ding Shujing was one of those. The YWCA would be her final career move: she would work for the YWCA from 1916 until her death twenty years later.

The Pathway to Leadership, 1916–1926

Ding's decision to leave the Bridgeman Academy and go to work for a women's service organization rather than another mission school was indicative of her quiet boldness. Mission schools were semiclosed worlds, safe and respected places to work because they replicated traditional Chinese society with a clear hierarchy, deference for age, and rules of female decorum. The YWCA was a modern institution, run by women for women. The organization chart that mapped out the Association's clear lines of authority and responsibility reflected the most recent thinking in business science, which extolled expertise, initiative, and achievement. Moreover, both the national headquarters and city associations provided women with a space of their own where they could experiment with new roles, learn modern approaches to social problems, and enter the public arena as women activists.

The Beijing YWCA singled out Ding for leadership training, send-ing her to America in 1919 to acquaint her with Association work and to present the "best" of Chinese womanhood to American women as a means of raising funds for China. Despite speaking little English, she traveled extensively, visiting fifty associations and experiencing first-hand the wide variety of Association work. The Beijing city association welcomed Ding home in 1920 as its first Chinese general secretary, although outgoing general secretary Theresa Severin remained as her advisor.[15]

Just as Ding assumed her new duties as head of the Beijing YWCA, national general secretary Grace Coppock identified Ding as the Chinese woman to train to eventually succeed her.[16] Then, in October 1921 Coppock died. The national governing committee selected first-term secretary Rosalee Venable to replace Coppock.[17] The choice was providential, as Venable knew of Coppock's intention and assumed of-fice in 1922 intent on having Ding replace her in time.[18]

Thus began Ding Shujing's meteoric rise. In late 1922 the national committee selected Ding as executive secretary for the first national convention committee. The holding of their first convention and the drafting of a constitution officially identified the Association in China as a Chinese organization run by Chinese women in the eyes of the World YWCA.[19] Only months later the national committee invited her to become associate general secretary and, after equivocating, she ac-cepted, stating, "It is because of your faith in me that I am doing it, and it is mostly because I realize I have no right to keep on refusing to take these positions of responsibility."[20] Then the national committee made Ding acting national general secretary when Venable went on furlough. Soon after, it presented Ding with a scholarship to the YWCA National Training School in New York.[21] They had clearly identified Ding as their future leader. That future, however, was closer than anyone thought.

Venable took advantage of Ding's absence to carry out her plan to have Ding succeed her. In February she peremptorily resigned and used her influence to convince the national committee to appoint Ding Shujing to replace her beginning January 1, 1926.[22] As Venable later wrote,

> I declared my intention of resigning and it seemed easier to the Committee to accept my resignation to take effect as soon as my successor can be found. That leave [sic] the position open, you

see, to call Miss [Ding]. There was not a dissenting note in the whole meeting. Surely if one can trust processes at all we all can have faith that we are being lead [*sic*] in the right way in this decision, and that Miss [Ding] is the right person for this place.[23]

Venable then encouraged YWCA secretaries in China and YWCA leaders in the United States to write and urge Ding to accept, in order to ensure that she would not equivocate this time. And Ding did accept, although not without expressing self-doubts about the awesome task of leading the largest Sino-Western women's organization in China.[24] After a year in the United States, she returned to Shanghai in late 1925.

5-1 Ding Shujing, general secretary of the Chinese YWCA, at national headquarters in Shanghai

Ding was taking the lead of an association dealing with several crises. Shanghai was still reeling from the shooting of antiforeign protesters gathered in front of a police station the previous May.[25] Antiforeign sentiment lent urgency to the organization's internal crisis over the issue of Chinese leadership. Despite the World YWCA policy to make the Association "as Chinese as possible," the transfer of authority to Chinese women had proceeded slowly. The first national convention had been a public declaration of the Association's "Chineseness" and an experience Ding Shujing described as Chinese women's "self-awakening."[26] But some Western secretaries viewed the situation differently. Publication department head Helen Thoburn noted in the Association's 1925 annual report that Western women had "finally" stepped aside and accepted the "chaos" that followed as Chinese women "found their way" as leaders.[27]

There were occasional disagreements, such as the one between prominent Western secretary Lily Haass and Ding in late 1927 over what direction the YWCA industrial program should take. Ding prevailed, leading Haass to express her exasperation to colleagues at the World YWCA headquarters: "To some of us who prefer to do a certain kind of advanced 'constructive' work it may bring a pretty definite choice as to whether we want to follow Chinese leadership . . . or go home!"[28] However, it is clear that by and large, Western secretaries, even powerful ones such as Haass, did give way to Chinese leadership, which was a testimony to the quality of that leadership. In fact, it would be Ding who limited the replacement of Western secretaries with Chinese women because she believed the expertise of Western women was needed and their presence highlighted the international character of the YWCA. To Ding, that was as important as, if not more important than, the Association's "Chineseness."

It was in this climate of change that Ding Shujing became the first Chinese national general secretary. To her own—and perhaps Venable's—surprise, Ding loved her new position. Six months after returning to China, Ding wrote Venable, "You remember that night when I told you how I should hate this job and how you said I had accepted it and I must therefore wait a little while before I made up my mind what to do about it? Well, I am not unhappy in it, I tell you privately I simply adore it!"[29]

Ding Shujing's Pathway for China's New Women, 1926–1936

The year Ding Shujing spent training in the United States provided her with the first opportunities to articulate her vision for the YWCA movement in China and her own ideas on leadership. She spoke of these when she addressed the World YWCA Service Council Meeting at the World's Quinquennial Convention in Washington, D.C., in May 1925. She noted the negative and divisive influence of nationalism in China, no doubt hitting a chord with women who still recalled how narrow European nationalisms had led to the carnage of World War I.

Ding proudly spoke about how the Chinese YWCA promoted international cooperation and friendship. At China's first YWCA national convention, she noted, delegates had voted not to limit membership to Chinese nationals. In addition, she pointed out, there were five nationalities represented on the YWCA staff, making the Association a model world community for others to emulate. "Is this not significant in its emphasis on internationalism? I do believe true international solidarity, which is our goal, can come only when the whole world can act together in a degree of cooperation more close and effective than we have as yet."[30]

She then talked about the spirit of unity and cooperation that came when "women have come to see the power of the group over the individual in accomplishing their desires." The YWCA, she argued, demonstrated the power of the group—and international cooperation—by bringing women of different social standings, different educational status, different religious denominations, and different nationalities together in an effort to develop international understanding.

Ding Shujing was just as articulate when discussing pragmatic issues, such as the recruitment and training of Western secretaries. Not only were Western secretaries necessary for the Chinese YWCA to be seen as a model of international cooperation, but they were also needed to provide expertise and to mentor Chinese secretaries, in short, to help harness the talent and energy of women.

In meetings with the Foreign Division of the YWCA of the USA, Ding insisted that the quality of Western secretaries was of paramount importance. Ding emphasized that a candidate should have a clear understanding of the purpose in her coming to China and understand that she "is not a traveler or a leisurely visitor; she has a real responsibility and business waiting for her there." Ding believed that anyone sent to China should have not only a deep-rooted Christian faith but also a clear understanding of the truth in other religions. A Western secretary should, above all, remain open-minded toward the new things she would experience in China.

She also had specific ideas on how Western secretaries should be trained. First, a new secretary should become thoroughly acquainted with every kind of Christian movement, because the Christian movement in China worked closely with those elsewhere. Next, she should study all kinds of women's movements in America and internationally because "Chinese women today, especially thinking women to whom we would trust our leadership, are very interested in international women's movements." Her third point was that all candidates for China should study comparative religions and the history and philosophy of China. Finally, Ding considered it very advantageous if, before traveling to China, candidates met with Chinese women studying in the United States, because "it is a loss both to us in China and to the Association here not to have close contact with such outstanding Chinese women." At her last meeting she summed up her thoughts with these words:

> In recruiting secretaries I think we should use the scientific way, and not merely propaganda or the emotional way. It should be made clear that in going they enter upon a world task to which they should give themselves wholly both in a study of the needs and in the service. They should go in the spirit of those who feel "The world is my country." I know that these things are already in your minds, but they are so strongly in my heart that I must say them to you in this last meeting with you.[31]

In speaking out so definitively on issues of leadership, Ding Shujing claimed these ideas as her own. They were, however, the product of nearly ten years of involvement in YWCA work, tutelage under two strong leaders, and two trips to the United States.

During her decade of leadership, Ding oversaw the second and third YWCA national conventions, numerous secretaries' conferences and, midway through her tenure, a critical but necessary reevaluation of the YWCA mission to China. Ding also gave YWCA secretaries great latitude in their work and, as a result, in the 1930s both industrial and rural programs established the Association as a force in the lives of Chinese women of all classes.

5-2 The "open door," suggesting new possibilities for women, was a popular YWCA motif

Uniting the Women of Shanghai

Ding's belief in the collective power of women is perhaps nowhere more apparent than in her involvement in the abortive attempt to create a Shanghai women's federation. The genesis of this effort was the resurgence of the women's movement in the wake of the United Front between the Nationalist and Communist parties.[32] In July 1926, the United Front launched a campaign to unify China. Marching from their bases in Guangdong province, the national army challenged the power of the regional warlords. Popular movements arose in the wake of these battles, as peasants, laborers, and women all were mobilized by United Front organizers.

Ding became acquainted with the resurgent women's movement on a trip south. When she returned, she met with local YWCA secretaries, allaying their fears of radicalism and sharing her enthusiasm for this tangible example of the collective power of women. YWCA industrial secretary Eleanor Hinder noted that "had we been a foreign institution" the YWCA would not have had the opportunity to become involved in the women's movement at all. Her final comments, referring directly to Ding, highlighted the opportunity the Association had to reach Chinese women who might have otherwise been leery of a "foreign" institution: "It is an enormous privilege to be under liberal Chinese leadership, and to feel in no way foreign to the spirit."[33]

Hinder's words suggest differing opinions over how the Association should position itself in relation to a women's movement with a political agenda, but they also testify to Ding's ability to allay fears and bring about consensus. Hinder's closing comment about being under "liberal Chinese leadership" is also telling. Most women on YWCA governing committees had chosen marriage to prominent men over career. They remained social conservatives, believing women's power and moral authority emanated from the home. Many hesitated to become involved in the radicalized women's movement when it arrived in Shanghai. Without Ding's ability to bridge the divide, the YWCA most likely would not have become involved in the attempt to form a united women's federation in Shanghai.

The YWCA played a prominent role. Its press release announcing the meeting identified the Association as moderate by claiming the federation's purpose was to coordinate the many organizations involved in women's emancipation.[34] Ding Shujing's presence as one of four cochairs at the federation's inaugural meeting on April 10 also lent the gathering legitimacy. Even the conservative lay leadership of the YWCA supported the federation, hoping their participation would be a moderating influence.[35] After the inaugural meeting, a second one was scheduled for April 12. Early on that morning, however, Chiang Kai-shek ordered attacks on Shanghai radicals, which forced many federation leaders into hiding. There is some evidence the remaining groups attempted to go forward with the federation, but nothing appeared to come of their effort.

Nonetheless, Ding remained involved in the women's movement by serving on the boards of different women's institutions and creating an informal women's network that, in a country where most educational and service work had traditionally been done at a local level, accomplished almost as much as national groups in the United States and England. Over the years Ding served on the board of directors or executive councils of Jinling College in Nanjing, Yanjing University and Bridgeman Academy in Beijing, McTyeire School for Girls in Shanghai, and the National Council of Women of China. She also served with leading groups that brought men and women, Westerners and Chinese, together in public service. These included the National Child Welfare Association, the People's Welfare Committee of the Municipality of Greater Shanghai, and the National Christian Council of China.[36]

Ding's enthusiasm for the women's movement, her willingness to participate in a coalition that included radical groups, and her commitment to public service outside of the YWCA illustrated the extent to which she wanted the YWCA to assume a wider leadership in the public sphere. Still, her YWCA work remained her priority, and she was determined to see the women working together in concrete programs that met real needs. She also wanted the Association to be more inclusive. The YWCA industrial program provided an opportunity to reach all social classes.

Working with Factory Women

The September following Chiang Kai-shek's purge of Shanghai radicals, YWCA industrial secretaries held their first conference to deliberate on new approaches to their work. Literacy training, these secretaries believed, would provide working women with the best means to effect their own emancipation.[37] Ding attended the meeting, lending her support and encouragement. Within twelve months, the YWCA had opened five night schools in five different industrial districts and a sixth that held late afternoon classes for girls on the night shift. Each school offered a basic literacy course that ran for six months, meeting for an hour and a half daily, five days a week.

These schools used the four texts in the "Thousand Characters" series developed by Yan Yangchu for use in mass education projects. Upon completing the series, students were able to read simple books and newspapers, and write letters. Once a literacy class was organized, one session per week was given to club work. Club work helped girls understand their place in relation to the entire industrial order, encouraged them to think together as a group, and acquainted them with organizational methods, all of which industrial secretaries considered essential to the labor movement. YWCA secretaries pointed out that this nucleus of industrial women, while negligible in the face of the entire labor problem, was vital in the production of leadership among industrial women.[38]

In February 1930, less than three years after the first industrial secretaries' conference, Ding spoke at the second one, emphasizing that "Our purpose in the YWCA is to work for *all* women. . . . Our function is to lead, to walk beside them, and to push them onwards." She continued,

> What kind of people ought we to be? First of all, we are a Christian movement. We may differ in methods—some may want to build character by thinking of Jesus as a great personality; others may get people to follow Jesus' way of life themselves. Secondly, since we ourselves have had the opportunity of education we should know how to educate others. We should be in the position of advisors to industrial workers—we need to be encyclopedias of knowledge regarding the labor movement. Fourth [*sic*]: We should make friends with all sorts of people. Fifth: First we need to know—then do. We should be willing to divide responsibility, share it with others, even though it might be easier to do things ourselves. Sixth: We should have initiative and constructive ability in order to extend our work. Seventh: Our special job is with industrial girls and women. The most talked about subjects these days in China are industry and agriculture; hence we are in a very important field. Finally, we should maintain the purpose of working *with* industrial workers, not *exclusively* for them.[39]

Ding's words hark back to her 1925 address to the World YWCA Service Council, where she also emphasized the important work of the YWCA in bringing all women together, both women of different nationalities and women of different social standing. Her goal of inclusiveness—of working with industrial women and not just for them—would not be achieved until the third YWCA convention in 1933, when both factory and rural women were welcomed as members. But the goal was advanced considerably when the national committee appropriated $3,000 for an industrial center the following September.[40]

The Ferry Road Center, as the project came to be known, included four houses on Ferry and Robinson Roads in the western district of Shanghai's International Settlement and combined an industrial center, a working girls' hostel, a demonstration project in health care and vocational services, and eventually a training center for new secretaries. Two YWCA secretaries and two teachers lived in the center, providing continual contact with working women. The goals Ding had outlined in her address the previous February now became a reality.[41]

Building a Model for World Community

Having YWCA secretaries and teachers live with working women also partially achieved her goal of having the YWCA provide a model of world community that bridged both nationality and class. Ding's staunch commitment to a fully international YWCA not only ran counter to official World YWCA policy to bring Chinese women into leadership positions but conflicted with the prevailing opinion of YWCA women in China that Chinese should replace foreign nationals as soon as possible. It is ironic that a woman who so benefited from that policy remained so steadfast in her belief that the international staff was absolutely essential to the YWCA movement in China. As early as 1924, before she took over as acting national general secretary, Ding discussed this matter with Venable: "I do not see why the foreigners should ever leave their staff as workers. The time ought to come when we ought to take for the jobs those who are best fitted for them whether Chinese or foreigners, and the time ought to come when China could share in the sending as well as the receiving."[42] This statement reflected her rejection of narrow nationalism.

Ding sought to make the staff even more representative of the world community, working through the national committee to broaden the Association's international base. In March 1929, in one of her regular letters to the YWCA staff, she wrote that the National Committee was considering writing directly to Denmark and Germany about sending staff; to Norway, Sweden, and Australia requesting that former staff members be replaced; and to Great Britain, Australia, and New Zealand urging them to increase their representation in China.[43] Two years later, Ding made a very clear statement of her vision for the YWCA movement in China: "Now our growing conception of internationalism leads us to believe that we shall draw no hard and fast lines which shall constitute artificial barriers to mutual sharing, and we look forward to a continued relation of cooperation and sharing for mutual benefit.[44]

The deepening world financial crisis in the 1930s frustrated Ding's efforts to maintain, let alone increase the number of foreign secretaries. The Third National Convention in 1933 provided her an opportunity to make one final appeal. The delegates had identified the development of rural cooperatives as important. However, veteran rural secretary Josephine Brown was being considered for reassignment to Korea. Ding pleaded with delegates to insist Brown remain in China:

> It takes a long time to get the knowledge, breadth of view and experience necessary for a Chinese secretary to lead in this difficult field . . . we look to Miss Brown for aid in finance, publicity, and recruiting. You may think we depend too much on Western Secretaries; yet what the situation is, it is. What has not been prepared for long since cannot suddenly be forced to the detriment of the work. All of this points to one inescapable fact, that the National Committee's request for Miss Brown as one of the twelve secretaries was based on a conviction of the need, and that for full time![45]

However, at that convention, the general opinion on retaining foreign staff went against Ding's vision. By October 1934, only twelve foreign secretaries remained out of a total of ninety-seven at the beginning of the 1930s.

Maintaining an international staff, however, was only part of Ding Shujing's commitment to building a world community. Ding also believed in the pursuit of peace, a cause taken up by transnational women's groups, including the World YWCA, during the interwar years. That cause took on urgency as Japanese aggression escalated in north China after 1928. In 1931 Japan invaded Manchuria, annexing it and establishing the puppet state of Manchukuo. The three-month Shanghai war in early 1932 brought Japan's imperial ambitions to the YWCA's doorstep, as its Ferry Road Industrial Center was among the buildings damaged.

In the coming months, more YWCA women came to accept China's need to defend her sovereignty. Ding's regular letters to Association secretaries, however, reflected her struggle to hold onto the vision of a world community. Her final demonstration of that belief was her decision to attend the national convention of the YWCA of Japan in November 1935 as a representative of the World YWCA. She came away with renewed hope, because the Japanese women she met had been eager to know the truth of the situation on the Chinese mainland, which their own press failed to report. She believed a spirit of fellowship had permeated their discussions of the difficult subject of Japanese aggression.[46]

Ding made the trip to Japan while she was on a one-year leave of absence attending international meetings in Europe.[47] While in transit in the United States in August, she met her longtime friend Rosalee Venable in New York City and confessed that she planned to resign. She thought that ten years was long enough to serve and that there were other women capable of carrying on in her place.[48]

The World YWCA invited Ding to work for them as a permanent representative to its World Council in order to launch "a new era of oriental collaboration." World leaders felt strongly that "Europe should have the benefit of more direct personal contact with Miss [Ding]."[49] As enticing as the offer might have been, Ding equivocated, not wanting to leave one full-time position just to take another.[50] Whatever her final decision may have been, her health gave way suddenly during the final months of her furlough. She was hospitalized with sepsis caused by a severe tooth infection and died in Shanghai at age 46 on July 27, 1936.

Ding Shujing's Legacy

Immediately upon Ding's death, dozens of memorial messages poured into the YWCA's national headquarters in Shanghai. Former national committee chair Mrs. Mei Huaquan (H. C. Mei) wrote of Ding's confidence in the potential of Chinese womanhood and the YWCA as the instrument through which that potential would "develop and assert itself in the national, civic and social life of modern China." Mei extolled

Ding for her vision: "She steadily held the view that the YWCA, as an institution, was not an end in itself, but always a means to a greater end." Lady Proctor, vice chair of the national committee of the YWCA of Great Britain, wrote in a similar vein, but connected Ding's character and leadership to her love of God: "There was something so understanding, so far-seeing, so statesmanlike about her, and one was so conscious that all that fine character was deeply rooted in the love of God, and in the realization of His great call to service, a service which she gave with such tremendous unselfishness and graciousness."[51]

Ding Shujing's legacy is difficult to assess, since shortly after her death a full-scale Japanese invasion engulfed China and Asia in a long and costly war that transformed the Chinese social climate. The YWCA's survival in both the Japanese-occupied cities and in unoccupied China, however, testified to Ding's success in strengthening the Association's base and developing Chinese leadership.

Ding's most lasting legacy was mentoring the two women who led the YWCA for the next thirty years. Although the choice of another Chinese leader, Cai Kui, as Ding's successor was not without its controversies, Cai served as national general secretary for a dozen years, stepping aside in 1949 to allow politically savvy Deng Yuzhi to lead the Association into the Communist era. Both of these women had joined the national YWCA staff in 1927 and worked under Ding during her decade of leadership.

Eulogies by many colleagues in 1936 emphasized Ding's internationalism, perhaps because one of her final acts was attending the Japanese YWCA national convention. Mrs. Matsu Tsuji, chair of the Japanese YWCA national committee, wrote,

> For us in other parts of the world also Miss [Ding] was a leader, an outstanding one; we all looked up to her as one who has given her all in consecration to God's work and who has abundantly imparted His spirit and grace in whatever circle she moved. And now at the time of greatest need when with her wisdom and experience she could have guided us through many difficulties she is suddenly taken away from us. The memory of what Miss [Ding] meant to us at our convention last autumn will long remain with our membership.

Talitha Gerlach, one of the few Western secretaries who dedicated their whole lives to China, commented,

[Ding Shujing], always an internationalist, remained confident that only by an honest facing of basic issues in the international scene could national antagonism be transcended and world peace be achieved. The YWCA, for her, continued to be a channel for arriving at such understanding and the means for working toward solutions. Her very being, though wrung with agony by the Sino-Japanese conflict, voiced her vision of the basis for genuine world peace in the words, "We love peace, but we love justice more." Love and goodwill would be accompanying factors, but to her only as justice is achieved in world relationships and international affairs can lasting peace and world brotherhood be realized.[52]

Sarah Lyon of the YWCA of the USA perhaps best summed up Ding's spirit. She described Ding as "no selfish nationalist, but a true patriot who loved her own country and was one of its best interpreters. She was no theoretical impractical internationalist dreaming of Utopia or making a conscious effort to remember other countries. She naturally lived in the whole world as a citizen of the world community."[53]

Ding's untimely death spared her from seeing the world community she so believed in shattered by war. She would have been gratified to know that the Chinese YWCA survived both that war and the revolution that followed. Today it is among the oldest women's organizations in China. She would have been equally gratified to know that the World YWCA continues to be a leader of women's internationalism, working to make the collective power of women a force in today's world.

MEI YIQI
University President in Wartime

by Stacey Bieler

As the years of World War II dragged on, desperation grew among the students and scholars of China's top three universities, who had sought refuge in southwest China. At the National Southwest Associated University, or "Lian Da," in Kunming, Yunnan Province, some professors were separated from their families, while others, living in a village a few miles from the university, wearied of feeding their families on inflation-depleted incomes. The students only had two meals of rice and vegetables a day, which were served in a large shed used as a cafeteria, with no chairs. "Starving students are taught by starving professors," reported a writer for the *Saturday Evening Post* in November 1943.[1]

Lian Da, close to the terminal of the Burma Road, consisted of eighty low hovels built of mud bricks and covered with straw thatch or corrugated-tin roofs. Since there was only one "desk" (a crate serving that function) in each drafty dormitory room for four students, many would study in the tea houses or line up outside of the library, another shed, ill-lit with a hard mud floor. Most students had to wait their turn for hours to get a book they wanted. A volume on aerodynamics had been mailed in from the United States as sheets of paper in a dozen envelopes. Some classes were filled to overflowing, with students listening through open windows and taking notes on paper pressed against one another's backs. The Young Men's Christian Association (YMCA) at the other end of town provided hot showers.[2]

Daisies grew in the craters left over from the bombing raids of 1938–41. Since it was impossible to build underground shelters due to Kunming's high water table, the only way to escape the bombs had been to run to the surrounding countryside.

President Mei Yiqi (pron. yee-chee) shared all the shortages and the dangers. Before he would leave his office, Mei always packed important documents and locked them up. Then he would flee with the teachers and students to the cemetery in the small hill behind the school. One time when they returned they found that the two guards who had stayed behind to guard the documents were killed and the office bombed.[3]

Classes were held from seven to ten in the morning followed by lunch so that the middle of the day could be spent "running the air-raid alarm." Classes resumed from three to six in the afternoon and some continued into the evening. The raids became monotonous after awhile, but bombs ruined some classrooms, laboratories, and dormitories.

In the midst of this tumult, President Mei's honesty, frugality, and generosity were highly respected. The basic diet for his family—wife, son, and four daughters—was rice seasoned with hot peppers, and his transportation was his two legs, not a university car.[4] Once when he returned from meetings at the wartime capital of Chongqing, he gave up a plane ticket to ride in a postal car, thereby saving the university two hundred dollars.[5] Though his son, Mei Zuyan, slept in the same room as his father, he rarely saw him. His son left early in the morning for school and his father had business engagements or hosted two or three events each night, since their home was the only place large enough for guests to be welcomed or professors to hold parties.[6] Often at the end of dinner, his wife, with a smile on her face, would bring in a large plate of dessert and show the four characters on the cake: "Victory is for Sure." Then everyone would stand up and toast victory.[7]

After the Japanese drove Allied forces from Burma in mid-1942, more refugees flooded into Kunming. Despite the panic, Mei announced that the university would stay in Kunming. "Thereafter, refusal to contemplate moving became a point of pride," observes one historian, "and enhanced the ethos of institutional survival as an end to itself."[8]

One of the First Indemnity Students

Mei Yiqi was born in 1889 in Tianjin, the eldest of five brothers and five sisters in the family of a salt administration official. In 1900 the family fled to Baoding to avoid the Boxer Uprising. When they returned to Tianjin that fall, his father lost his job and the children went hungry.[9]

Mei was one of the first students at Yan Fanshu's family school, which became a Western-style middle school in Nanjing and later grew into Nankai University under President Zhang Boling. After winning one of the first forty-seven Boxer Indemnity scholarships in 1909 to study in the United States, he and several other students went to Lawrence Academy in Groton, Massachusetts. The next fall Mei began his studies of electrical engineering at Worcester Polytechnic Institute (WPI) in Worcester, Massachusetts. During his college years, he was elected vice president of the Electrics Club and lived in the Cosmopolitan Club house his last two years, where he served as secretary, treasurer, and president. He also served as English Secretary of the Eastern Section of the national Chinese Students' Alliance from 1912 to 1913.[10]

After becoming a Christian at a YMCA summer camp, Mei was active in WPI's YMCA and Chinese Students' Christian Association and was a delegate to the Student Volunteer Convention in Kansas City in December 1913. He served as the treasurer for the national Chinese Students' Christian Association during his senior year.[11]

After returning to China in 1914, he fulfilled his pledge to serve with the YMCA in Tianjin for one year before becoming an instructor of physics and mathematics at Tsinghua School. During the summer vacation, Mei returned to Tianjin and met with Zhang Boling. When Mei told him that he had no interest in teaching, Zhang replied, "You don't want to teach after only six months experience. How do you know you have no interest? Young people have to learn to be patient. Go back and teach!" Many decades later he joked, "The patience lasted for several decades, even a lifetime."[12]

In 1919 he married Han Yonghua, the oldest of the brilliant and beautiful Han sisters, at the Eastside YMCA in Beijing. She had gone to Yan Fanshu's family school at the same time as Mei, but had to be disguised as a boy. After graduating from college, she taught kindergarten at two schools and worked at the YWCA in her spare time. They had six children in eight and a half years. After they were married he sent one-third of his monthly salary to his parents and one-third to his three brothers for their college expenses, and his own family lived on the last third.[13]

After Mei received an MA in Mechanical Engineering from the University of Chicago in 1922, he became the dean of faculty at Tsinghua School in 1926. Though he did not have a PhD like many professors at Tsinghua, he was elected dean because of his trustworthiness and his democratic style when working with committees.[14]

Mei encouraged students to do service projects. He suggested to one of his students, Zhi Meng, that he teach general science on the weekends in orphanages in Beijing. Mei would teach Zhi various topics, such as electric light or telephony, help him explain and demonstrate scientific phenomena, and let him borrow the apparatuses that were needed. In 1918 the YMCA held a conference for two hundred middle school and college students from north China in the ruins of the imperial Summer Palace, next to Tsinghua. The various speakers included Sherwood Eddy, a YMCA evangelist in Asia for seventeen years, Sidney Gamble, who was doing social survey research in Beijing in support of reform programs, and Mei, who urged students to participate in voluntary charity work and to contribute their time and money faithfully.[15]

Mei served as the director of the Chinese Educational Mission in Washington, D.C., from 1928 to 1931. Required to make inspection trips to various institutions and to meet the students supported by the Boxer Indemnity and their professors, Mei got rid of his chauffeur and drove the car himself. Then he fired the cook, and his wife cooked for the staff.[16] His office became a second home for students. Those in the area came for wholesome recreational activities and rest, and students from farther away stayed there during school vacations.[17]

When Mei's former student, Zhi Meng, was trying to decide which of three job offers to accept, he asked Mei for advice. Mei replied, "Some young men start out seeing their careers only as stepping stones, without any dedication. I rather like to see you choose wisely some work you believe in and stick to it." Zhi became the director of the China Institute in America for thirty-seven years and Mei served on the initial board of advisers.[18]

6-1 Mei Yiqi and family at Mount Vernon, 1930.

Mei was called back to Tsinghua in 1931, to serve as president (the school had become a university in 1928). Tsinghua's students had rejected the previous three presidents, and the campus had been in turmoil for several years. At the inaugural ceremony he said,

> It is of course a very happy thing for me to come back to Tsinghua. But I feel unconfident because of the weight of the responsibility. Since I was asked repeatedly to take up this post, considering also the fact that I was educated by Tsinghua and had worked at the institute for over ten years, it seems naturally to be my obligation to serve Tsinghua. So I am determined to do my job the best I can. I only hope not to be blamed for what I have not done enough to help the university in its development.

Later he often would describe his love for Tsinghua using the old Chinese saying, "I love my dwellings as I was born and raised here."[19]

During his seventeen-year presidency he cultivated a spirit of liberalism in education and in politics. He prodded engineering students to become more than skilled technicians and encouraged all students to transcend class and party cliques.

By 1935 Tsinghua offered ten graduate departments, more than one-third of all the graduate departments in China. Students doubled in number from six to twelve hundred, and in stature Tsinghua was second only to Peking University in humanities and social sciences.

After developing its engineering departments, Tsinghua became the equal of Shanghai's Jiaotong University. Besides initiating an ambitious building program (chemistry building, five dormitories, a dining hall, faculty and staff housing), Mei annexed some land from the neighboring ruins of the Summer Palace, so that the biology department could conduct experimental work on agriculture. He continued the tradition of inviting American and European scientists to give lectures and was the first president of a Chinese university to financially support faculty furloughs. Two-thirds of the full professors had studied in the United States and used science and engineering textbooks from MIT and the University of Michigan.[20]

Mei's administrative skills included the ability to discern what was essential as well as the willingness to delegate power. Once a policy was determined, members of the faculty or staff could carry on with considerable freedom. "It is this spirit of genuine trust that has prompted many to do their best."[21] He also had infinite patience as a peacemaker and mediator. His seriousness and caution prompted his students to create a humorous motto for him: "perhaps, probably it may be so, but, nevertheless, not so necessarily." He was no stern moralist, but rather was modest and sympathetic, with a sense of subtle humor.[22]

Mei's educational principles were a mixture of the East and the West. The Chinese approach was to form talented men who would cultivate themselves, be in harmony with their families, serve their country, and achieve peace in the world. Western liberal education emphasized equality and freedom: freedom for the university administration to be independent from any politics, freedom for professors and students to be independent in their pursuit of studies, and freedom of belief. "These two principles . . . originated from Christianity. Because it is said that God endowed mankind free will and that before Him, all men are born equal."[23]

During the thirties, the atmosphere on campus became tense over the Japanese encroachment on Chinese territory and the government's weak response. After the Japanese army took Manchuria in late 1931, Tsinghua students urged an immediate declaration of war. The faculty supported them by suspending classes for three weeks so that the students could take military training. Other campuses in northern and central China followed suit. Two years later some students from Tsinghua went to the Great Wall to aid Chinese troops fighting the Japanese.

6-2 President Mei Yiqi at Tsinghua's 24th anniversary, April 1935

The *Tsinghua Weekly* observed that the government's response to criticism and growing Communist party influence was to suppress civil liberties and academic freedom through predawn raids, surprise searches, and secret arrests on the campuses; it was thus producing more student radicalism than it was destroying.[24] At first light on December 9, 1935, students from Tsinghua and Yanjing marched to Tiananmen Square, only to be dispersed by police, who beat some of them. A week later, more than seven thousand students from twenty-eight schools, led by the National Salvation Committee from Tsinghua, marched to the Foreign Ministry building to ask why the authorities were selling out the nation. After staging a sit-in, the students dispersed due to the cold night, whereupon soldiers assaulted some of them brutally.[25]

The radical and conservative students at Tsinghua clashed openly. The conservative students called for a united front against Japan, a year before the Chinese Communist Party (CCP) advocated the idea. When several hundred police stormed Tsinghua's gate, the students attacked them, smashing their vehicles and chasing them from campus under a barrage of steamed bread that was to have been the policemen's breakfast. Despite these episodes, Mei maintained a relatively normal campus environment and encouraged the students to build a new China through studying rather than by political action. Tsinghua was described as the only place to find a "calm and peaceful study desk" in north China on the eve of the Japanese advance.[26]

Protecting the National Treasures

For several years, Mei planned for the eventuality of a quick evacuation of Tsinghua.[27] When John King Fairbank, who had been a visiting professor at the university in 1933–34, saw faculty and students removing books from Tsinghua's library, he commented sadly, "The best college library in China is being scattered to the winds."[28]

During the summer of 1937, most of Tsinghua's students and teachers fled south, taking lab equipment and five hundred cases of books with them. They first went to Changsha in Hunan Province, but the Japanese bombed the city. Linguistics professor Zhao Yuanren, a graduate of Cornell and Harvard, joked during one of the air-raid alerts, "Do not put all your intellectuals in one basement."[29]

The students and faculty then traveled southwest to Kunming, Yunnan's provincial capital. Poet and professor Wen Yiduo, seven other professors, and two hundred students walked one thousand miles across mountains and through rivers for two months. Most took a train to Guangzhou and then entered Yunnan via Hong Kong and Vietnam.

Governor Long Yun, a member of the Yi nationality, was proud to have all the "best brains in the country" in his province. He had enough money from the sale of opium to support an army that kept the Kuomintang (KMT) secret police from making arrests in the area. In the provincial capital, horse carts and rickshaws still far outnumbered bicycles.

Tsinghua, Peking, and Nankai universities joined as the National Southwest Associated University, or "Lian Da." On May 4, 1938, classes began in makeshift lecture halls, twelve large cattle sheds built on top of an ancient cemetery, about half a mile from the city's North Gate.[30]

Mei and Tsinghua dominated the school. Jiang Menglin was tired after years of overseeing fractious students at Peking University, and Zhang Boling, the founder of Nankai University in Tianjin, was heartbroken after his son died in the war and his school was bombed and burned by the Japanese. So Mei, the youngest of the three school presidents, became the chief administrator. More than half of the student body was from Tsinghua, and more books had been brought from there than from the other two schools. Mei nonetheless divided the senior positions fairly among the staff and faculty from the three schools. The student body of three thousand enrolled in twenty-six departments, two special training programs, and a preparatory division, making it the largest Chinese institution of higher education at the time.[31] (Yanjing University, the Christian college in Beijing, was closed by the Japanese and relocated to Chengdu from 1942 to 1946. Mei's younger brother, Mei Yibao, served as acting president and chancellor.)[32]

In 1940 Mei's alma mater, WPI, gave him an honorary Doctor of Engineering degree in absentia for his years of service to Tsinghua. The citation noted his training of research students "in the hope that when peace comes again to his stricken country, they may be the more adequately prepared to play their part in the gigantic task of reconstruction." It also stated that his former teachers and associates remembered his "rare qualities of heart and mind" and "his indomitable persistence in the face of every discouragement, his unswerving loyalty to the ideals which even as a youth upon our campus he had begun to cherish."[33]

Later that year, the Alumni Association of Tsinghua held a special meeting in Kunming to honor Mei's twenty-five years of service to the university. He responded, "The accomplishments of Tsinghua in the past years cannot be said whether [sic] it was from any particular person. What we have accomplished today is the result of joint efforts from many, many persons." He went on to compare his role as college president to the role of wang mao (King Crown), the Yellow Emperor in Beijing opera. Whenever King Crown enters the stage he is fully costumed and escorted by many attendants. He is very solemn and upright "like a dignified mediator." Though seated at the center of the stage, he does not draw attention to himself, for he is not required to sing. "When the stage is cheered by the audience he feels he is 'also honored.'"[34]

In May 1941 Mei and two others went on an inspection tour of four campuses in central and southwest China. On the way back they were held up for three months due to bombing, floods, and other un-expected difficulties. One of the men lost his temper one day. After his rage subsided, Mei said patiently, "I had thought about joining you in the tantrum. But that won't help us resolve the problem." Because of Mei's sincerity, the other man was mollified.[35]

In the same year, when bombings caused severe damage to already insufficient facilities and inflation was taking its toll, Mei gave a speech that showed his perseverance.

> Tsinghua is like a small boat tumbling on the raging waves. A person who happens to be at the helm must not shirk from fear but should gather up courage and man the ship. Although the night seems long and dark, we are certain daylight will come soon. He must navigate this ship back to Tsinghua Garden and proclaim to all persons of the university that he has done his deed.[36]

Tsinghua's traditional rigorous teaching atmosphere was impeded by lack of books, paper, and equipment, but the students benefited from being able to take classes from 179 specialists from the three campuses. All but twenty-three of the full and associate professors had studied abroad in the United States or Europe.[37] Professors used English in their lectures and, if possible, continued to assign American and British textbooks.

The standards remained high at Lian Da despite the horrendous circumstances. Only 3,800 of the 8,000 students who passed through the gates graduated. Worldwide acknowledgment of the school's role of cultivating leaders came in 1957 when two graduates, Yang Zhenning (C. N. Yang) and Li Zhengdao (T. D. Lee) won the Nobel Prize in physics.[38]

Though the plant physiology labs of Tang Peisong, a graduate of the University of Minnesota and The Johns Hopkins University, were bombed out three times, moved to four different locations, and rebuilt of mud bricks, they were full of eager students who went on to serve in the Academia Sinica, Peking University, and Fudan University.[39]

Tsinghua essayist Zhu Ziqing and Tsinghua poet Wen Yiduo dominated the Chinese literature department. The lectures of Wu Mi, a graduate from Tsinghua in 1916 who went to Harvard, "dazzled his undergraduate audiences as he moved back and forth from one culture to another, leaping across centuries, often following the recitation of an English poem with a comparable verse from the Tang dynasty."[40]

Tsinghua fostered talented people who introduced Western learning to China. Besides Wen and Wu, prominent Tsinghua graduates who served as Lian Da faculty included Chen Da (sociology, class of '16), Pan Guangdan (sociology, '21), Liang Sicheng (architecture, '24), and Wu Han (history, '34).[41] Mei also recruited promising young scholars into the faculty: Chen Xingsheng and Hua Luogeng (mathematics), Zhou Peiyuan (physics), Tao Baokai (engineering), and Chen Daisun (economics).[42]

The role of education during wartime continued to be hotly debated. Peking University ("Bei Da") brought with it an atmosphere of academic freedom known as the "Bei Da winds of learning," created under the leadership of Cai Yuanpei, who had studied in Germany and served as the university's president from 1917 to 1919.[43] Some believed that the students were "national treasures" who needed to complete their education for the sake of China's future rather than be squandered in battle.[44]

In contrast, the government sought to control Lian Da through the hiring and firing of faculty, standardizing the curriculum, requiring a course on Sun Yat-sen's "Three Principles of the People," and enforcing an examination system for graduation. With the help of Yunnan's Governor Long, the faculty and students successfully opposed most of the restrictions, causing the campus to become known as a "bastion of democracy."[45]

When John King Fairbank visited Kunming in 1942 he first met with President Mei, who was even more emaciated and worn-out than he remembered, but still very cordial. Fairbank wrote to his superiors in the Office of Strategic Services in Washington, D.C., that the American-trained faculty of Tsinghua, who represented an "American investment and asset in China" and were "living agents of American educational influence," were seriously threatened with extinction. A year later, he concluded that the faculty members were in a contest "to see how long they can survive in the face of the government's hope that they will die off, disintegrate and remove the chief concentration of returned students from the Chinese intellectual landscape."[46]

Mei's wife sold her "victory cakes" through a local shop as a way to supplement their income. She would wear cheap cloth and call herself by her maiden name, Han, but everyone knew she was the president's wife. Once when it was her turn to prepare a meal for the Kunming YMCA, she did not have any money to buy food. So she put a tarp on the ground outside the west gate of the campus and sold some of her children's clothes, some crafts, and some of her own clothes. Once she had ten yuan, she bought and prepared the food.[47]

As inflation rose, Mei pledged at a meeting of the school's standing committee that efforts would be made to ensure that no faculty member or student would go hungry. Lian Da would supply eighty kilos of rice to each faculty family. Purchasing agents were sent into the countryside for this difficult and dangerous work. University graduates working in government departments also helped. After Tsinghua sold some of its surplus engineering equipment in order to subsidize needy students and faculty members, Mei gave an extra month's salary to the faculty of the other two schools as well. During those eight difficult years, as people often observed, President Mei Yiqi was always identified with the common good.[48]

The campus became even more divided when the Japanese Army's Ichi-Go offensive (April–December 1944) broke China in two, bringing the war and the accompanying inflation, corruption, and injustice closer to Lian Da's doorstep. The Nationalist government's failure to deal with either the external threat or the internal problems caused the faculty and students to become greatly disaffected. More joined the Communists or other opposition groups, such as the Democratic League.[49]

When the school's protector and patron Governor Long was removed in a coup in October 1945, the right wing of the KMT was finally free to take action, smashing furniture, threatening professors, and removing books to see if they contained subversive thoughts. After a student strike on December 1, 1945, the collision between the government and the students led to the deaths of "Four Martyrs" (a middle school teacher, one middle school pupil, and two university students).[50]

Navigating the Ship Back to Home

Mei's wise leadership had helped direct Tsinghua during the turbulent 1930s and China's top three universities during the trauma of war in the 1940s, but once the war ended in August 1945, new challenges lay ahead. For the first year, Mei Yiqi oversaw the rebuilding of the gutted campus in Beijing in preparation for a return from exile. During the war Tsinghua had served as a hospital, bar, brothel, and stables for the Japanese army. More than 90 percent of the furniture and equipment was lost, and most of the school was seriously damaged, especially the shelves in the library and the floor of the gymnasium.

After eight years in exile, Lian Da closed with a ceremony attended by two thousand students, professors, alumni, and local guests held in Kunming on May 4, 1946, the twenty-seventh anniversary of the May Fourth movement of 1919. They erected a stele commemorating tolerance and democracy adjacent to the graves of the Four Martyrs, with an inscription by Wen Yiduo, who was famous for his calligraphic masterpieces. He had almost ruined his fingers by carving seals late into the night to earn extra money to support his family during the war. The exiles joined millions of war refugees in the arduous trek back north to home.[51]

Mei did "navigate the ship back to Tsinghua Garden." The campus reopened on October 10, 1946. The student body of over three thousand was more than double its prewar size, with the greatest increase in the engineering division. Though money from the accumulated interest of the Boxer Indemnity fund helped buy books and equipment, high inflation made daily life for students and faculty difficult, since the KMT turned its attention and finances toward fighting a civil war with the Communists.

The recent assassinations of Democracy League leaders Li Gongbi and Wen Yiduo, the Tsinghua professor, in July 1946 had sent people reeling. The democratic liberalism for which Tsinghua was noted, with its emphasis on individualism, personal quest for truth, and tolerance of various eccentricities and ideas, was helpless in the face of the terror dispensed by members of the right-wing KMT.[52]

The intellectuals were indecisive. Some were fleeing to the Communist "liberated areas" while others were fleeing from them. The KMT's censorship of the press, interference with education by promoting the government-approved version of Chinese history and KMT ideology, and mass arrests caused ninety professors from four Beijing universities to issue a statement demanding a guarantee of human rights.[53] The CCP began moderating its class war slogans in order not to frighten people.

One liberal remarked in 1947, "The question with the KMT was how much freedom, while with the CCP the question was whether there would be any."[54] Like Qu Yuan, the upright and patriotic poet-scholar of old, many felt that staying in China was impossible, but going away was unbearable.[55]

Despite Mei's calm but firm attitude toward students, they boycotted classes thirteen times in two years, adding up to nearly two months of lost class time. When the authorities attempted to force all institutions of higher education to move south as the People's Liberation Army approached from the north, the underground Communists opposed moving the school.[56]

Building Yet Another Campus

On December 13, 1948, Communist forces swept past the gates of Tsinghua to lay siege to the city of Beijing. Mei, who had gone into the city the night before, flew out of Beijing on December 21 with other intellectuals on a special plane sent in by the KMT. He went to Paris as the chairman of the Chinese delegation to the 1949 meeting of the United Nations Educational, Scientific and Cultural Organization (UNESCO).[57]

Mei spent the next six years in New York City conferring with the China Foundation about how the Boxer Indemnity fund could help subsidize the almost four thousand Chinese students and scholars stranded without financial support in the United States. Congress approved of allocating $6 million for the Program of Emergency Aid of Chinese Students three weeks before the outbreak of the Korean War in June 1950. These funds helped students complete their degrees, and new laws allowed them to remain in the United States. Funds were also used to donate books and journals to colleges and universities that had moved to Taiwan.[58]

Some Chinese students in the United States returned to China. After finishing his degree at Tsinghua, Mei Zuyan graduated in 1949 from his father's alma mater, WPI, and then went to Illinois Institute of Technology in 1951 for his master's degree. Though he planned to return to the mainland, he did not discuss the issue with his father.

After a long journey back to China by way of Europe in 1954, he taught hydraulic engineering at Tsinghua until 1998. It was only in 1996 that he was able to make a trip to Taiwan to present a bouquet of flowers at his father's tomb.[59]

In 1955, Mei was asked to come to Taiwan to create a nuclear science research institute in order to supply Taiwan with power. He chose a site, directed the construction of the buildings, bought the books and equipment, and oversaw the laboratories and workshops. In his search for researchers, he made several trips to the United States to convince scientists to come for several weeks or months to supervise the installation of the laboratories. At the inauguration in Xinshu, seventy kilometers from Taipei, the minister of education said, "The Tsing Hua reactor writes a new page on the history of science development in the Republic of China. . . . It also signifies the crowning success of Dr. Mei's dedication to education and science."[60]

When the institute became the National Tsing Hua University in 1956, Mei assumed the presidency. He pledged his "sincerity" and called upon all members of the university, including the students, to do the same. He won another generation of students' genuine love and respect.

Three years later he was appointed minister of education by the Nationalist government in Taiwan. Mei served as vice chairman on the National Committee for Long-Term Scientific Development under the chairman Hu Shi, one of the 1910 Boxer Indemnity scholarship recipients, who was serving as the president of Academia Sinica. After an operation for cancer, Mei was too weak to leave the hospital. He died in Taipei on May 19, 1962, at the age of seventy-three.[61]

After Mei passed away, his secretary sealed the handbag that Mei always carried even when he was seriously ill. Two weeks later, his wife and others gathered to unseal the bag. Inside were the Tsing Hua fund accounts, all recorded carefully. Though Mei had been encouraged to write a will, it was not necessary because he had no personal property. His treatment fees, hospital expenses of two years, and funeral expenses were paid off from the gifts sent earlier by Tsinghua alumni in the United States, Hong Kong, and Taiwan to celebrate his seventieth birthday.[62]

Each year faculty and students at National Tsing Hua University, one of Taiwan's most prestigious universities, pay respect to Mei Yiqi at his grave in the university's Mei Garden. Tsinghua University in Beijing held a memorial service in 1989 on the hundredth anniversary of Mei's birthday, during which a bronze bust of Mei contributed by overseas alumni was unveiled.[63]

On January 25, 2005, another ceremony was held at Tsinghua University in Beijing. Ms. Liu Ziqiang, daughter-in-law of Mei Yiqi and widow of Mei Zuyan, donated a painting, seals, furniture, and photos used by Mei before his death. Today, as Tsinghua pursues the goal of becoming a world-class university, Mei's wise words are still quoted: "A university is great not because of its tall buildings but because of its great scholars."[64]

7

LIN QIAOZHI
The Steady Pulse of a Quiet Faith

by Guowei Wright

On December 23, 1901, the third child in the Lin family was born on Gulangyu Island near Xiamen, Fujian Province. After giving birth alone, cutting off the umbilical cord by herself and wiping off the blood from her second daughter, the exhausted mother had no energy left even to wrap up the baby, but instead fainted with a gush of her own blood. When the baby's father came home from work, the naked new-born baby couldn't even cry anymore. Mother Lin blamed herself for giving birth to another girl, while the father held the tiny body close to his chest to warm her up. Father Lin, a believer in God, told his wife that the next day was going to be Christmas Eve, so this child was a special gift from God. He rubbed the tiny hands and feet and named her Qiaozhi (pron. chow-jer), meaning skillful and innocent.[1]

Lin Qiaozhi (Lim Kah T'i) became a famous obstetrician, known and loved by Chinese people from the 1940s to the early 1980s, from Premier Zhou Enlai and his wife down to the poorest common people. In fact, she was called a "living Buddha" by a large number of women patients who received her care and treatment. While her love for and devotion to her patients and her brilliant medical skills were apparent to all, her Christian faith was largely unknown to most people, given the political situation of her time. Yet there is evidence of this steady pulse that carried all through her life, beginning with her father's welcome at her birth.

A Doting Father

Lin Liangying had gone with his grandfather to South Asia as a child, learning English while attending a Christian school in Singapore.[2] After his grandfather passed away, he came back home and married a local girl from Gulangyu, a very important seaport throughout history. According to the Nanjing Treaty of 1840 at the end of the first Opium War, Xiamen was one of five ports forced to open to British residents. The earliest arrivals found the island a very pleasant place to live. Therefore, the United Kingdom and many other countries established their consulates on the island, and foreigners opened banks, factories, churches, schools, and hospitals. By 1899, Gulangyu Island had become multi-national property.

Lin Liangying and his wife settled down and he worked as a translator and a teacher. Qiaozhi had one brother and two sisters (one adopted). When she was five years old, her mother died.[3] Father Lin had promised his wife he would take good care of their daughter, the youngest. He poured out extra love on this motherless little girl. He treated her as well as a son, making sure she had a good education and a happy life. Lin was a faithful believer and brought his whole family to faith. He took his little daughter to the beach to watch the sun set over the horizon and told her stories from the Bible and his overseas experiences.

She attended one of China's first kindergartens, run by a British missionary who taught the children Christian nursery rhymes in Chinese. Sunday mornings, they went to the nearby Gospel Hall with their father. While the adults held their worship service, the children played outside and read Bible picture books. Christmas Eve every year was unforgettable. Fellow believers sang, candlelight reflected on the walls, and organ music echoed under the high arched ceiling together with the singing: "Silent night, holy night. . . ." Qiaozhi did not want to go home even when she could not keep her eyes open. At midnight, bells from far and near rang, and believers greeted each other in peace.

From the time Lin was ten through her high school years, she attended a Western-style girls' school that included elementary, junior high, and high school. Chinese pastor Zhou Shouqin founded the school in 1900. The campus included two small buildings and a couple of one-story houses.[4]

The school's principal, Mary Carling, was a graduate of the British Advanced Teachers College and was sent to China by the Anglican Church. She was humble, passionate, and rigorous in all she did. She established school rules covering not only academic requirements but also character and conduct, with a strict dress code. She taught the senior grades English, geography, and piano. She taught the girls to "love your neighbor as yourself" and also how to obtain peace and joy in all circumstances.

This was a new type of school, quite different from traditional Chinese schools at the time. English was the major course, which took up many of the school hours. Lin Qiaozhi was very good at English and learned to read English language books very early on, because she already had learned English from her father at a younger age. She was also fond of math, with its rigor and clarity. She spent a lot of time explaining math problems to her fellow students, who found math rather a headache. She also began to talk about a love for medicine that was inspired by biology lessons at school. Her biology teacher was a foreigner who took the students to catch butterflies and dragonflies in the mountains and sea creatures in the ocean to make specimens.

Lin spent ten happy years there. She loved school and learning, and was baptized in the Christian faith. Every year during the Easter, Thanksgiving, and Christmas holidays, school had all kinds of special activities. Students volunteered practical help to their fellow believers at church. They learned to enjoy being together and serving each other, experiences that shaped Lin for the rest of her life.

A Mentor's Influence: Mary Carling

To her curious girl students, Miss Carling was a romantic legend. She once had a very handsome and loving fiancé. During World War I, he died on the battlefield in Spain just before the war ended. After that, Carling decided that she would not get married, and came all the way to Gulangyu Island to teach. She was surprised by the isolated and unsophisticated lifestyle at first, but became fond of the simple rural customs, the empty beach, and the sweet sunshine. And she came to love her students, who lived with her every day. She knew them even better than her sister Jenny, whom she now had not seen for many years. She watched them grow from innocent little girls to elegant and refined young ladies. And she knew that it was not simply time that had changed them; it was education.

Lin was not the most spectacular student of hers, but Carling loved her with all her heart. Besides Lin's excellent academic achievement, her diligence, honesty, and sense of responsibility demonstrated real Christian character. On top of that, Lin's outstanding English enabled casual and spontaneous communication between the two of them and brought them closer.

Mary Carling had the biggest impact on Lin in her formative years. Her strong faith, her humble and considerate approach to people, and her lifestyle revealed a completely different life as a woman. Most women Lin had seen up to this point had married and taken care of their in-laws, husbands, and children. All their lives revolved around men, restricted within their own courtyard. What she witnessed in Miss Carling was how a woman could manage with her own learning and faith to live independently and with dignity, even when she was away from her family members and homeland.

Lin often went with Carling into the city of Xiamen, visiting families from the church. Rich or poor, they were treated the same. Sometimes people called Carling "female foreign devil" or "foreign old woman," but she bore insults with equanimity, without any complaint about the hardships or inconvenience of living in a foreign country. Carling's favorite saying was "God first, others second," taken from the spiritual biography of a French nun.[5] Lin Qiaozhi was also very moved by this book. She read it many times until she could repeat whole paragraphs from memory. She told Miss Carling that this book helped her understand the biblical message that we must become humble like a little child to enter heaven. Carling explained to her that this ordinary nun had showed how a real Christian could do extraordinary things when doing everything with kindness and love, showing God's love while sharing the gospel.

Lin learned that it was faith that gave Carling her direction for life and her sense of morality and order. Next to an old picture of her fiancé, Carling placed a famous prayer from St. Francis of Assisi:

> *Lord, make me an instrument of Thy peace;*
> *Where there is hatred, let me sow love;*
> *Where there is injury, pardon;*
> *Where there is doubt, faith;*
> *Where there is despair, hope;*
> *Where there is darkness, light;*
> *And where there is sadness, joy.*
> *O Divine Master,*
> *Grant that I may not so much seek to be consoled as to console;*
> *To be understood, as to understand;*
> *To be loved, as to love;*
> *For it is in giving that we receive,*
> *It is in pardoning that we are pardoned,*
> *And it is in dying that we are born to Eternal Life.*
> *Amen.*[6]

The relationship between the two women not only helped Lin find a part-time job during her senior year at school but also shaped her heart for eternity.

A Test of Ability and Character

Lin Qiaozhi stayed on as a teacher at the girls' school after she graduated. It was a highly admirable job, but she had something else in mind. She wanted to continue learning instead of getting married and settling down in Xiamen. Her father and older brother, Lin Zhenming, had always encouraged her to study abroad. Unfortunately, by the time she graduated from high school, her family could no longer afford to send her overseas. Her father had remarried and now had six more children. Her older brother was also married, with children of his own. When she heard one of her brother's friends talking about an American medical college in Beijing, she immediately was very interested.

7-1 Young Lin Qiaozhi (center) and friends on Gulangyu Island

Lin Qiaozhi thought there was no better life for her than to become a doctor. She had read many stories in the Bible's book of Acts about how the followers of Jesus practiced healing power while they spread the gospel. They took care of people's souls while relieving their physical pain. When she told Mary Carling what was on her mind, Carling recalled hearing from her friends that the medical college in Beijing was going to recruit twenty-five students from all over the country.

Lin very much wanted to take the examination, which would be held in Shanghai, but she was unsure whether she could succeed. Carling told her, "You should receive a more complete education. When you face big decisions like this, you need to keep praying and do your best rather than wondering whether or not you can do it. Give it to the Lord, obey him and he will make your path straight." Lin listened and prayed as always, and she could feel that her burden was lifted. Peace and confidence filled her heart.

After obtaining approval and support from her father and brother, Lin Qiaozhi was filled with gratitude. She was thankful for her heavenly father's guidance, her understanding family members, her accepting stepmother, and her teacher's help. The rest was up to her now.

It was already near the date for the exam when she decided to enroll. Her sister helped her prepare her luggage, while her brother arranged for her traveling tickets and companions. This was the first time for her to leave Gulangyu Island and Xiamen. She knew that Xiamen was only a small dot on the map of China. She was full of longing to see the outside world.

The three-day examination took place at a Christian school in Shanghai, where the weather was especially hot and sticky that summer. Through Carling's connections in the Xiamen church, Lin was able to find a place to stay at the Young Women's Christian Association (YWCA) building. During the testing, she began to gain more and more confidence after her initial nervousness. The English written test was the final one, following the oral test. Though it was not as hard as she had imagined, she had to keep writing in order to finish on time.

One word tripped her up when she translated English into Chinese. She searched for a Chinese word corresponding to "bike." She knew from the context that it was a transportation vehicle. After eliminating power-driven vehicles, ox and horse carts, and tricycles, she wrote "a two-wheeled vehicle for one person to use." She was unsure about it, but she could not think of anything better. She had never had the chance to see anything like the vehicle described, let alone ride one.

During the testing, there suddenly was a noisy disturbance in the back of the examination hall. The test monitor went back to check. Lin had no time to look back. She had to write the English essay, the major part of the test, and she had to concentrate. But the noise was growing louder. What had happened? She then saw that a student had suffered heatstroke and was being carried out. Lin knew her; they were staying at the same place. Because this was a female student, the male monitor did not feel comfortable taking any action and instead inquired of the students how to contact her family.

Lin Qiaozhi could not concentrate any more. She put aside her paper and ran over to help. The student had been carried to the restroom. Her eyes were closed, her cheeks red. Lin dispersed the crowd around her and untied the collar of her Chinese dress, put a wet towel on her forehead, helped her drink some water and take some Chinese medicine, and then fanned her carefully. After a while, the student groaned, took a deep breath, and started to sweat on her forehead and neck.

By then, the test time was up. Lin went back to Gulangyu. She had to tell her family and friends what happened. English was her favorite subject and normally would have given her the best chance to do well. But she had not finished. She was told that of the 150 people who took the test, only 25 would be selected. It looked as if she had no chance. But her father was rather proud of what she did. "You did the right thing taking care of the sick person first; don't worry about what's next."[7]

One month later, she received notice of her admission to Peking Union Medical College (PUMC). Later she learned that the test monitor had written a special report on her to the college administrators. He praised her for her beautiful character in helping others and her calmness and proper manner in handling the situation. He also affirmed her clear and poised English oral communication. The report was attached to Lin's unfinished paper. After reading the report and her test scores, the college decided to enroll her.

Lin Qiaozhi was twenty years old. Many years later, she recalled how special that summer was. Her father seemed to become much younger overnight. Many people from the island, both friends and strangers, congratulated him. He could not hold back his pride and joy. Even Mary Carling, who was normally very levelheaded and restrained, hugged her with excitement, and kept saying: "Thank God! Praise the Lord! I knew you could make it!"[8]

Study and Work at PUMC

Peking Union Medical College was founded in 1906 by several missionary organizations and run by the China Medical Board, an independent subsidiary of the Rockefeller Foundation, from 1915 to 1949.[9] The goal was to train high-quality medical doctors and administrators. In order to ensure high standards, the school required three years of preparatory courses and then five years of courses for a bachelor's degree. After eight years of study here, students were qualified for a medical degree as a doctor from both PUMC and New York State University.

The challenge to succeed was tremendous for Lin. Physics and chemistry were major parts of the curriculum; she had studied neither of them and had to start from the beginning. English was easy for her,

but not Chinese. Growing up she was used to speaking either the local dialect or English. Learning to speak Mandarin was like learning
another language: one word at a time to pronounce and memorize.

Finances were also a challenge. Students who came to the college
had to have considerable financial support. Almost no one, especially
any female student, was in Lin Qiaozhi's difficult situation. However,
her upbringing and early education had instilled in her not only qualities fundamental for making a good doctor, such as love and faith, but
also fierce determination. When her father died midway through her
study, she wanted to continue, and her older brother was willing to support her financially. Later, Lin would in turn help his children through
school. In June 1929, Lin graduated with the highest honor, the Wenhai
Award, for both her outstanding academic achievement and her compassion for others. She became the first woman hired as a resident physician in the PUMC hospital. By this time, Lin had made the choice of
devotion to her work over marriage; female hospital physicians were
required to be single.[10]

During her work-study program, Lin realized that Chinese women
patients who came for obstetric and gynecological (ob-gyn) treatment
would wait in long lines to see her simply because she was the only
Chinese female doctor. She understood completely how they must feel.
She thought of her own mother. It might have been the same hesitancy
that caused her mother to delay treatment until it was too late. At the
same time, she had witnessed many infant congenital diseases that
came directly from the mothers. Lin was determined to become an
obstetrician.

Friend and Mentor Dr. Yang Chongrui

Lin started her work-study program at the First Medical Clinic in
Beijing, with other students under Dr. Yang Chongrui's leadership.
With her, the students visited local families to investigate epidemic disease prevention, checked hygiene at public places such as restaurants
and bathing houses, provided checkups and treatment for prostitutes,
sterilized homes with contagious patients, and promoted preventive
health knowledge.

Dr. Yang was an earlier graduate of the school that preceded PUMC and had then studied in the United States in the Public Health Department at The Johns Hopkins Medical College. In 1929, Yang started the first midwife training school in Beijing and invited Lin to teach about the science of childbirth. The school was located at Qilin Hutong, which was known as a gathering place for midwives in Beijing. According to a local legend, Qilin, the Chinese unicorn, delivered babies.

Dr. Yang was one of the early advocates for birth control in China, hoping to reduce the surprisingly high percentage of obstetric diseases compared with other diseases for Chinese women. Yang told Lin that according to her statistics, the majority of women had four or five children, and some as many as fifteen. After consulting with Lin, Dr. Yang invited the eminent speaker Margaret Sanger to China to give lectures on birth control in order to draw society's attention to the issue. Unfortunately, the speaking tour was not well received by the wealthy Chinese men with high social status, who took pride in multiple wives and concubines and a houseful of children and grandchildren, and the lower-status Chinese did not even hear about it.

Yang was ten years older than Lin, a believer in Christ herself, with the same PUMC background and equally devoted to women's health and birth control. Lin enjoyed a special relationship with her for thirty years until 1957, when Yang was labeled a political "rightist" and disappeared from the medical field. In 1958, motivated by a desire to honor her friend as well as a continuing concern for women, Lin mobilized all the medical forces in Beijing to conduct an obstetric survey of nearly eight hundred thousand women. As the focus of the survey, she chose cervical cancer, the most common killer among Chinese women. It was a huge project and the impact of the survey was highly significant. In a culture where women were treated as secondary humans or worse, the attention paid to their health was indeed a tremendous breakthrough. Soon after that, big cities like Shanghai and Guangzhou followed suit. The surveys raised awareness of the problem, and the ratio of cervical patients dropped from 646.17 to 90.46 per each hundred thousand women. Expectant mothers began to receive medical supervision and enjoy maternity leave.[11]

"At All Times and in All Places, a Doctor on Duty"

In 1941, the Japanese army occupied American institutions, including PUMC. The hospital had to close. Patients had to leave, as well as professors, staff members, and students. Showing her enterprising spirit and also needing to support her relatives, Lin opened an ob-gyn clinic at No. 10 Dongtangzi Hutong. This was the first time she came in close contact with the lives of regular people's families and with women from the bottom of society. She often reduced fees or charged nothing for her services, at times riding a donkey to distant villages to see poor patients.[12]

As an ob-gyn doctor, Lin Qiaozhi had done in-depth research about women's bodies and their physiology. She understood that childbearing was a natural function of the body, not the source of disease. However, in her everyday work, she was shocked to come across so many gynecological diseases: repeated inflammation, chronic sexual diseases, and many pathological and painful conditions that were eating away women's health, destroying their dignity, and corroding their sense of happiness.

Many of these problems resulted from poverty, frequent childbirth, and lack of basic knowledge of hygiene. Women had no control over their own lives and bodies. Men and the elders of the family made decisions on everything, including childbirth, as if a woman was just a tool for reproduction. Most of the time women delayed treating their sicknesses for too long. They never went to a hospital, let alone the prestigious medical college hospital.

Now, however, Dr. Lin had become their neighbor. She was not only gentle and highly skilled, but her fees were low. Lin would always think of ways to save their money. If she could use medicine, she would not use shots. Patient and kind, she told them how to look after themselves to prevent more problems. These women had never received such concern and tender loving care, not even from their own mothers. They could not help but tell Lin their most private concerns.

Obstetrics, like gynecology, involves hard work, but there is the added joy of welcoming new lives. Obstetrics is also unpredictable, since every woman in labor has a different experience. Some cannot make it to the delivery room before their babies arrive, others have to suffer long labor. Waiting right next to a woman giving birth, Lin would be there to catch the brand-new baby with her own hands and listen to its first cry. She thus experienced the wonder of a new life and was filled with awe and gratitude.

Dr. Lin approached women in labor with a mother's heart, though she was never a mother herself. In her diagnosis and treatment, prescriptions and advice, she poured out not only her experience and wisdom, but also mercy and compassion. The comfort and care she offered these women day in and day out brought doctor and patient closer. They did not know what to do with the gratitude they had for Lin except to share the news with their sisters, relatives, and neighbors. They said there was a "living Buddha" in eastern Beijing. Lin's name spread throughout the city.

One evening when she was getting ready to close the clinic, she saw a man completely soaked by rain standing outside. He said he feared his wife was not going to live. She had been in labor for two and a half days and the baby still had not been delivered. The midwife had left. After someone mentioned Dr. Lin, the man came to her place, desperate for help. Lin asked some questions, got a cup of coffee, grabbed her bag, and went into the rain without delay. Hard labor could often last a whole night, so a cup of coffee was necessary to stay awake. It was already midnight by the time they got there. The woman lay on a bare bed; her eyes were closed, with wet hair stuck to her face, and she groaned periodically. Lin gave her a quick check. The position of the baby was horizontal and its heartbeat was weak. The woman had no energy left after such a long struggle.

The rest of the world disappeared for Lin. All she saw was this suffering woman in difficult and painful labor. She asked a family member to make some boiling hot water. She cleaned the woman's face and body, put a clean sheet on the bed, and gently adjusted the position of the baby. At the same time, she whispered to the woman to encourage her, offering detailed guidance and listening to the baby's heartbeat. In between contractions, she fed the woman a bowl of porridge to give her some energy. Gradually, the baby's head emerged and Lin brought him out with obstetric forceps, held him up upside down, and patted him on the back until he cried out loud. "It's a boy," said Lin. "Congratulations!" The loud crowing of a rooster was heard; it was dawn.

Dr. Lin looked around at the empty home and opened her bag. She took some money, left it on the bed, and said to the man, "She is exhausted. Buy some food for her to eat after she wakes up." The baby was giving out loud and short cries. A healthy boy, Lin thought to herself as she was leaving. Only then did she feel the sopping wet shirt sticking to her back; her legs were almost too weak to move.[13]

Thus Lin practiced and modeled what she taught the students who came for her work-study programs. She asked each of them to write reports on delivery procedures. After reading all of them, she gave only one student a grade of "Good" and asked the rest of the students to rewrite their reports. The students came back with more detailed reports, but Lin was still not satisfied. So they read the "Good" report and realized that there was one special sentence: "The woman in labor had pea-sized sweat on her forehead." "Don't think this one sentence is not a big thing," Dr. Lin admonished them. "Only when you pay attention to these details will you know how to observe them, and recognize the specific unpredictable changes during any regular delivery. You need to learn to respect life before you can protect it."[14]

Lin's memorial in Xiamen includes a stone tablet highlighting her pledge, "I am, at all times and in all places, a doctor on duty. No matter when and where, it is my obligation to save the seriously-ill pregnant women."[15] Somehow, in a sixty-year career, Lin not only did research and taught medical students, but personally delivered many thousands of babies. Many grateful women named their babies after Dr. Lin, using the character for "lin" meaning "forest."[16]

Whenever Lin had to wait for labor to start or to watch postsurgical developments after her work hours, she liked to do needlework. She would buy white cotton fabric, cut it into small T-shirts with an opening in the front, then sew them into baby undershirts and decorate them with embroidered flowers. She gave these to the new mothers. On the birth certificates, she wrote "Lin Qiaozhi's baby" in English. This heartwarming signature was very touching to a well-known woman writer, Bingxin (Xie Wanying), whose three babies were delivered by Lin. Whenever they saw each other, they would talk about "our babies." Bingxin wrote, "With nimble hands, Lin helped give birth to thousands of babies; she not only helped the babies see the world, but she also guided their parents on how to nourish their children with limited food supplies. She helped nurture numerous fighters of the nation."[17]

Honors for Outstanding Medical Research

At one point in Lin's medical career, one of her American colleagues ridiculed her for the way she related to her patients. "Dr. Lin, do you think you can turn into a professor by holding hands with the patients and wiping off their sweat?"[18] She did not have to say anything to prove him wrong. Despite the medical field's very strict and heartless promotion structure, Lin made significant progress each year: from assistant doctor to resident to general resident.

In 1932, after Lin had served as a general resident physician for a year, PUMC sent her to Manchester Medical College and London Medical College's Gynecologic and Obstetric Hospital as a visiting scholar, and the following year to Vienna. She participated in research for a project on the breathing of fetuses in the uterus. This gave her a taste of the frontier of research in her area and a sense of direction for her own future research. After she came back, she worked with Prof. Zhang Xijun to study how the chemical element acetylcholine interferes with uterus contraction. Zhang and Lin later published their research results. (In her publications, Lin Qiaozhi used the variant spelling of her name, Lim Kah T'i.)

In 1939, Lin went to Chicago University Medical School to continue her study on fetus physiology (the relationship between a mother and a fetus). She knew this was an important issue for the many poor mothers in China with bad health, since the health and growth of the fetus depends on the nutritional condition of the mother. After she finished her study in 1940, she was granted honorary membership in several U.S. science associations, but she turned down offers to remain in the United States.

Upon return to PUMC, Lin became the first woman in China to be appointed director of a hospital department of obstetrics and gynecology. Other "firsts" were to follow in the 1950s, when she was the first woman appointed vice chair of the Chinese Medical Association, director of the new Beijing Maternity Hospital, and a deputy director of the Chinese Academy of Medical Sciences. She also was elected a representative to the National People's Congress and the Chinese People's Political Consultative Conference.[19]

During the 1940s decade of war, there had been no opportunity for Lin to continue her research. But by the mid-1950s, she started to pursue her long-term vision: developing several different research teams in PUMC's ob-gyn department to study key subjects. She also advised or edited major professional journals. Because of her rich clinical experience and the academic environment she created, there were high-quality medical research teams in her department. With this solid foundation, PUMC's and other ob-gyn departments and hospitals continued to flourish many years after Lin had passed away.

Dr. Lin and Premier Zhou Enlai

During the mid- and late 1950s, many well-known intellectuals joined the Chinese Communist Party. Like most educated Chinese, Lin Qiaozhi experienced the challenge of trying to identify with the new government. She went from a distant observer to an enthusiastic supporter, however, when she saw how the new government transformed prostitutes. Many of them had sexual diseases, and the government provided free treatment for them. After recovery, and equipped with job training and life skills, they were sent back to their hometowns or helped to find a job where they were. Being a gynecologist, Lin had more reason than most to hate the disgusting system of prostitution. The boldness of vision and strength to make changes that the new government had demonstrated were very convincing to her.

Deng Yingchao (Mrs. Zhou Enlai) was one of Lin's patients from the early 1950s. Lin did not realize who Deng was until Deng called to thank her. Lin then became close friends with the family. Sometimes, Premier Zhou would ask Lin to host special overseas visitors. When she encountered a situation in which she had to explain her attitude toward the party, however, she took the opportunity to share her faith openly with Zhou. She told him, "An honest person can't lie to either the organization or herself." She stressed that her Christian faith had a long history and deep impact on her life. She explained that it was probably not a good thing for the party if she claimed herself a Christian yesterday, and then tried to join the communist party the next day. Zhou told her clearly that there was no need to worry about this. The party trusted her. She could do a lot of things for the party by being an outsider, maybe even more than what she could do otherwise. Zhou's words were a big relief to Lin.[20]

It became common belief that as a result, Lin was protected during political campaigns such as the Anti-Rightist Movement and the Cultural Revolution. PUMC, with its earlier American affiliation, was a target of the Red Guards, who replaced the name plaque on the hospital with "Anti-Imperialism Hospital."[21] They took over one floor of Lin's house for use as their office, and she was forced to cut her long hair and stop wearing the traditional Chinese dress. Forbidden to work as a doctor, she was assigned as a nurse to give shots, deliver medications, and wash bedpans. She then recalled what she used to tell the young nurses: do these daily ordinary things out of love. What she had not told them was that in the early years of the profession, most nurses came from Christian families, because Christ's love enabled them to sacrifice their pride and serve others. Although she had not been involved in church activities since 1949, it was in these most helpless situations that she realized her deeply buried faith had never left her.[22]

To the Countryside: Life-Saving "Grandma Lin"

In 1966, Chairman Mao Zedong called for a shift of focus in medical and health work to the needs of the countryside. He criticized the health ministry officials as just city bureaucrats. Responding to Mao's instruction, the ministry put together a traveling medical team composed of impressive medical experts to show their determination to change their image. Lin, 64 years old by then, had never been to the countryside in her life. Team members were supposed to eat, live, and work together with the farmers. She was more concerned about how well she could perform the medical work in the new environment than any discomfort it would bring. She went out and talked to people to understand the common diseases of the area. When she heard that an eye disease was common, she spent time in the ophthalmology department to learn how to cure it. She also went to traditional Chinese doctors to learn how to use acupuncture to treat headaches and arthritis.

Lin ordered a plain padded jacket made for her and packed a pair of rubber-soled shoes in her bag, along with coffee, of course. After some controversy over this "luxury" item, an exception was made for her. With their simple clothes, assigned medical equipment, and state food coupons, the medical team arrived at a commune in Hunan, where over one thousand farming families were living next to Dongting Lake. With no electricity, telephones, or cars, the farmers lived on the cofferdam, where they also grew their rice. When floods came, the crops, houses, and human lives were at risk.

The medical team started by cleaning up a small room, painting the walls, putting gauze on the window, and hanging a bamboo screen in the doorway. The room seemed brighter after that. They bought a bamboo food steamer for sterilization and oil lamps and flashlights for surgical lighting. A door plank on top of two medical chests served as a counter for examinations.

In Beijing, these prestigious doctors had been in charge of departments and programs instead of practicing in clinics. Many people had to use social connections in order to see them. Now, however, very few people came to see them. The farmers could not afford to visit a doctor, nor could they even imagine the idea. They put up with small illnesses, and delayed seeing a doctor for bigger problems. In many cases, minor diseases became major ones over time and caused farmers to lose labor time. To deal with this situation, the medical team decided to divide into two groups and pay home visits.

One day a family brought to the clinic a twenty-year-old woman in labor with pregnancy toxicities. She had high blood pressure and edema all over her body. She was vomiting and twitching. It was a high-risk situation. The relatives who had brought her there were sighing and shaking their heads, afraid it was hopeless. Calmly, Dr. Lin started the delivery procedure. With the help of Lin and her assistants, the woman was able to deliver the baby safely and the baby's heartbeat was revived with mouth-to-mouth artificial breathing. Finally he cried out loud.

As such stories spread, others became convinced of the benefits of visiting the doctor. After that, some women started to come to the clinic for life-saving "Grandma Lin" to cure their diseases. Many husbands also started to bring their wives for checkups and treatment.

Within three months, Lin had seen and treated thirteen hundred farmer patients. Yet three months were not enough to change the medical and health situation of an entire area. After putting their heads together, the medical team came up with the idea of developing a rural health network. They selected local youth with middle school educations and trained them to become rural health workers and midwives. They were possibly the first group of "barefoot doctors."[23] Soon after that, the government set up clinics at the commune level, with health workers for production teams and "barefoot doctors" in the villages who could give simple shots and acupuncture to take care of headaches or fever.

Although there was still a huge gap between urban and rural areas, China's progress through the 1970s was praised by the World Bank and World Health Organization as a model for a revolution in rural health, wherein "the most health benefits occurred with the least investment." By 1980, 90 percent of China's villages practiced cooperative medical service. There were 630,000 rural midwives, 2,360,000 health workers, and 1,460,000 "barefoot doctors." These unromantic but exciting numbers cited by the World Health Organization brought tremendous pride to Lin.

7-2 Dr. Lin Qiaozhi

Her Last Years and Lasting Legacy

In 1972, Lin helped lead the first People's Republic of China medical delegation to visit North America and from 1973 to 1977 served as a consultant to the World Health Organization. In 1978, Lin became a vice chairwoman of the National Women's Federation and visited Europe as deputy head of a friendship delegation. While in Britain, she suffered a brain hemorrhage and was hospitalized for six months before she could return to China. She told her British friends, "I know my sickness is serious, but medicine alone cannot cure me. I need the sunshine, the air and the water of my own country."[24]

In 1980, Lin had another such attack in China, and she spent much of her last few years sick in bed. Even then, however, Lin was involved in advising and editing publications, including *Gynecological Tumors*. Her earlier book, *Family Health Advice*, had been so well received for its answers to general health questions that she organized the writing of two more books: *Encyclopedia of Family Child-Rearing* and *General Knowledge for Rural Women and Children*.

Before her eightieth birthday in 1981, Lin was not doing very well physically. From the hospital bed she told a journalist from the *China Youth Daily*, "I am a doctor, I have witnessed too many births and deaths. I am not afraid of death. The Bible says 'I will go to see Him.'"[25] After she died, Lin Qiaozhi willed all her savings to the kindergartens and nurseries in Beijing.

Her last request was that she be taken back to Gulangyu Island. Her fellow townspeople built a beautiful garden with a white marble statue of Lin to remember her. The Lin Qiaozhi Memorial displays the history of her life, and one of the stone markers along the road contains a quotation from Lin that reads, "I am a daughter of Gulangyu. In my dreams I often go back to my hometown by the boundless sea, where the water is so blue, so beautiful."[26]

On the hundredth anniversary of her birth, December 23, 2001, many well-known doctors, public health officials, and senior officials gathered in Beijing to honor her memory. At the Great Hall of the People, a copper statue of Lin was unveiled. The Chinese Academy of Medical Sciences opened an ob-gyn institute named after Lin, fulfilling her longtime dream for excellence in the care of women and infants.[27]

8

WEI ZHUOMIN
Bridging National Culture and World Values

by Peter Tze Ming Ng

A pioneer in comparative cultural studies, Dr. Wei Zhuomin (also known as Francis C. M. Wei) became a channel for the cultural exchange between the Western world and China. The famous American historian Kenneth Latourette expressed his high regard for Wei while writing a foreword to Wei's book, *The Spirit of Chinese Culture*:

> We have here a subject of central importance treated by a master. . . . Toward the comprehension of the spirit of the Chinese and their culture, Dr. Wei is a superb guide. A Chinese by birth and nurture, he knows his people and the unseen forces which have molded them. . . . At the same time, he knows the Occident and so is able to bridge the gulf between that part of the world and China. . . . Sympathetic with the deepest insights of the Chinese spirit, he is also a Christian. Few can equal him and none can surpass him as an interpreter of the Soul of China to the English-speaking world.[1]

Among Chinese Christians in the late 1940s and early 1950s there was a popular saying, *"bei Zhao nan Wei,"* meaning, "For Protestant theologians in China, we have Zhao Zichen (T. C. Chao) in the north and Wei Zhuomin in the south."[2]

Behind the achievement of such recognition at home and abroad was a remarkable man, Dr. Wei Zhuomin. Although he lived most of his life in the Wuhan area on the Yangtze River in central China, Wei became a citizen of the world through education, work, and travel abroad. He was not only a dedicated and influential educator but also a creative philosopher and theologian. He was an outstanding Chinese intellectual, yet unlike many of his contemporaries, he did not despise Christianity or Western culture. Early on, he had a great interest in the study of Christian religion and Western philosophies, and he was baptized into the American Protestant Episcopal Church. He possessed a strong sense of Christian identity, yet he did not forsake his own Chinese identity, instead maintaining a keen interest in the exploration of his national culture. As a pioneer in comparative cultural studies, Wei became a bridge between Western and Chinese cultures.

Life and Work in International Education

Wei Zhuomin (1888–1976) was born on December 7, 1888, in the village now called Zhongshan, in Guangdong Province.[3] He received his education from Boone College, a mission school run by the American Protestant Episcopal Church in Wuchang, Hubei Province, where his father had some trading business. Wei gained his Bachelor of Arts degree in 1911, and in the same year he also became a Christian and was baptized.

Wei received a scholarship in the same college to work on the degree of Master of Arts, which he completed in 1915. In September 1918, Wei had a rare opportunity to go abroad through a scholarship offered by the American Episcopal Theological School in Cambridge, Massachusetts, where he spent one year studying theology before completing an MA in philosophy at Harvard University. In July 1920, he returned to Boone College, where he became a professor.

In 1924, Boone College was renamed and expanded as Central China (*Huazhong*) University (CCU), which today is Central China Normal University.[4] Wei was appointed Dean of the Faculty of Arts and Sciences. In 1927 he traveled to Europe, completing a PhD degree in 1929 at the University of London, after which he returned to become the first Chinese president of his alma mater. There he served as president for twenty-three years until 1952, thereafter serving as a professor.

CCU was founded by the joint efforts of various Protestant denominations: the London Missionary Society and the Wesleyan Methodist Mission from England, and the American Protestant Episcopal Church, American Reformed Church, and Yale-in-China Mission from the United States. The members of the management board were representatives from the various denominations. In this way, the university itself provided a global context for Wei, who had to run an internationally linked Christian university for the benefit of Chinese students, of whom most were from local regions in China. Hence, Wei had to seek his own ways to integrate the Christian faith with the Chinese social context in order to serve as a Chinese president who could be both a true Christian and a truly Chinese educator. He had to be concerned with the realization of the Christian vision and its universal values in a localized Chinese context.[5]

Despite his major administrative responsibilities, Wei was actively involved in the expansion of the Christian faith, both locally and internationally. American historian Miner S. Bates, who worked in China for thirty years, listed Wei as one of China's prominent Christians.[6] Wei's many public activities from the 1920s through the 1940s provided him a worldwide context for comparing Christian movements around the world and exploring how Christianity could help in the development of his own national culture.[7]

In the first decade after his return to China, Wei was appointed a delegate of his own church to attend the inaugural conference of China's National Christian Council held in Shanghai in 1922. At the conference, he was then elected as one of the one hundred members of the NCC, and thereafter, he gave addresses at several of its conferences from 1922 to 1928. In 1928, he was appointed one of the Chinese delegates attending the International Missionary Conference in Jerusalem. While studying in London between 1927 and 1929, Wei kept in close touch with the London Missionary Society and the Wesleyan Methodist Missionary Society, which supported his study and his work at CCU.[8]

In the 1930s, after his return to China, he became a Chinese representative in the Christian World Movement, which led to the launch of the World Council of Churches (WCC) in 1938. Here, too, Wei became an active leader as well as representing China.[9] In 1946, he was elected president of the National Committee of the Chinese Anglican Church. That August, he attended a World Council of Churches (WCC) conference held in Cambridge, England, where he served not only as a Chinese delegate but also one of only three vice chairs of the conference.[10] In 1948, he was invited to attend a WCC international conference in Madras, India.

Being Chinese, Wei Did Not Reject Western Christianity

Wei was raised in a fairly traditional Chinese family in South China. Wei's uncles and their family members were mostly bankers and merchants. His own father was a tea merchant as well as a Confucian scholar. Wei was brought up with a Confucian education at home, being taught the Chinese classics at the age of seven. As a merchant doing business in Hankou, however, Wei's father also understood the importance of learning the English language, so he sent Wei away from home at the age of twelve to a mission school in Wuchang (across the river from Hankou). Wei was told by his parents that the aim of his study in a mission school was to learn as much English as possible from the missionaries but to close his ears to their religious teachings.[11] Wei spent eight years at Boone School in Wuchang, and as an obedient child he dared not proclaim himself to be a Christian until he graduated at the age of twenty-one.[12]

Despite his parent's admonition to learn only English, Wei was much enlightened by the holistic education he received from the missionaries. As he recalled later, the mission school provided him the great opportunity to learn about Christianity, despite his initial unwillingness to attend mandatory worship services. The school stimulated his thinking about his own culture, and he started to study the Confucian classics again. Gradually he discovered that the teachings in Christianity and the Confucian ethics were not contradictory.[13] By then, he had developed a keen interest in not only the Christian religion but also Western culture and philosophy. In 1919, after one year of preparatory study in Cambridge, Massachusetts, Wei moved on to Harvard University, where he studied comparative philosophy under William E. Hocking, a renowned philosopher.

8-1 Wei Zhuomin and a colleague

In 1927, Wei had another chance to go abroad, this time to Europe for more advanced research on comparative studies of Eastern and Western cultures. He was fortunate enough to work under L. T. Hobhouse at the University of London and B. H. Streeter at Oxford University. While he was pursuing his study in England, Wei was invited to write for the series *China Today through Chinese Eyes*, and he contributed a treatise in English entitled "Synthesis of Cultures of East and West."[14] Wei explicitly stated his own understanding of cultures, as well as the possible approaches to cultural intercommunication and ways of "synchronizing" Eastern and Western cultures. He sought to provide important insights regarding modern society.

On the subject of synchronizing Eastern and Western cultures, Wei proposed adopting a sympathetic and appreciative attitude toward the different cultures, not to conquer one by the other, but rather to conserve the good elements of both cultures and integrate them into an organic whole.[15]

At that time, there was a rising tide of nationalism in China, and most intellectuals were cautious about Western culture and wanted to guard Chinese culture against being eroded by Westernization. On the contrary, Wei advocated an open attitude toward Western culture.

He affirmed first of all that a nation could never exist without its own culture, and that a people could never totally forsake its own culture. A culture was organic by nature; it grew by absorbing or being transformed when interacting with other cultures.[16] Cultural change would not destroy the country as such; rather, it would help the nation grow. Since culture grows like a living organism, the best way to preserve culture was not to protect it from encountering other cultures, but to help it grow well, by adopting an open attitude to different cultures, preserving their valuable elements, and seeking ways to help develop their growth into an organic whole.[17]

Being Christian, Wei Did Not Despise Chinese Culture

Wei was educated and baptized at a missionary college, where he had been taught much about Christianity, but he also spent much time studying Chinese classics in order to compare Confucian and Christian teachings. Even though Wei was interested in Christianity, he still valued highly his own national culture. He had written an excellent graduation thesis entitled "Religious Beliefs of the Ancient Chinese and Their Influence on the National Character of the Chinese People."[18] This was probably the first undergraduate thesis in a Chinese university on the religiosity of the Chinese people. Besides being published in 1911 in the college magazine, *The Boone Review*, it was quickly reprinted by the *Chinese Recorder*, an influential magazine printed by the missionary community.[19]

In his thesis, Wei explored ancient Chinese religious beliefs, especially Chinese conceptions of God and of ancestor worship. He quoted references from *The Book of Rites* and *The Book of Books* and argued that those religious beliefs had long been in the minds of the Chinese and had become part of the national character of the Chinese people. Hence, Wei's in-depth exploration of the religious elements of Chinese culture led him to affirm the significance of such beliefs.

Just after Wei began his postgraduate study at Boone in September 1911, he witnessed the start of the 1911 Revolution in Wuchang, which was just across the Yangtze River.[20] The birth of the new Republic of China had a great impact on Wei. He chose to write his master's thesis on "The Political Thoughts of Mencius," revealing his keen interest in studying traditional culture with a very specific political dimension.

He retained this focus on Chinese tradition even in 1929, while pursuing a doctoral degree at the University of London, with a dissertation entitled "A Study of the Chinese Moral Tradition and Its Social Values."[21] Even though Wei was educated in a Christian college and trained in both American and British contexts, his research interests remained focused on a wide range of aspects in Chinese culture, including ethics, politics, philosophy, and religion. Thus, his early research already highlighted the interplay between Western and Chinese cultures.

He was highly respected by foreign academics because of his ability to produce such scholarship on Chinese culture and clearly share his knowledge with Western audiences. Wei was invited to attend a conference at Yale University in 1934 and lecture at Yale University Divinity School, Columbia University, the University of Chicago, and Oberlin College while he was attending the General Conference of the Protestant Episcopal Church in the United States. In 1937–38, he was appointed Adjunct Professor of Ethics at Yale Divinity School.

The appreciation of American scholars became more evident when Wei was appointed Visiting Professor of Comparative Philosophy at Union Theological Seminary, New York, a position he held from 1945 to 1946, and when he, as the first Henry W. Luce Visiting Professor of World Christianity, presented a series of Hewett Lectures, later published as *The Spirit of Chinese Culture*.[22]

A New Understanding of Christian Mission as a Bridge between East and West

Besides introducing the spirit of Chinese culture to American scholars and religious leaders, Wei took upon himself the challenge of developing an alternative understanding of the Christian mission in China, which he unveiled during his series of lectures in New York.

Wei began with an emphasis on the antiquity of Christianity in China, with which most of his audience was unfamiliar. While most of his Chinese as well as Western contemporaries assumed Christianity came to China from the West in recent centuries, Wei pointed out that it arrived much earlier, and from Persia in West Asia, not from Europe or America.

He followed Prof. Chen Yuan's analysis of Christianity's arrival in China in four distinctive periods.[23] Wei explained that according to Chen, Christianity first came to China by the early Tang Dynasty, when Alopen, the first Nestorian missionary, arrived in Chang'an in A.D. 635, in response to an official court invitation. The Chinese emperor, Tang Taizong, had shown great respect for and welcomed Christianity most graciously. But because the Nestorians were perceived as one of the Buddhist sects in China, they were suppressed when the later emperor Tang Wuzong ordered a ban on Buddhism in 845.

The second period was during the thirteenth-century Yuan Dynasty, when the Mongols favored Nestorian Christianity. After the destruction of Mongol rule in 1368, however, the religion's influence quickly dissipated, since it had been so closely affiliated with the foreign rulers. The Mongols had been indifferent to Chinese culture and there had been little Mongol evangelism among the Chinese, and thus there was no broad Christian impact upon Chinese life and thought during Mongol rule.

The third period was the coming of Roman Catholicism in the fifteenth and sixteenth centuries during the Ming Dynasty. Great Jesuit missionaries such as Matteo Ricci and his successors had significant influence on the imperial court. Later, however, the Dominicans and Augustinians quarreled with the Jesuits, which gave rise to the Chinese Rites Controversy concerning the practice of veneration of ancestors. The ensuing challenge to such central tenets of Chinese state orthodoxy led to the expulsion of Catholic missionaries from China in the early eighteenth century.[24]

The fourth, modern period began with the coming of Protestant missionaries in the early nineteenth century. In retelling the history of Christianity in China, Wei concluded that as far as Chinese life and thoughts were concerned, and at least for the first and second periods, the missionary "had failed to understand the essence of Chinese culture and to make a real impact upon it or to utilize it as a medium for presenting Christianity to the Chinese."[25]

Wei then expounded on the Chinese perspective regarding the modern Christian mission in China, usually conceived of by Westerners as part of the "expansion of territorial Christendom."[26] This was especially so during the late nineteenth and early twentieth centuries, when Protestant missionaries were consumed with the zeal "to evangelize the whole world in this generation."[27] The idea was manifested at the World Missionary Conference held in Edinburgh in 1910, during which the world was defined in terms of two categories: "lands fully missionized' and "lands not yet fully missionized."[28]

By the 1920s, there was growing resentment of such thinking in China, which surged after the publication of Milton Stauffer's book, *The Christian Occupation of China*, the title of which suggested the conquest of China by Christian powers.[29] The Chinese people strongly reacted against such imperialistic conceptions of Christendom, and intellectuals began to criticize the missions as "tools of Western imperialism" and the "means of cultural imperialism by Western powers in China."[30] One famous Chinese scholar captured this sentiment when he said, "When Buddha came to China, he was riding on an elephant, but Jesus was riding on gunboats."[31]

Following widespread incidents during an anti-Christian movement throughout China, culminating in the damage of mission property in Nanjing during the Northern Expedition of 1926, nearly half of the missionaries left China. Shortly after this, Wei was asked to give an address on January 5, 1928, to church leaders at the National Christian Council in Shanghai. He spoke on a very timely topic: "Projecting the Future of Mission Policy in China."[32]

Wei observed that Chinese Christians did not like to see their conversion to Christianity interpreted as being "called into Christendom" in the way the missionaries had understood this, that is, merely to be transferred from a "heathen" world into the Christian kingdom. Rather, they would prefer to be invited to join and share in the Christian worldwide movement without losing their own national identity.

Expressing sorrow over the withdrawal of the missionaries, Wei gave three suggestions regarding the future of Christian missions in China, namely to (1) emphasize Christian nurture rather than "Christian occupation" in China, (2) be more concerned with the training of Christian leaders so that churches could move ahead toward self-governance and self-support, and (3) move beyond Western denominationalism.[33]

Over a decade later, in 1939, Wei spoke on a similar topic, "(World Christian) Missions in This Age," in an address at the annual conference of the American National Women's Auxiliary Association.[34] He affirmed the work of the missionaries who had devoted their lives to China in the past century, and he stressed that since the Chinese population constituted one quarter of the world's population, it was essential and significant to help Chinese people understand the Christian message and revelation.

Then he expounded on the four necessary stages of development for missionary work in China. The first stage occurred when the pioneer missionaries came and explored new ways to start work in China. The second stage was when the missionaries consolidated foundational missionary activities and began schools and churches. The third stage was when the missionaries expanded their work by setting up mission stations and management networks throughout China. This was also the time for training local people and building up "self-governing" and "self-supporting" native churches. In the fourth stage, the Chinese churches would stand on their own and become fully autonomous.

Wei explained that mission work in China had reached only the third stage and was just beginning to move into the fourth stage. "The building of the Chinese churches had to be accomplished by the help of the missionaries, with the support from their 'mother church' and the 'universal church.'" Yet the work had to be completed by the Chinese people themselves. In other words, the missionaries had to prepare to hand over authority to the Chinese churches.

In his 1945–46 Hewett Lectures, Wei stated his views even more clearly:

> It is because the Christian believes that the Christian Church needs all people in the world, as much as all people in the world need the Christian faith, that the world wide Christian missionary movement is supported and kept going. When this is explained and understood in China the missionary movement will no longer be regarded as Western arrogance and presumptuousness, and the missionary will not be considered as exercising his prerogative of making known what he has in himself and what others lack, but (rather) as doing his duty in seeking for a more adequate expression for the Faith which is intended for the whole of mankind.[35]

Wei was suggesting that only in this way could the Chinese (and other non-Western peoples as well) feel respected as a people and as individuals, maintaining their own national identities. They could thus feel honored to be part of the Christian worldwide movement by joining as members of the universal church.[36] This mutuality would be essential to both the appreciation of global values in Christianity and the respect for the spiritual heritage of Chinese culture.

A New Conception of World Christianity

Besides cultivating a new understanding of Christian missions for American scholars and religious leaders, Wei also attempted to develop a new conception of world Christianity. His opening lecture in New York in 1945 addressed the issue of "Rooting the Christian Church in Chinese Soil."[37] While affirming Christianity as a worldwide movement, Wei believed that only with an in-depth appreciation of the spirit of Chinese culture and rooting the Christian church in the Chinese soil could Christianity and Chinese culture be mutually benefited. In order for Christianity to be properly understood and received by the Chinese, Wei argued, Chinese culture needed to be utilized "as a medium for the presentation of the Christian religion to the Chinese, [and] that Christian teachings must be put, at the initial stage at least, in terms of Chinese thought-forms and according to the Chinese philosophical, religious, artistic and social genius."[38] Wei even suggested that development of a Chinese Christian theology could supplement Western Christianity and enrich the worldwide Christian heritage.

Wei also suggested that if one took the idea of world Christianity seriously, one should be clear that without Asia or China, Christianity could in no way be a world religion.[39] In other words, the "local" (Asia or China) should be seen as an indispensable part of the "global" (world Christianity). For Christianity to be recognized as a world religion, it needed to find its full expression in all cultures. Thus, when the Chinese accepted and gave expression to their Christian faith in the Chinese culture, they were at the same time bringing about the realization of Christianity as a world religion. This was by no means a rejection of Western Christianity; rather, Christianity would become more welcome in China the more its Western form was not presented as the only perfect form of Christianity.

Wei suggested that his approach was a new way of interpreting Christianity in the context of all the various cultures it encountered.

> In this way the special strength and virtue of all the religious traditions (including the Chinese religions) may be brought into the Christian Church, each as a new emphasis to supplement the 'empirical' Christianity which we at present recognize as predominantly western, and we may have an entirely fresh vision of the glory of our Faith. . . . For we see clearly that not only do those peoples need the Faith of the Christian Church, but also the Christian Church needs their cultures in order to give it a fuller expression that it may become more ecumenical.[40]

The task of mutual enrichment was not easy to achieve, and indeed it would require a long process of mutual adaptation, maintaining the consistency of each culture and yet working for constructive assimilation. Thus, on the one hand, Wei believed that Christianity could help fulfill the spirit of Chinese culture by making it more complete. For example, it brought a more profound understanding of the nature of God and the way human beings could communicate with and relate to God. To the Chinese people, God was a judge, not a father, much less the loving father in Christian teaching. Similarly, the doctrine of grace could enrich the spiritual dimension of Chinese life.

On the other hand, Wei argued that Christianity needed China in order to move beyond Western denominationalism to become more inclusive. Wei explained, "We may not have to give up our denominational characteristics, but what we ought to learn is to respect and tolerate one another's differences."[41] Ever since Protestantism came to China, the various denominations had been fighting against one another for their own territorial dominions. "The astonishing thing to the Chinese is that the Christians do not respect each other. . . . It is denominationalism rather than denominations that has been a hindrance to the Christian enterprise in China."[42]

Wei pointed out that the Chinese people were peace seeking and practical, with concerns that were predominantly ethical and political rather than metaphysical and epistemological, as in the West.[43] Because of this spirit of pragmatism, the Chinese people were more ready to accept a plurality of religious traditions. They were apt to accept that

Christianity embraced various denominations, as there was also a divergence of sects among Buddhism and Daoism in China. However, the strong "spirit of denominationalism" in Christianity had created great divisiveness and had kept the Chinese people away.

Wei once recalled a conversation with an American that went as follows:

"Are you an Episcopalian?" (Wei was asked.)
"No. But I abide by the Episcopalian doctrines and services."
"Are you a Presbyterian then?"
"No. But I serve as an elder in my church."
"Are you a Baptist then?"
"I was baptized. But I was not baptized by immersion."
"Then, which denomination do you belong to? Are you an Anglican—a member of the Church of England?"
"Oh! Dear Brother in Christ. I am a Chinese, how can I be a member of the Church of England?" Wei replied.[44]

Wei strongly suggested that the Christian churches in China needed to advocate the virtue of tolerance if they wanted to "make Christianity live in China."[45] In other words, an attitude of respect would be more congenial to the spirit of Chinese culture than ostracism. This critique of the spirit of denominationalism in Western Christianity from the higher plane of world Christianity was unique. Wei was among the first Chinese Christians to tell Westerners so precisely what the Chinese thought of the Christian world mission.

Wei's ideas both reflected and shaped the Christian ecumenical thinking of his times. He had been actively involved in the formulation and the early years of the World Council of Churches (WCC). Wei attended both the Life and Work Conference at Oxford University and the Faith and Order Conference at Edinburgh University in the summer of 1937, which laid the foundational work. At both conferences, Western Christians were critically rethinking the old territorial conception of "Christendom," and there was a strong urge to develop a new understanding that could replace the idea of "foreign mission" with "world mission" and sectarianism and denominationalism with Christian ecumenism. The formation of the WCC in 1938 was viewed as one concrete way to work out a radical reformulation of "Christendom" that was "non-territorial," "non-racial," and "non-political."[46] And Wei's new understanding of Christian missions helped to introduce the

Chinese point of view into this reformulation, with special relevance to the Chinese understanding of universalism (*datong shijie*) and the spirit of inclusiveness (*baorong xing*) in Christian ecumenism.

After World War II, there emerged a new conviction that Christian ecumenism should proceed even further, to define and construct a proper role for Christianity as a world movement and make a Christian contribution to the new international order. These issues shaped the Cambridge WCC Conference in August 1946, where Wei was appointed as one of the conference vice chairs. Out of the discussions came the creation of the Commission of the Churches on International Affairs (CCIA), a working relationship with the United Nations on religious liberty and human rights issues, and contributions to the establishment of the Universal Declaration of Human Rights.[47]

Exploring World Values from Christianity

In his Hewett Lectures, Wei proposed a Chinese Christian intellectual's understanding of world Christianity. Wei was perhaps the first scholar to attempt something akin to today's concept of cultural globalization as the interplay among cultures. Though the term "globalization" was not used in his time, Wei was developing his own conception of world Christianity in such a way that required more attention to the interplay between the globalization and localization of Christianity in the Chinese cultural context.

As the first Visiting Professor of World Christianity, Wei explained to the Western audience that a good sense of world consciousness would not hinder one from affirming one's own cultural heritage. As a Chinese, he could also apply a "typically Chinese Christian" point of view by trying to elaborate this "Chinese Christian" understanding of world Christianity, that is, the Chinese way of seeking the "middle way" ("the Mean" or "keeping the balance") between the universal religion and the specific, cultural context in China. In Wei's words, "Even when we are taking Christianity as a world religion, the full expression of Christian faith needs to be in congruence with its specific contexts."[48] On another occasion, he said, "We are sure of one thing, and that is, if

Christianity is to take root in China, it must assume a Chinese form, congenial to the Chinese cultural heritage."[49]

Wei understood that as human beings, we are bound by the localized culture we represent. On the one hand, Chinese culture was the same as Western culture in that each was but a representation of local cultures. Wei thought that world Christianity, to give itself a fuller expression of the universal Christian faith, needed people from all cultures to give expressions of that faith through their own traditions. This was precisely the global vision found in Christianity.

On the other hand, Wei had the conviction that since world Christianity had survived interaction with a multitude of various cultures in different parts of the world, it could help all local or regional cultures to move forward and become more inclusive if they were to adopt its world values and global vision. Hence, Christianity could be beneficial to the exploration and enrichment of Chinese culture in the following ways:

1. As a world religion, Christianity would help the Chinese to open up and learn to embrace people of other cultures, other countries, other races, and other religions.

2. Christianity was concerned with not only the material world but also the spiritual world, so it would help the Chinese people to care more for their spiritual well-being.

3. Christianity conceived of a world beyond the present world and the existence of a transcendental world; this perspective would help provide more meaning for life in the existing world.

4. The orientation toward the future opened yet another new perspective on human existence, a new form of expression for any existing culture, including all Chinese and Western cultures.

5. As a worldwide culture, Christianity introduced a new sense of communal relationships among world civilizations, especially in an era when different cultures were encountering one another more fully and regularly.

6. Christianity paid great respect to both history and present reality, with a strong historical consciousness and an appreciation of cultures worldwide.[50]

Wei proposed that Chinese culture would benefit by learning from Christianity because it had all these elements. The cultivation of "a universal and ecumenical culture" (*shijie datong wenhua*) would involve the lifting up of Chinese culture to the spiritual dimensions of human life, to the transcendental elements that go beyond the present world, and to the sense of communal relationships that would help the Chinese people embrace other cultures.[51] Wei recalled many instances from the history of intercultural exchanges that demonstrated how the modification of local cultures would often enrich, rather than endanger, one's local or national characteristics. In his view, this was the fundamental principle underlying all forms of organic life.[52]

To illustrate the proper interplay between Christianity and Chinese culture, Wei suggested that the best way to preserve Chinese culture was to offer it to God and make it sanctified.[53] In other words, Wei believed that Christianity might help to bring Chinese culture to the altar of God and let it be purified and sanctified as it was brought closer to truth.

While world ecumenical leader John R. Mott was visiting China in January 1926, Wei was asked to give an address to a group of church and missionary leaders at the National Christian Council conference in Shanghai. Wei chose the topic "Making Christianity Live in China." In his speech, while admitting the fact that Chinese culture was not Christian, Wei urged efforts to achieve mutual enrichment in the interplay between Christianity and the Chinese culture, including "the Christianization of China" and "the indigenization of Christianity in the Chinese soil." The spirit of Christ could transform the Chinese culture by giving it "a new soul;" it could be "Christianized."[54] The Christian faith, Wei added, could then be given the chance for expression through the lives of Chinese people in their families, their churches, their society, and even the whole nation.[55] Moreover, as all good things came from God, Christianity might help reveal all truths and all good deeds within Chinese culture and make them all manifestations of God's good deeds.[56]

Wei sought to implement his views within China's academic world, even setting forth "the sanctification of Chinese culture" as one goal of the redevelopment plan for his university after World War II. Speaking from his own experience as a university president, Wei pointed out that Christian colleges in China had provided a successful platform for an educational encounter between Eastern and Western cultures. In a speech at Jinling College, he reminded the students that it was their duty to know clearly the roles of Christianity and Chinese cultures in the world today.[57]

For Central China University, he planned to recruit as many missionary educators as he could from overseas, in order to bring about more interaction with local Chinese students. He aimed to employ one third of his staff from overseas, and for the rest, to seek as many Christian professors as he could from local sources.[58] As professors and students met face to face in the Christian college, they were bound to encounter one another's different cultures. They thus were given daily opportunities to cross over the barriers that usually divided individuals and groups. Students and faculty were encouraged to get down to the bedrock of their own cultures by careful observation, open discussions, and their own serious academic studies.

Wei's vision was that in the Christian colleges, missionaries and local people would work and live together, and by the Christian spirit of appreciation and learning from each other's cultural peculiarities the synthesis of Eastern and Western cultures could be more easily achieved. Wei emphasized, "The synthesis of cultures is, therefore, an educational necessity."[59]

8-2 Prof. Wei Zhoumin in his study

A Legacy for Bridging Cultures Today

Few could understand fully what Wei was saying in his time, although his appointment as the first Henry Luce Visiting Professor of World Christianity affirmed his theoretical contributions. The process some call "glocalization" involves interplay between "globalization" and "localization." Wei's ideas are still relevant more than sixty years later to debates about such processes, as well as to current discussions about world Christianity. Scholars of the twenty-first century are in a much better position to understand Wei's views as precursors of today's concepts and to appreciate the real meaning and value of Wei's discovering world values in Christianity while preserving the uniquely Chinese culture.

On March 26, 1976, Wei died in Wuhan at the age of eighty-eight. Wei is still remembered and highly respected in China. In 1984, the alumni of Central China University, together with leaders from the Hubei provincial government and the Provincial Protestant Three-Self Patriotic Movement held a special memorial conference for him and honored him as "a great scholar of China."[60] Prof. Zhang Kaiyuan, former president of Central China Normal University, recalled in 1995 that he had been a friend and a colleague of Wei's for thirty years. He greatly appreciated Wei's service and leadership at CCU, especially his work in the exploration of as well as the bridging between Chinese and Western cultures.[61] Zhang stressed that as an educator, Wei taught his students not only by what he said, but more importantly by what he did and how he behaved.

Zhang affirmed a description of Wei by Prof. Jessie Lutz, an American historian, who called him "a Christian, a scholar and a patriot."[62] When asked whether Wei had given up his Christian faith during the Cultural Revolution, Zhang stated firmly that Wei had not, even though he had been labeled a "rightist" in 1957 and had gone through very difficult times.[63]

CCU alumni living in Taiwan remembered and honored President Wei in 1980 by establishing a memorial hall and publishing *Dr. Francis C. M. Wei's Writings on Education, Culture, and Religion*. Alumni in mainland China compiled *The Selected Writings of Francis C. M. Wei*, published by the Central China Normal University Press in 1997. Indeed, Wei is held in such high esteem that the university erected a granite statue in his likeness and held another international conference in honor of his achievements at the ninetieth anniversary of the founding of the university in 1993. The conference proceedings were published by the university press (in 1995) as *A Giant Bridging Over the Gap between the Chinese and Western Cultures: A Collection of Theses at the International Symposium on Dr. Francis C. M. Wei*. The university community saw this as the most appropriate way to show respect and honor to Wei, their model as a patriot and a Christian educator.

As a Chinese intellectual in early twentieth-century China, Wei skillfully brought together Christian world values and his own national culture. His contemporaries promoted either "complete Westernization" or the use of "Chinese culture as the essence; Western learning as the means" in response to contact with Western cultures. But Wei attempted a new way of synthesizing Eastern and Western culture by interpreting Christianity in terms of Chinese culture (a process of localization) and by transforming Chinese culture with Christian world values (a process of globalization), hence demonstrating an interplay of cultures (the process of glocalization) and the construction of "an ideal, universal and ecumenical culture" (*shijie datong wenhua*). These concepts have yet to be fully explored and developed. Wei was indeed a great scholar who proposed new ways of understanding Christian missions and a more creative interplay between Christianity and Chinese culture.

9

WU YIFANG
Abundant Life in Training Women for Service

by Mary Jo Waelchli

At 10 a.m. on November 3, 1928, Wu Yifang was formally inaugurated head of Jinling Women's College in Nanjing, becoming China's first female college president. The thirty-five-year-old Jinling alumna had just returned from the United States after finishing a doctoral degree in biology from the University of Michigan. Audience members included presidents of other Chinese universities as well as Jinling faculty, alumnae, and students. China's first lady Soong Mei-ling (Madame Chiang Kai-shek) was one of the speakers.

In her inauguration address, Wu told the audience that the "opportunity that arrives when the times produce heroes is now here." She emphasized the college's role in cultivating female talent conversant in both Chinese tradition and Western science to serve China, a theme she was to stress throughout her tenure at Jinling and beyond:

> Jinling was established to meet the needs of the time following the 1911 Revolution, to train female leaders for society. Today the college is also cultivating talent to do various kinds of work for the new China ... for Jinling, studies of Chinese ancient civilization and science are both equally important, cultivating the

thinking of Chinese scholars who will then go out into society and be able to meet various kinds of new needs, applying what they have learned to contribute to various kinds of new work. . . . Currently there are still very few women getting a higher education, so they have a kind of responsibility to society as leaders. The most critical qualification for a leader is moral integrity.[1]

Wu's voice trembled as she gave her address, but the students in the audience were proud of their "young pretty president" and felt the speech was "beautiful and moving."[2] Wu Yifang was to remain as Jinling's president until the Christian colleges disappeared in a reorganization of higher education institutions in the early 1950s. She was also to become a prominent leader of educational, women's, church, and government-sponsored organizations during the Republican period and in the People's Republic of China. Yet it was Jinling College and the training of women for service to the Chinese nation that remained dearest to her heart. On her deathbed in 1985, her last words were to inquire about the establishment of the new Jinling College.

However, as Wu Yifang stood on the podium for the inauguration ceremony, this was all in the future. In fact, she had walked a long road to even arrive on that stage in 1928. Only a person of Wu Yifang's steadfastness and determination—resting on a strong inner strength and solid personal Christian faith—would have made it so far.

From Family Tragedy to Graduate Study Abroad

Wu Yifang, the third of four children, was born on January 26, 1893, in Wuchang, Hubei Province, as China's final imperial dynasty tottered on its last legs and the country was on the cusp of great change. Wu's early life illustrates the changes in women's lives in late nineteenth- and early twentieth-century China. The custom of foot binding, for example, was beginning to decline, and Wu Yifang's feet were first bound and then unbound.[3]

Typical of her era and class, Wu—the daughter of a Qing Dynasty minor official—received her early schooling at home, studying along with her brother from age seven.[4] Traditionally, China's schools and academies were not open to women. However, new-style schools that offered Western learning were opening in China's large cities, and Yifang and her elder sister Yifen set their sights on attending one.

When a relative brought word of a new girls' school in Hangzhou, where their maternal grandmother and other relatives lived, the two sisters saw their chance and begged their parents to allow them to go. Their father flatly refused. He and the other adult family members, like most Chinese of this time, considered education outside the home to be unacceptable for girls. Their paternal grandmother commented that it was "not right" for girls to show their faces outside the home. Strong-willed Yifen, however, refused to give up. Desperate to attend school, she attempted suicide in protest. Shocked, the girls' parents finally gave permission for the sisters to attend school in Hangzhou.[5]

In 1904, Yifang, 11, and her sister Yifen, 15, journeyed to Hangzhou to study at Hangzhou Girls School.[6] This was the first in a succession of modern schools—some, like Hangzhou Girls School, run by reformist Chinese, others by Christian missionaries—in Hangzhou, Shanghai, and Suzhou that the sisters attended from 1904 to 1909. Wu Yifang's life changed abruptly and tragically, however, when her father committed suicide in 1909. The sisters were forced to leave school because of stress on family finances. In 1911, their elder brother also committed suicide. Their mother, who had been in ill health for some time, died shortly afterward, and Yifen hanged herself before her mother's funeral. Therefore, within two years, four of Yifang's closest family members were gone—three within a month of each other. At eighteen, the grief-stricken Wu Yifang was left with only her paternal grandmother and her nine-year-old sister Yiquan as surviving family members.

A maternal aunt and her husband, Chen Shutong, who lived in Hangzhou took them in. Chen treated them as members of his own family, which was quite prominent. He had passed the highest level of the Chinese civil service exam and entered the Imperial Academy, then studied abroad in Japan. He returned to China in 1906 and later became a member of the short-lived Qing Consultative Council. After 1911, he served in the Republic's first House of Representatives.[7]

In 1913, with the support of this progressive uncle, Wu Yifang returned to school in Hangzhou. The next year, she moved north to Beijing with Chen and his family, where she taught English at Beijing Girls Normal School—ironically, using the schooling that the family had so strongly opposed to help support her grandmother and younger sister.

In 1916, Chen Shutong moved to Shanghai as one of the directors of the Shanghai Commercial Press and again made it possible for Wu to return to school—this time to Jinling College in the Republican capital, Nanjing. A Christian mission institution, Jinling was one of the first schools in China to offer a full college course to Chinese women. In 1919, Wu became one of China's first college-educated women, when she and four others graduated in Jinling's first class.

Although some of the schools that Wu attended were run by missionaries, her family was not Christian. She became a Christian during her junior year at Jinling College. Her conversion to Christianity helped fill the emotional and spiritual void of losing her family members. Wu later recalled that when she was suffering "deep sorrow from a family tragedy," it was a classmate's "Christian life" and "her loving sympathy for me" that "uplifted me out of self-imposed isolation." She remembered, "Gradually I understood the real meaning of life and learned to aim at a worthy life purpose."[8]

Wu's Christian faith was one of the many influences that helped shape her worldview and steered her in the direction of service to others and to the nation as her "worthy life purpose." Another important influence on Wu was the concern of Chinese intellectuals with saving the nation. Convinced that far-reaching change was necessary to ensure China's survival, educated Chinese by the late Qing period had begun questioning centuries-old cultural and educational precepts. From an early age, Yifang and her sister Yifen had read books and pamphlets advocating reform, by authors including Liang Qichao.[9] Like many of the educated Chinese of her generation, Wu through her years of schooling in China came to believe in the power of education to save the nation.[10]

Furthermore, Wu and her fellow female students also came to believe in the equality of the sexes and were convinced that by having a profession they too could play a role in leading China out of its national crisis.[11] In the early years of the twentieth century, when Wu Yifang began attending school, these ideas were nothing short of revolutionary.

Wu Yifang and the other members of Jinling's first graduating class felt a special obligation and responsibility to other Chinese young women. In a book authored by the members of the first class—aptly named *The Pioneer*—one of them wrote,

> Our friends and families were proud of us, and told us that we
> could have the right to be proud of ourselves, since we are the
> selected few who have acquired a regular college education in
> China. Can we be proud of that when we learn that in every
> thousand girls of school age there are only three who can go to
> school? Can we feel rested and happy over our fortune at having
> received more than the other 180,949 girls have? Our college
> education would not amount to anything if we selfishly rejoiced
> for our own privileges and opportunities.[12]

In addition to other new ideas, nationalism, by this time a major
force in China, permeated the teaching in the schools Wu attended. In
1905, when she was only twelve, Wu accompanied a Chinese teacher
to a rally protesting the treatment of Chinese workers in the United
States.[13]

In 1919, as Wu and her fellow students were about to graduate
from Jinling, students in Nanjing's schools went on strike. They were
following the example of their counterparts in Beijing, who took to the
streets on May 4 to protest the unfair terms of the Treaty of Versailles
(which allowed Japan to control Shandong) and the government's
weak foreign policy response. Jinling students, including senior class
president Wu Yifang, joined in protest activities. After two weeks, the
students, including the seniors, decided that the national emergency
was so great that it took precedence over examinations and graduation.
The situation changed, however, when three pro-Japanese government
officials resigned. The students decided to return to classes to finish the
year's work.[14]

Ultimately, Wu was deeply affected by her encounter with another
culture through her part-Chinese and part-Western education. She
came out of her years of school in China imbued with strong nationalist purpose, a belief in the Christian spirit of service to others, a sense
that women should take their place beside their male counterparts, and
a belief in the power of education to change people and to save the
nation.

After teaching for a brief time at the National Beijing Women's
Higher Normal School—previously the Beijing Girls Normal School,
where she had taught before attending Jinling—in 1922 Wu was offered
a Barbour Scholarship from the University of Michigan. She left China

for Ann Arbor, eventually earning master's and doctoral degrees in biology.

While in the United States, Wu's abilities as a leader, seen in her early years at Jinling, were more clearly developed. She worked to introduce China to Americans through activities in Chinese and Chinese Christian student associations. During the 1925–26 academic year, for example, Wu was president of the nationwide Chinese Students' Christian Association in the United States. Her various concerns are illustrated in her president's message in 1925:

> We have often been told that coming to the States for higher education is such a rare opportunity that we have a big responsibility to take up after our return. This is true indeed and it is what we desire to do, but besides, there is an immediate obligation for us right here and now—an obligation toward our Fatherland and the world at large. It is up to us, China's educated sons and daughters, to make known to the Western World our civilization, our past history and our modern developments. It is up to us, while meeting different races in American institutions, to remove racial prejudices and secure mutual understanding.[15]

While Wu was abroad, a movement to put educational institutions in the hands of Chinese leaders had gained momentum. Chiang Kai-shek had also unified most of China, making it possible for the new government to enforce its will. American Matilda Thurston, Jinling's first president, was forced to resign to make room for a Chinese. Finishing her doctoral work in the United States in 1927, Wu was unexpectedly offered the presidency of her alma mater in China. After some initial hesitation, Wu put her original plans for a career in teaching and research aside to answer the call—and thus came to be on the stage in Nanjing in November 1928, inaugurated as Jinling president.

Wu Yifang remained at the helm from 1928 until 1951. The context in which she worked, a turbulent Republican China wracked by Japanese aggression, war, intellectual upheaval, and revolution, made this job exceedingly difficult. Wu never married, and she put all her energy into Jinling and other activities. For her, the college served as a kind of surrogate family. As she lay dying in the Nanjing hospital in 1985, it was Jinling alumnae who kept vigil by her bedside.[16]

9-1 Wu Yifang, president of Ginling College

Abundant Life

The college motto, chosen by Jinling's faculty and its first class (Wu's class) was "Abundant Life," taken from John 10:10—"I came that they might have life, and have it abundantly."[17] Wu emphasized the service to humanity she believed inherent in this passage, constantly exhorting others to serve the greater good. as she later explained in her short history of Jinling:

> At the time the college used "Abundant Life" as its motto with the implication that the goal of life is not just to live for oneself, but to use one's intelligence and ability to help others and benefit

society. This is not only beneficial to others; one's own life is enriched as a result. The college used this as its objective to guide students and in addition, by means of a silent transforming influence in various aspects of college life, guided students to exert themselves in this direction.[18]

Wu worked to instill this service ethic in her students and encouraged them to serve the community, China, and the Chinese people, particularly Chinese women. As a starting point, she provided students with concrete opportunities to serve, encouraging them to become involved in social service and educational work with the local community. As Jinling president, Wu continued and expanded the college's community programs. The college established a rural service center in the countryside near Chengdu, Sichuan, in 1939, for example, offering education, health care, and industrial work among local women and children.[19] (For most of the Sino-Japanese War of 1937–45, Jinling College joined other refugee institutions in Chengdu.) After the return to Nanjing in 1946, the college opened another rural service station in a town nearby. Wu proudly wrote in 1950, after the establishment of the People's Republic of China, that the station was considered the best in the area and would serve as a model for the county.[20]

Many students were inspired by Wu's emphasis on service. One outstanding Jinling alumna, botanist Hu Xiuying, later recalled how Jinling had "deepened" her habit of sacrificing her own interests for the sake of others, which she had already developed in her village and in her training in a Christian middle school. "The world's different places and different languages articulate the same ideas," Hu wrote. "The highest realm of morality is to forgot oneself and to serve others."[21]

Wu also encouraged graduates to take jobs in rural reconstruction work. She hoped to further the rural work by sending Jinling personnel overseas for advanced training.[22] For example, Wu urged a PhD candidate to consider rural education as a dissertation topic, pointing to the importance of rural reconstruction to China's larger reconstruction efforts.[23]

Interpreted more broadly, Wu's life itself epitomized "Abundant Life." She was unfailingly generous to her students, co-workers, and the college itself. Discovering that one member of a group leaving for the rural service station did not have a raincoat, Wu loaned the student her own.[24] As Jinling president, Wu generally turned over her own income from special sources such as speaking engagements to the college. In 1942, she informed the Board of Founders that, through such sources, Jinling had actually *made money*.[25] Years after the college closed, Wu sold jewelry inherited from her mother to give some money to a former college employee who was having trouble making ends meet.[26] In 1979, Wu went to the United States to accept an "Athena Award" (for outstanding alumnae) from the University of Michigan. The Chinese government allocated $25,000 for Wu's visit, but Wu and the two people accompanying her used only $3,500 and returned the rest to the government.[27]

One Jinling alumna suggested that Wu's qualities of "giving generously of her time and energy to be of service to others" and "putting to good use every available moment of her time" may well have been one of the "secrets" of Wu "being able to accomplish so much" for Jinling and for China.[28] Indeed, Wu was ever busy. For example, during the Sino-Japanese War, time spent in a bomb shelter during air raids was used to write letters or have conferences.[29] During the Chengdu years, one student, going out very early one Sunday morning, was amazed to find President Wu cleaning the corridor of the dormitory. Wu simply said that she had some rare spare time and was looking for something to do.[30]

Another factor in Wu's success was her extraordinary speaking talent. Even as a student, Wu could easily speak extemporaneously, with no need for a written speech.[31] A student who attended Jinling with Wu recalled,

> She was very quiet, poised, and reserved, and was more like the daughter of an old-fashioned family than a pioneer in women's education. I remember her especially as the president of the Student's Self Government and admired the way she conducted the meetings and the beautiful, literary expressions she commanded.[32]

In 1919, Xie Wanying, who later became famous as a writer under the pen name of Bingxin, was among audience members listening to Wu give a speech at North China Union Women's College. Bingxin recalled years later how impressed she was as Wu, dressed in "simple and elegant" attire, "calmly" walked to the stage and gave a presentation that was "distinct and clear" in a voice that could be easily heard. Bingxin felt the school had never before had such an outstanding speaker on its stage, and she decided to take Wu as a role model.[33] In 1937, when a scheduled speaker failed to show, Wu gave an excellent unprepared baccalaureate address at a school set up for Jinling students to practice teaching.[34]

Wu, however, was unfailingly modest about her abilities. Her explanation of why she was chosen to give a report at the first meeting of the Chinese Women's Association for War Relief in 1937 is typical: "I speak loudly and in good Mandarin."[35]

Wu was also a strong person who faced adversity with an admirable steadfastness. A Jinling faculty member once called Wu a "great and fearless general" and observed that Wu's "foundation" was "solid rock through and through."[36] A clue to the origin of this "foundation" can be found in her comments to a group of Jinling freshmen. It is necessary, Wu told them, to pay attention to the soul. "It is not true," Wu emphasized, "that when you have education, you do not need religion." She told the students "we must pay attention to the training of the unseen part of ourselves" and "not only to our classroom education." "If service is the aim of our lives," she continued, then we will be able to give "better service" if we have "this inner strength to draw upon."[37]

Wu drew upon her own inner strength throughout her life, employing it to face personal family tragedy, from the early deaths of her family members to the sudden and unexplained disappearance of her younger sister in the early 1930s. (Wu Yiquan was never seen again.) She also relied on this strength to make it through the difficult years of Japanese aggression and civil war in the turbulent Republican period, and later through the political campaigns of the People's Republic.

In addition to the spirit of public service that Wu worked to instill in her students, she also urged them to fulfill their obligations to their country. Wanting her students to serve China and help it out of its predicament, Wu promoted nationalism and patriotism. In 1932, Wu chastised students, who, frightened by (false) rumors of an impending Japanese invasion, were ready to leave the campus, by saying, "Are you forgetting the nation as you think about saving your own skins? . . . Patriotism is not just talk—it has to be translated into action."[38]

Wu herself, however, was deeply emotionally affected by the Japanese aggression of the 1930s. In 1937, with the Japanese advancing on Nanjing, Wu left the city just before shipping was stopped on the

Yangtze River. She was greatly disturbed at having to leave and later referred to "running away" from Nanjing as "the most agonizing experience."[39] She recalled that "as soon as we got on the boat you could not help having the deepest sense of pain, leaving your own college, leaving the capital of your country which was threatened or sure to fall within a few days."[40]

A Jinling supporter once told Wu she appreciated her "gift" of "controlling and guiding young spirits in a hard world."[41] Wu had to tread a fine line, however, since she only approved of certain types of "action" for her students. As a student, Wu had joined classmates in the May Fourth demonstrations. However, despite her previous activism and her personal feelings about Japanese aggression, as the administrator of a women's college—and like many of her counterparts among Chinese Christian leaders—Wu advocated gradual reform and social service. She generally opposed the more strident forms of student political activism, such as protests, strikes, demonstrations, and boycotts, and did her best to channel her students' patriotic energies into their studies or into practical activities in the community.

Students recalled their president telling them during the Sino-Japanese War that by studying hard, they were doing their part to resist the Japanese and save the nation.[42] But by 1944, with a turn for the worse at the war front, students wanted to do something directly for the war effort and questioned why they should remain at their studies. One chemistry student asked Wu why Jinling could not suspend regular chemistry courses and give instruction on poison gas and explosives instead. Partly in response to such sentiment, the faculty began organizing some war-related extracurricular activities for students, including training in first aid.[43]

"Controlling and guiding young spirits in a hard world" became increasingly difficult. By the late 1940s, with civil war raging, Wu's continued advocacy of gradualism did not go over well with some of her students, and she found herself fighting a battle to stem the student tides. In 1948 the unprecedented happened—a student openly challenged President Wu at an assembly, saying, "How can we students study quietly with our minds at ease while the government concerns itself only with fighting a civil war and the people are in deep misery?"[44]

Although Wu did not agree with the strident political activism of her students, she did her best to ensure that nothing happened to them. In 1948, for example, Wu, worried that students would be hurt, firmly told authorities they were not to cause trouble at the women's college by making arrests—and no Jinling students were arrested.[45] A former faculty member recalled that when she had been in trouble with the Nationalist authorities, Wu had her check into a hospital until the Communist forces arrived.[46]

On May 20, 1947, Wu was sitting at the same table as Chiang Kai-shek during a lunch for government advisors. According to later accounts, she took the opportunity to sharply question Chiang about police action against students during a demonstration earlier that day. The two exchanged harsh words and Wu walked out.[47]

Wu, however, seems to have largely kept such incidents to herself. In fact, Wu was generally a very private person and as a rule was likely to emphasize the positive and to downplay any event she believed reflected poorly on China or the Chinese people. She was disinclined to criticize the Chinese government—whether the Kuomintang (KMT) or later the Communist government. For example, Wu glossed over the difficulties she experienced during the Cultural Revolution. She told a British visitor in the early 1970s that she "had not suffered hardships."[48]

The truth was that she, like most other Chinese officials of the time, had her house raided by the Red Guards. She had already burned her diaries, letters, and other papers in anticipation. Wu, in her seventies at the time, was also forced to participate in struggle sessions and "study classes" and later sent to do manual labor and undergo thought reform.[49]

Public Leadership

A pioneering female leader who herself challenged traditional gender norms, Wu looked for an expanded role for women in the public sphere and exhorted her students to work for women's interests. She saw education as the most important preparation for China's future female leaders. "Only as women become educated," Wu was quoted as saying in a publicity pamphlet, "can we expect them to step into their places as leaders."[50] To Wu, these female leaders, who would stand beside men in national reconstruction, were best cultivated in women's colleges such as Jinling.

Wu told one of Jinling's classes that there was no difference between men and women, and that women should rely on their own abilities to establish themselves in society. She urged the students to respect themselves, stand on their own two feet, and to ask for less and contribute more.[51] She also reminded the class of 1947 that they were one out of two thousand—the one Chinese woman out of two thousand with a college education.[52]

While quick to point out the changes in the position of women in the early decades of the twentieth century, Wu also noted that the new improved status posed a challenge. In a 1934 newsletter, she was quoted as saying that the position of women was equal to men politically, legally, and economically. Typically, in the spirit of "Abundant Life," she asked, "Will we use our rights as opportunities for giving our best to others?"[53]

When students and faculty wanted to contribute to the war effort by working at an American airbase located near Chengdu in 1944, conservative local gentry who "could not conceive" of the idea of "girls from good families going to work in an army camp" voiced their opposition. Wu, however, stood behind their decision and encouraged the women to take the jobs. Chinese college girls, she wrote, "should take part in more direct war work," just as did college women in America and England.[54]

Wu took great pride in the accomplishments of Jinling alumnae. In "Forty Years of Jinling College," written in 1983, she reflected on the college's achievements and noted,

> Although the number of Jinling College graduates would not be considered large, however, at that time when there were not many female college graduates, they occupied a certain percentage of China's senior female intellectuals, a good portion of whom made contributions to Chinese education, science and technology and other fields.[55]

Wu's activities outside Jinling College included many national and international women's organizations. In 1933, for example, she represented China at the International Women's Congress in Chicago, speaking during the same program as American social reformer Jane Addams. In 1936, Soong Mei-ling, chairman of the Committee on Women's Work of the New Life Movement, appointed Wu vice chairman.[56] After the Sino-Japanese War began in 1937, Wu became involved in various types of war relief efforts, working with Soong Mei-ling on the Chinese Women's Association for War Relief and the National Association for the Children of the War Areas.[57]

Among the many local, national, and international organizations with which Wu became involved upon her return to China in 1927 were Christian organizations, such as the National Christian Council (NCC). With missionaries and Chinese Christians in its ranks, the NCC served as a coordinating body for various Protestant churches, helping give direction to the Protestant movement in China. Wu became the organization's first female chairman in 1935 and served as chairman until 1947.[58]

Wu also participated in numerous international Christian conferences and meetings. For example, as NCC chair in 1938, Wu headed the forty-nine-member delegation from China, consisting of both Chinese Christians and missionaries, to the International Missionary Conference in Madras. At the end of the conference, Wu was elected a vice chairman of the International Missionary Council for the following six-year term.

Wu was also sent by the KMT government to represent China abroad. In April 1943, Wu and five other prominent educators went to the United States to study the international situation and then advise on planning for postwar reconstruction. Included in this assignment was the important task of fostering better understanding among the Allies and drumming up support for China in the United States.[59]

Wu may have been on assignment for the government, but Jinling was never far from her thoughts. When invited to the White House in December 1943 for lunch with First Lady Eleanor Roosevelt, Wu presented her with a piece of embroidery from Jinling students.[60]

Wu was also the only woman in the ten-member Chinese delegation, led by Premier Song Ziwen, to the 1945 San Francisco conference in which delegates from fifty nations drew up the United Nations charter. On June 26, 1945, she was one of only four women to sign the UN charter.

Wu declined opportunities to serve the KMT government directly as an official, however, including two offers to head the Ministry of Education, in 1946 and 1949.[61] She did agree to serve on the People's Political Council (PPC), an advisory body consisting of public figures appointed by the government. In spring 1938, Wu was appointed to the

9-2 Wu Yifang signing the United Nations charter, 1945

first PPC, one of only ten women in a body of two hundred.[62] Wu hoped for democratic political reform and she believed that the PPC was a step in the right direction. She acknowledged that the council was "not a real legislature" but argued that it served a "good purpose" since members brought "the people's opinion" to the Central Government and in return were able to hear about "the policies and actual accomplishments" of government departments.[63]

In 1941, Wu was elected the only female member of the five-person PPC presidium, rotating as chair. A reporter who covered the PPC sessions recalled that Wu as a PPC member and chair was capable, practical, and familiar with the democratic process, dealt with the motions in a closely reasoned and well-argued fashion, and got right to the point.[64] Writer Bingxin, who served in the PPC when Wu was a presidium member, remembered that during the discussions Wu presided over she calmly and precisely indicated the order of speakers, remembering every member's name and background. Bingxin also recalled veteran Communist Dong Biwu—later a high-level PRC leader—commenting that there were "very few men [as] keen-witted and capable" a chairman as Wu Yifang.[65]

Wu, who insisted that women were as capable as men and that gender should not be an issue, was not particularly impressed by such comments on her abilities. Writing to a Jinling alumna in the United States in 1941, she complained, "The thing that amused me as well as annoyed me was the undue praise given to my ability in presiding. It appeared to me as if the men never expected a woman to be able to have a clear head about parliamentary procedure, and to preside at a large gathering."[66]

Although privately Wu apparently had some early misgivings about Chiang Kai-shek's leadership—in 1930, for example, she wrote that Chiang was "not building his government on substantial foundations"[67]—she later supported Chiang and became friends with his wife, Soong Mei-ling, working with her in various organizations. By the early 1930s, Wu began receiving invitations for social events at the Chiang residence.

By the late 1940s, however, Wu, like many Chinese, had become dissatisfied with the Nationalist government. In personal letters, she became increasingly critical of Chiang's government and also of Madame Chiang. Yet she was apprehensive about a Communist victory in the Chinese civil war—particularly how it would affect Christian work in China and Jinling College as an institution largely funded by overseas donations. Despite her concerns and her connections with the KMT government, she did not seriously consider leaving China as the Communist forces advanced in the late 1940s. By November 1948 she wrote that she had made the decision to remain in China "regardless of what may happen" and would try to keep Jinling College open under the new government.[68] She would not consider a suggestion that Jinling be moved to Taiwan.[69] Indeed, Wu refused to take Soong Mei-ling's telephone calls on the eve of the KMT withdrawal from the capital in

April 1949, and when Soong sent a courier to Wu's residence with a plane ticket to Taiwan, Wu simply returned it.[70]

Wu Yifang and Jinling College after 1949

After the establishment of the People's Republic of China, Wu worked to find a place for Jinling College in the new China. She told a group of educators in 1949 shortly after the Communist victory that "under the principle of religious liberty," Jinling College "with its idea of Christian education would continue to train young women to serve the people."[71] Wu envisioned the college training Christian students and strengthening their faith at the same time it trained talent for the new China. In short, she saw her role and Jinling's as the same as before 1949.

However, with the change of political atmosphere in 1950 occasioned by the outbreak of the Korean War and Chinese involvement, the days of American-funded institutions such as Jinling were numbered. Wu's pre-1949 vision was ultimately not to be realized. In 1951, Jinling College was merged with another nearby Christian institution, the University of Nanking, to form National Jinling University. Wu was appointed vice president of the new institution. A year later, the new Jinling and the remaining Christian colleges were eliminated completely in a national reorganization of higher educational institutions. Eventually, Jinling College campus became the site of Nanjing Normal College (now Nanjing Normal University).

The only means of fulfilling Wu's desire that Christianity find a place in the new China was through involvement in a new government-sanctioned Protestant association. In May 1950, after a group of Chinese Christian leaders met with government and party officials to discuss the role the Protestant church could play in the new China, a public "Christian Manifesto" spelled out a pro-government political stance for the church, exhorting Christians to support the policies of the PRC government. Issued in July 1950, just as the Korean War began, by the mid-1950s it was said to have been signed by over half the number of Chinese Protestants, many under duress.

Wu joined the CCP-orchestrated "Three-Self Patriotic Movement" (TSPM), which rejected all foreign involvement, emphasized patriotism as loyalty to the party-state, and worked to implement the three goals of self-governance, self-support, and self-propagation. These three aims had originated with missionaries and were long-standing objectives of the Chinese church, but they were far from being realized at the time. The transformation from foreign control ultimately took place within official, registered churches subordinate to the Communist government. Wu served as one of the TSPM vice chairmen for the first (1954) and second (1961) TSPM national committees, and as Honorary Chairman of the third (1980). Through this organization, Wu hoped to continue the propagation of Christianity in China.

After 1949, Wu quickly gave the new government the same support she had given its Nationalist predecessor and served the government in various capacities. She attended the new Chinese People's Political Consultative Conference (CPPCC) that met in Beijing in September 1949, as one of seventy-five special representatives that included Sun Yat-sen's widow, Soong Ch'ing-ling. On October 1, 1949, Wu watched with great pride as Mao Zedong proclaimed the establishment of the People's Republic of China from the rostrum above Tiananmen Square.[72] Wu was particularly enthusiastic about the new government's emphasis on service.

In the 1950s and early 1960s, Wu also became involved in other state or state-sponsored institutions and continued to represent China to the outside world, including in the World Peace Conference in Helsinki in 1955. She held positions in national organizations such as the National People's Congress (NPC), the All-China Women's Federation, and the China Association for Promoting Democracy (APD), a minor political party subordinate to the Communist Party, composed mainly of teachers. After a stint as education commissioner for Jiangsu Province, Wu became the first woman to serve as a vice chairman of Jiangsu's provincial government. Her uncle, Chen Shutong, was also prominent in many national organizations, serving as vice chairman of both the NPC and the CPPCC, as well as chair of the All-China Federation of Industry and Commerce.

These activities ground to a halt during the Cultural Revolution, but by the late 1970s, Wu again was recruited into much of the same work. It was as though, as her Chinese biographer suggests—the octogenarian wanted to "make up" for the "loss" of the Cultural Revolution period.[73]

Wu remained particularly concerned with education. She gave this advice to educators who continued to dwell on the Cultural Revolution:

> Ordinarily, doesn't everyone talk about patriotism? Actually, loving one's country is not empty talk. Loving one's country is having a deep love for the work you are involved in and having a deep love for whom you are educating—the young—because they are the future and the hope of the motherland. Only with the healthy growth of the next generation will the nation be able to flourish more with each passing day.[74]

After the reorientation of Chinese policy in the post-Mao period, foreign connections became acceptable again. Wu was convinced that Jinling's alumnae again could help build a better future for China, and she quietly exhorted alumnae to establish branches of the Jinling Alumnae Association both in China and abroad.

When Jinling alumnae gathered to visit her in the fall of 1984, an ill Wu Yifang urged them to open a girls' middle school in China named after Jinling. The alumnae considered her suggestion, then came back with a counterproposal: a higher-educational institution for women. In the year before her death in September 1985, Wu supported efforts to start such a new "Jinling College" in China.[75] Her final instructions were "to establish Jinling College and to make it even better than the old Jinling."[76] After her death, a "Jinling College" for women was opened as part of Nanjing Normal University in 1993, offering courses in a limited number of programs.

Wu's emphasis on service and self-sacrifice and her firm belief in the transformative power of education echoed elements of Confucianism, Christianity, and Communism and served as her compass through an extraordinary life that spanned three major changes of Chinese government. Maintaining a strong personal Christian faith throughout her life, Wu continued her commitment to Christian service and to achieving national salvation in post-1949 China, meshing it with the Communist ideal of service to society.

Wu both promoted and embodied the spirit of "Abundant Life." She was selfless, always thinking of the good of others and of the nation. Although she was well known internationally, it was local concerns—particularly Jinling College and its alumnae—that remained closest to her heart. As one Jinling alumna put it, Wu "received 'Abundant Life' from Jinling and devoted her life to Jinling, represented the Chinese people, and shone toward the world."[77]

10

YAN YANGCHU
Reformer with a Heart for the Village

by Stacey Bieler

At the 1928 annual dinner of the China Society of America, held in New York City, Yan Yangchu (also known as James "Jimmy" Yen) described how his rural reconstruction program was turning illiterate Chinese peasants into citizens of a strong and democratic China.

> I don't know if the Chinese people are fitted for democracy or not, but they want it. I have been told by friends in this country and in Europe, "How could your country, with the great masses of her people illiterate and uneducated, unschooled, be fitted for democracy? Democracy and illiteracy cannot stand side by side. One of the two must go. And which shall it be?" And we said, "Illiteracy must go and democracy must stand."[1]

Yan, a wiry, athletic young man with an energetic smile, was back in the United States for the first time since his graduation from Princeton in 1920. As head of the National Association of the Mass Education Movement (MEM), he was raising money for a new program that he had begun in 1926 in Dingxian (Ting Hsien), a county of four hundred villages with four hundred thousand people in Hebei Province 120 miles north of Beijing.[2]

While interspersing jokes about the imperfections in American politics and the size of the honorary diploma he had just received from Yale, he explained how mass education associations had sprung up across China, with four to five million students enrolled. Yan had reduced the Chinese vocabulary of forty thousand characters to the *People's* 1,000 *Character Primer*, after which inexpensive sets of four readers were prepared. Since workers did not have much time or money, classes were held one hour a day, six days a week, for a total of ninety-six hours. A "people's pocket dictionary," containing about two thousand additional Chinese characters, was prepared, and it allowed each citizen to read anything in colloquial (*baihua*) literature. Many groups such as the YMCA, YWCA, and faculty at universities eagerly used the new resource. Mao Zedong and his colleagues worked with Yan's literacy campaign in Changsha, Hunan Province, in 1922. They then wrote their own 1,000 *Character Primer* that introduced Marx and attacked the militarists, bureaucrats, and capitalists.[3]

Yen's concrete results had captured the attention and imagination of Zhu Qihui, the wife of a former premier of the Republic of China. At a graduation ceremony in Shandong in the early 1920s, she was moved to tears while handing out diplomas to people who represented a wide range of ages and class backgrounds. Though she had been involved in many kinds of organizations, she resigned from them all, because she had found her life work in the literacy project.[4] This formidable woman supported Yan's work by giving her own finances, raising support, and calling upon leaders of every province to send delegates to the second annual mass education conference at Tsinghua University in 1923. The MEM was formally organized with Zhu as chairwoman, Yan as vice chairman, and Tao Xingzhi, a former student at Columbia University, as secretary. A year later, after the MEM appeared to be self-supporting, Yan became general secretary. His family lived with the Tao family in a sunny courtyard in Zhu's old-style Beijing home near the Forbidden City and the diplomatic quarter.[5]

After three years, Yan and the MEM headquarters moved from Beijing to the county seat of Dingxian, a walled city on the flat, coastal plain. The focus was expanded from literacy alone to broader rural reconstruction in order to address the four interlocking problems of village life: poverty, disease, illiteracy, and misgovernment. Yan told his New York audience how practical equipment that fit local conditions

10-1 Yan Yangchu (front center) and colleagues at Dingxian, mid-1920s

had been introduced. One Cornell graduate, who specialized in farm engineering, had spent five or six months improving native water wheels, an important implement in dry northern China. Instead of replacing them with a large water pump driven by electricity (which poor farmers could not afford), the specialist built one that took one person instead of two to operate, irrigated three acres of land instead of one each day, and cost two dollars less than the traditional water wheel.

Yan described China as a place where "forces of amazing power are operating . . .both for good and for evil, struggling for supremacy." He told how democracy would only become a reality if the common people were given a chance for education and citizenship training. He warned his New York audience that because of external aggression, an increasing number of young people were advocating that China become a militaristic nation, but that "those of us in the mass education movement are resolving to play our little part in China that will help us to make possible an education and modern citizenry . . . ever striving to achieve the ideal of Confucius, . . . 'Under heaven there is but one family.'"

Yan's speech, in his usual style of an exhortation rather than a talk, was broken throughout by laughter and applause as he shared his dream with the prosperous audience. After catching their imagination and opening their pocketbooks, he also connected with leaders in the YMCA and the Institute of Pacific Relations to create the American Cooperating Committee of the MEM. Yan returned to China with

money from more than 150 contributors, including John D. Rockefeller III, and major companies, including General Electric, RCA, and
Standard Oil.[6] These sources were more stable than the Chinese government and less dangerous than getting backing from the latest warlord
or faction that would likely soon fall.[7]

Patriotism and Faith

Yan was born October 26, 1893, in Bazhong, a small town in northern
Sichuan Province. Yan's father, a scholar, poet, and writer, named his
youngest son "Yangchu," meaning "the start of the sunrise," in order to
convey the family's desire to build a new China. His mother was kind,
but strict. Once when his older brother got drunk with his friends, his
mother called all of the family members together in the courtyard and
whipped him in front of the family in order to set an example for his
younger siblings.[8]

After his father accepted a job teaching Chinese to missionaries in
the local China Inland Mission (CIM) station, the missionaries urged
him to send his ten-year-old son to a CIM school in Baoning, ninety
miles from home. The headmaster, Rev. William B. Aldis, dressed in
Chinese clothes and wearing a queue, did not lecture about the Bible
to his students but instead set an example of a pious life for the twenty
boys in the school. Although Aldis's Chinese was not easy to understand, Yan and his classmates "understood his love for us." Having been
inspired by Aldis's example, Yan became a "follower of Christ" (*Jidutu*).
He found in Christianity the love and power to serve China.[9]

After four years, Rev. Aldis encouraged Yan to attend a middle
school run by American Methodists in Chengdu, Sichuan's capital.
Because there were no dorms for the students, two young English missionaries organized a boardinghouse. James Stewart, whose parents and
two siblings had been murdered during antiforeign riots in Fujian in
1895, had come back to China after finishing schooling in England. Yan
often served as interpreter when Stewart gave lectures on street corners.
Yan recalled, "I learned to face crowds, and while I only interpreted, I
heard fine and sincere speaking."[10]

Stewart encouraged him to go to Hong Kong for further education,
so Yan hired a tutor to prepare for the college entrance examinations in

the fall. When the results were posted, Yan placed first, but he declined the tuition scholarship because it required him to become a British subject. During his three years at Hong Kong University he became friends with Fletcher Brockman, the national secretary of the YMCA in China from 1898 to 1915, who inspired his confidence and affection.[11]

Finding His Life's Purpose

In the summer of 1916 Yan was headed across the Pacific to Oberlin College in Ohio, but a Yale-in-China teacher on the ship encouraged him to go instead to his own alma mater because of the good teachers and libraries, as well as the proximity to New York and Boston. So Yan entered Yale University as a junior, and his Beta Theta Pi fraternity brothers helped him find two jobs, as a cashier in the Commons and as a member of the choir, which paid one hundred dollars.

Yan wrote Brockman in Hong Kong about his life at college: "I have not known any institution so high in scholarship and at the same time so democratic in spirit and in life as Yale. The Christian tone here is high and inspiring—the chapel, the worship, the Christian professors, the Christian students make the whole Yale Christian in spirit and in practice." Yan became a member of the Jonathan and David Society, the Chinese Christian fraternity that later combined with the Cross and Sword fraternity to become the Cheng Zhi Hui (Association for Realizing One's Ambitions).[12]

Two days after finishing his bachelor's degree at Yale in 1918, Yan joined with forty other Chinese students sailing for France, where thirty thousand Chinese laborers were working in munitions plants, doing farm work, loading military supplies, and building or repairing roads in order to release Frenchmen to fight the Germans. Earlier in the year, *The Chinese Students' Monthly* (a journal published from 1906 to 1931 in English by Chinese students in the United States) had published an article mentioning that the American YMCA had funds to send Chinese students to France to offer football, wrestling, boxing, running, movies, lectures, concerts, and evening classes to the workers as alternative diversions to liquor, gambling, or prostitution.

In Boulogne, Yan became so busy writing letters for the dozens of homesick illiterate men each night that he asked for volunteers who would be willing to be taught one thousand basic Chinese characters. His eager students skipped their dinners so as not to miss class, even after digging trenches all day. Yan began publishing a newssheet called the *Chinese Workers' Weekly* after they ran out of material for the new readers. Yan wrote out the paper with Chinese brush and ink on large sheets of cardboard, which were then lithographed. In early February 1919 they printed ten thousand copies of the four-page paper, which included news from Versailles, London, Washington, and China.[13]

When thirty-five of the forty trainees passed the simple test of writing a letter home and reading *Chinese Workers' Weekly*, Colonel G. H. Cole, the head of the Chinese Labor Corps, who had been with the Canadian YMCA in China for twelve years, ordered Yan to set up and direct an ongoing educational program. Yan responded by asking that the Chinese YMCA student volunteers be sent to Boulogne to observe his classes for a week. After they returned to their own camps, they started classes with three thousand students.[14]

After the war was over, he stayed in France for several more months. Just before returning to the United States, Yan wrote a series of articles in the *Weekly* diagnosing China's problems.

> The reason that China is poor and weak is that we are too selfish. We can not blame the Mandarin-Qing Dynasty for all of our poverty and weakness. From the bottom, our Chinese hearts are rotten. When roots rot, the tree would not have new leaves and fruits. The people are the substance of the nation and when people lose their heart, how can the nation be strong?[15]

> [What is] most needed today is not training armies, not more schools, not mining, not making another revolution; our people need to change our hearts, to get rid of the sick hearts, and find a new heart. When we have a new heart, we become new people, and then we have a new society, then there is a new nation. . . . To treat the heart problem, we have to ask the divine doctor. In other words, we need religion to cure our sick heart.[16]

The next two issues of the *Weekly* addressed who could cure these problems.

> It is not because American people are better than Chinese, and have no selfishness. In fact, selfishness is the nature of human kind. . . . But American people have the doctor who can treat their soul to cure them. That is why American citizens care for

the public more and their country is getting richer and stronger day by day. . . . The doctor who cured Americans is Jesus Christ. . . . Men and women of any race, he will treat all of them. His heart is for everyone.[17]

Just before he left, Yan gave the reason why the seventy Chinese students from the United States and Britain had come to France to be with the laborers.

They put their studies aside, and risked losing their lives to the enemy's submarine attacks to come here to be servants of Chinese laborers . . . because their hearts have been treated and changed by the Doctor Christ; thus they all have high standards of social ethics, love their fellow countrymen and want to serve them.[18]

When the ship with the Chinese students had sailed to France, the ship ahead was sunk and the one behind torpedoed, but their ship arrived safely.

Recognizing the potential power of peasants to build a nation, Yan made a vow that upon his return to China he would not go into politics or business. Instead, he would devote the rest of his life offering not relief but "release of the pent-up, God-given powers in the people."[19]

After he returned to the United States in 1919, Yan studied history and politics at Princeton, in order to understand how political and economic changes occurred. After graduating with a master's degree in June 1920, he attended a conference at Silver Bay, New York, where he was elected president of the Chinese Students' Christian Association in the United States. He wrote Brockman, "The Association offers the greatest opportunity thru [*sic*] which a Chinese youth can help together with others to regenerate his nation. God help us to be equal to the task."[20] At about the same time he received a letter from his brother saying that his mother was not well.

Yan decided to return to China, but he first visited Brockman, who had moved to the YMCA headquarters in New York. Brockman hoped he would become a leader among the educated scholars, but Yan told him that he wanted to eliminate illiteracy so that China could have a foundation for democracy. Yan hoped that by advocating Christian popular education, public opinion would become an "intelligent and patriotic" one. Though Brockman at first tried to convince Yan that his plan was unrealistic, he advised Yan to contact Yu Rizhang, the secretary of the Chinese YMCA in Shanghai. On the ship home in July, Yan wrote Brockman about the camaraderie among the ten returning Chinese students on board, all Christians, because they shared the same hope of serving China.[21]

Yan planned to begin his mass education work in western China in order to be near his seventy-year-old mother, but Yu Rizhang convinced him that Shanghai would be a better place to establish the headquarters for a mass literacy project because of the facilities and the personnel found in the more progressive province. While visiting his mother, Yan quoted a Chinese proverb, "It is difficult to be a filial son and a patriotic citizen at the same time" (*zhong xiao nan neng liang quan*). Yan successfully lobbied to become head of the Department of Popular Education, a new autonomous department in the YMCA.[22] Yan wrote Brockman to tell of the news and express again "my heartiest appreciation for the great confidence you have in me and my profoundest gratitude for your fatherly advice and inspiration. It will always be my hope and prayer that I may live up in some measure to the great expectations you have of me."[23]

While Yan was in the United States, he had met Alice Huie (Xu Yali), the second daughter of Huie Kin, the pastor at the Chinese Presbyterian Church in New York City, and Louise Van Arnan, the daughter of a Dutch American manufacturer. For decades the couple, with their two sons and six daughters, cared for the many needs of Chinese in Chinatown and provided a "spiritual home and social center" to Chinese students on the east coast.[24] After Alice graduated in physical education from Teachers College, Columbia University in 1917, she went to China to teach.

After Yan had secured his position, he asked Alice to move to Shanghai and marry him. They were married in Shanghai on September 23, 1921. They wanted their lives to reflect a verse they had memorized from the Gospel of John (1:14): "The word became flesh and made his dwelling among us. We have seen his glory of the One and Only, who came from the Father, full of grace and truth."[25] They had five children. Yan named his first son William, after his teacher, Rev. William Aldis, and named his youngest child, James, after his friend James Stewart, who had died during the war while serving as a chaplain in France.

Down to the Countryside

After several years of doing urban literacy work, which was reproducible and relatively cheap due to the use of volunteers, Yan looked for a site where the MEM could begin a rural reconstruction pilot project combining education, agriculture, public health, and self-government. After he met Hugh Hubbard, an American missionary, who was using Yan's *People's* 1,000 *Character Primer* in the rural suburbs of Baoding in 1924, Yan spent three days on-site with Fu Baozhen (Paul Fugh), a recent Cornell University PhD in rural education and the MEM's first Director of Rural Education. They were encouraged by the model, but felt that the city was too far away from Beijing. Two years later the Mi family, who had overseen educational reform in a village a few miles from the county seat of Dingxian since the 1890s, but were then floundering financially, urged Yan to come and set up a model village. The location was much better, since a nearby train allowed one to get to Beijing, but it was still located away from the political center.[26]

Besides recruiting American-trained Chinese graduates in agriculture from Cornell or Ohio State University, Yan convinced educators and dramatists from Columbia and a Harvard-trained political scientist to live in Dingxian, despite offering small salaries. He had to reeducate the professionals to "step down their high tension knowledge to the simple voltage of the village."[27]

> It is not easy or simple to get first-rate men to work together. Because they are creative they are individualistic, stubborn, and think all the world of themselves and little of others. . . . I would say that one-fourth of my own time was spent in lubrication. . . . You must . . . instill into them the spirit of service and self-sacrifice.[28]

The MEM team sought to build Dingxian as a model center for scientific research for the rest of China. From 1926 to 1933 the MEM's Department of Statistics and Survey researched many aspects (population, taxes, wells, industry, festivals, etc.) of village life. The organization's Ten Year Plan of 1929 had three phases: 1) literacy, 2) agriculture, health, and economic reconstruction, and then 3) village self-government and general citizenship. The work of regenerating a Chinese village was done solely by Chinese. They practically and carefully adapted the best methods that modern scientific (Western) study had achieved to actual local (Chinese) needs.[29]

The MEM's survey served as a pattern for other non-MEM rural reconstruction centers elsewhere in China.[30] Though Yan never allowed any organization of his to be identified as Christian after the Anti-Christian Movement in 1922, he encouraged the Chinese church to reach out to the villages. In 1930 the National Christian Literature Movement held its conference in Dingxian.[31] When the National Christian Rural Reconstruction Seminar was held in 1933, 180 delegates from fourteen provinces came.[32]

When Yan and his colleagues first told the peasants that they had come to teach them how to read, the peasants laughed at them and said it was impossible. After Yan started classes in several large villages, many villagers came to watch out of curiosity. After the first class gradu-ated, village heads wanted schools in their town. By 1931 all 453 villages in Dingxian had their own schools, in which twenty thousand students were being taught by volunteer teachers.[33]

Rui Feng, who had studied at Cornell, became head of the depart-ment of Agricultural Science. The local farmers had to be convinced that these returned student scholars knew more about agriculture than they did. The farmers were impressed by scholars working with their hands, an unprecedented demonstration of the compatibility of learning and labor. On the strength of the friendship won by the mass education work, the farmers gave the MEM 15 *mou* (one-sixth of an acre) of land. When the results demonstrated that the newcomers did have some good ideas, the farmers gave one hundred *mou* and offered several local farmer boys to help cultivate the land. The following year the farmers gave twelve hundred *mou* because they saw the practical value for themselves.

In December 1929, Yao Xunyuan, a graduate from the Peking Union Medical College (PUMC), became the head of the MEM's Department of Health. He turned down a Rockefeller fellowship to study in the United States to come to Dingxian. His first goals were to reduce the death rate due to typhoid, dysentery, infant mortality, and smallpox. With support from the Milbank Memorial Fund (co-led by Edgar Sydenstricker, brother of Pearl Buck), Yao built a twenty-five-bed hospital. The medical needs were so great due to the large population that another, less costly approach was tried by Chen Zhiqian, also a graduate of PUMC, who had a master's degree in public health from Harvard Medical School. Chen created a three-level health care program with village health workers who were graduates of the village schools. They were trained to use a first-aid box of various medicines. By 1934 eighty workers covered one-fourth of the county's population. After Chen's work was recognized by the Chinese vice minister of health, Chen went on a tour of Russia, Poland, Yugoslavia, and India that was arranged by the League of Nations Health Organization.[34] As further testimony to the program's success, Mao Zedong and his associates may have adapted the MEM's model in creating their "barefoot doctors" program.[35]

Training citizens was also an important focus of the MEM, which published a book about national heroes in Chinese history, using simple pictures and language to educate the peasants.[36] After Hubei became a Japanese puppet province in 1935, Yan promoted solidarity and patriotism through speeches, storytelling, and drama, which led to Dingxian becoming a source for guerrillas and leaders allied with the communist border region government.[37]

Though Yan tried to avoid involvement in political struggles, political turmoil occasionally threatened to disrupt his work, requiring delicate diplomacy. During the 1920s, when northern China was divided among warlords, he ran literacy programs for several of them, but he did not want to be connected or indebted to any one person. In 1926 Zhang Xueliang, the son of the warlord in Beijing, gave him a new French automobile after he saw Yan fall off his bike when its wheel caught in a trolley track. But Yan let the car rust unused in a garage for years. In 1927 Yan was treated for an ulcer and told to take time off. In 1928 he returned from a trip to the south and learned that two hundred police had ransacked MEM headquarters and arrested Chen Zhusan, his closest advisor. After two days of negotiation and a telegram to Zhang Xueliang at the front, Yan went to jail with the release papers and found the door unguarded and Chen teaching the *People's 1,000 Character Primer* to the guards. In the midst of so much political and economic uncertainty, Yan went to the United States for ten months in 1928–29; recuperating from a health problem, he also used the opportunity to raise money.[38]

Thus Yan learned to walk a tightrope of remaining autonomous without angering people more powerful than himself. In the summer of 1931 a general from Shandong marched through the countryside. Dingxian would have been overrun if Yan had not used his connections to persuade the general to detour.[39] His brother-in-law and fellow rural reformer, Zhang Fuliang, wrote that Yan was "highly respected and widely acclaimed throughout the country, but being apolitical, he was not generally accepted by those in power."[40]

The Yan household was the heart of the community of thirty scholars and their families. Many visitors found warmth and hospitality there. Most of the families had never lived in the country town and complained about the lack of flush toilets or hot baths. Mrs. Yan would visit the wives and explain the meaning of the Mass Education Movement; she also founded a school for children of the MEM staff. Alice had complete responsibility for the five children when Yan traveled.[41] George Shepherd, a New Zealander who worked with the American Board of Commissioners for Foreign Missions, wrote, "Those of us who called upon Dr. and Mrs. [Yan] and their children found them dressed in plain blue cloth living joyously amongst the people."[42]

10-2 Yan family in Dingxian, 1933–34

Every morning the staff met in the Yans' living room to discuss (or argue) about the next step. In the winter they would pace back and forth, holding steaming tea cups to keep themselves warm, and in the summer they would fan themselves. Despite counseling and encouragement, only about one-third stayed on for more than a year, since they could find better-paying jobs elsewhere.[43]

In the 1930s Yan welcomed thousands of visitors to Dingxian. The historian and journalist Chen Hengzhe arrived in 1933 after a six-hour train ride from Beijing. After being met, she and Mrs. Yan rode in a rickshaw, while Yan rode a donkey to the village. In an article for the *Independent Critic*, Chen described the health clinics, the associations to stop gambling and opium smoking, and the broadcasting stations that could quickly spread local and national news. She admired the women volunteers, who taught household management and cooperation, helped with handicraft art, and improved spinning and weaving. She found that students were very serious, enduring both poor conditions in classrooms and walking to and from their villages for evening classes held from 9 to 11 p.m. She was impressed by the sacrifice and cooperation found among the MEM's leaders, the emphasis on science in the textbooks or in the research on population, and the significant reforms that met the immediate needs of the common people. She concluded, however, that the experiment at Dingxian would be meaningful only if it spread to the rest of China.[44]

Though Yan had many invitations to "put on a literacy campaign here, help start a big Mass Education program there, send a man for special work or even organize a country wide experiment" similar to Dingxian, he purposefully limited the program to Dingxian. He wanted to "prove by definite results that they have solved some of the problems of working with farmers, have worked out a technique that will be applicable to country work in general and have been able to train enough workers so that some can be spared for work in other centers."[45]

Despite his aversion to politics, Yan was appointed president of the Hebei Institute of Social and Political Reconstruction (IPSR) in 1933 and given de facto political control of the Dingxian government. The local economy was in distress due to global depression, local wars, starvation due to the hard winter of 1932, and eight thousand people dying during the flood of 1933, all of which led to the number of beggars doubling to 5 percent of the remaining population.[46]

Cotton textiles, one of several local handicrafts, were the most important village industry. IPSR standardized weights and measures, supported cooperative production, and encouraged new materials, but new sources of credit, new markets, and innovation were also needed to make a difference. The IPSR also established village co-ops so farmers would not be forced to sell at a low harvest price. By the middle of 1935, there were more than seventy buying co-ops, seven production co-ops, and five savings co-ops that put two hundred local moneylenders out of business.

War Years

As the Japanese army extended its control from Manchuria into Hebei Province, they allowed the spread of opium, terror, and extortion. When Hebei became a Japanese puppet province in 1935, the MEM's national headquarters was forced to move to Changsha, Hunan.[47]

After war broke out with Japan in 1937, Dingxian was lost and regained seven times due to mass mobilization of first-aid and self-defense teams. However, the Japanese were only able to occupy the county seat and the dozen villages along the railroad line, leaving the other four hundred villages under control of two teachers in the MEM's schools. Though several thousand local youth had already died in the fighting, a guerrilla division of some twenty thousand youth from Dingxian continually attacked Japanese positions.

When Hunan, China's "rice bowl province," was threatened, the governor invited Yan to organize a resistance movement. Yan said that he would do it for no pay as long as the corrupt local officials were first cleaned out. All county officials were called in for interviews and many of them were replaced. Since Hunan was an inland refuge for educated people, Yan was able to recruit thousands of students. They, along with higher officers and village heads, were trained and assigned to teams. The system was used in Hunan until 1944, when the Japanese took Changsha.[48]

Yan wrote about the plight of the "forgotten man," the tiller of the soil, who was at the front, fighting and bleeding for his country, and at the rear, toiling and producing food and clothing for the army and the people.

> The danger in war times is that the government will look upon
> the farmer merely as a tool for the winning of the war and not

realize his inherent worth. . . . The masses are beginning to feel their strength. We must direct their awakening to constructive ends. The communists in the Northwest have shown ability in organizing the masses and in challenging intellectual youth to serve the people. The most important thing, however, is not the triumph of one or another political or social theory but the release of new life for the rural masses. New tyrannies must not take the place of the old. The new nation must be built upon the incontrovertible strength of the people.[49]

In 1940, the MEM opened the National College of Rural Reconstruction near Chongqing. It was a difficult time, with Japanese bombing, diminishing grants, opposition from the Ministry of Education, and the loss of twenty members from MEM families when the boat carrying them, along with their personal items, MEM records, and equipment, capsized. Mrs. Yan's steadiness and courage, gained through her morning and evening prayers, inspired many of the students and staff to keep at their work. When an air raid occurred, she would always supervise finding a safe place.[50]

In 1945 Yan sent his regrets that he could not be at the college to give a speech to the graduating class, since he was in the United States. He told of the many pessimistic and often untrue reports being sent back to the United States by American soldiers in China. "So for the sake not only of our collaboration with America now in winning the war but particularly because of our cooperation in winning the peace later, men like myself should do everything possible to help enlighten the [American] people, particularly the leaders, both in and out of the government." He told of his series of lectures at the University of Havana and said that during the postwar period, mass education and social reconstruction would become internationally important. He closed, "The more I see of America, the more I realize that the foundations of this whole nation are not the specialists or the scholars but the masses of educated, enlightened people."[51]

In early 1945, Song Ziwen, as acting president of the Executive Yuan (a branch of the government), sent a confidential telegram from the war capital in Chongqing to Yan in New York City, asking if he would lead a government-sponsored program of local self-government and mass education. Though Yan declined the offer in a cablegram, he quickly followed up with a letter outlining the necessary steps. In his description of creating self-government, he told how his experience in Dingxian and in other areas of China showed that once "people have learned to run their own schools, their own modern farms, their own cooperatives, their own clinics, they do not only *demand* to run their own government, but they also *can*."[52]

In 1946, when Yan returned to China after three years of raising funds in the United States, he met with Chiang Kai-shek to ask for support for a publishing house and a national training network for rural reconstruction. Chiang promised that as soon as the war against the Communists was won, Yan could have his rural projects. Yan replied that since the Communists were fighting both on the military front and the people's front, the minds and hearts of the masses must be won. "If you see only the power of the army, and not the power of the aroused peasant masses, then China will be lost." Chiang replied, "Dr. Yan, you are a scholar and I am a soldier. We cannot see eye to eye." Yan stood up and shook Chiang's hand and said goodbye. He never saw Chiang again.[53]

In the face of continuing disruption by the civil war in China, Yan and three close associates in the MEM signed an oath in March 1947. Having the conviction that the power of nation building lay in the villages, they resolved to commit themselves "to develop the power of the people to build together with them our nation" through working together, agreeing to make decisions together, and by encouraging each other and sharing their difficulties and hardships.[54]

Yan came to the United States the following month to encourage the establishment of a rural reconstruction commission that would produce a strong and democratic China. Though President Harry Truman offered to put all of U.S. aid to China under Yan's direction, Yan deferred in order not to anger Chiang Kai-shek. Yan told Truman that he would take only 10 percent of U.S. aid, which was later known as the "Jimmy Yen provision" of the 1948 aid package to China. The Joint Commission on Rural Reconstruction (JCRR) became the most effective non-Communist rural program in China before 1949, though it spent only $4 million U.S. dollars of its total allotment ($27.5 million), supported only a small number of workers, and lasted only a little over one year.[55]

As the Communist army pushed south during the spring of 1949, Yan held private meetings with politicians, including the acting president Li Zongren, as well as the several commissioners of the JCRR˙ such as Jiang Menglin, former chancellor of Beijing University. They discussed how Chiang's arrogance, loss of prestige, and unwillingness to change his attitude, combined with the Americans' feeling of being suckered into giving aid in the past, meant that there was not likely to be any more aid to create a "last ditch stronghold of free China" in Sichuan.[56]

A Family and Nation Divided

Yan, his wife, and two daughters went to New York City in December 1949. Though the JCRR moved to Taiwan, where its land reforms formed the basis for the economic success of the island in the 1950s and 1960s, he chose not go to Taiwan himself in order not to give the Communists, who accused him of being a slave to American imperialism and a conspirator with Chiang Kai-shek's regime, more of an excuse to persecute his numerous colleagues remaining on the mainland. In December 1950, two months after China entered the Korean War, the MEM office and the College of Rural Reconstruction in Sichuan were dissolved.

Yan's three sons, who stayed in China, had promised to send their sisters a picture of themselves. They had agreed that if they were seated, it would be safe for the sisters to return. When the picture arrived, it showed all three brothers standing. Fred, who joined the Chinese Communist Party because he believed that they carried out his father's goals effectively, was persecuted and died during the political campaigns that followed the Korean War.[57]

The political environment in the United States was inhospitable as well, however. During the anti-Communist scare, scapegoats, including some of Yan's friends such as Edward Carter of the Institute of Pacific Relations, through whom Yan had many American financial connections, were blamed and sometimes jailed for "losing China."

So Yan moved back to Asia to establish the Philippine Rural Reconstruction Movement (PRRM) in the summer of 1952, building its headquarters in Silang, Cavite, about twenty-five miles south of Manila. He chose the Philippines because "they are blessed with abundant resources, a responsive people, four centuries of Christian heritage and in President Magaysay, a forceful leader close to the masses." The PRRM improved rural health by cleaning up the villages, setting up garbage sites, and providing basic medical attention. They set up show-case farms that grew dual harvests and promoted rural credit coopera-tives. They educated the rural people and trained the youth to become local leaders.[58]

Yan founded the International Institute of Rural Reconstruction (IIRR) in 1960. He spent the next thirty years encouraging rural recon-struction in the Philippines, Africa, Central America, and Southeast Asia. In 1980 Alice Yan passed away and was buried at the IIRR head-quarters in the Philippines.

Yan later honored his wife for her contribution to their work, saying that there were three reasons why the rural reconstruction movement had been able to accomplish so much: first, the creative research and dedicated service of hundreds of college-educated men and women and the active participation of millions of peasant men and women; second, the generous support by American, Canadian, and European friends; third, the lifelong partnership of his wife, whose "laboring, struggling" he noted, adding, "She fought a good fight. She kept the faith. Her memory a benediction, and her life, to many, an inspiration."[59]

How did Yan continue his work despite so many obstacles? His early influences were William Aldis's humble example, Fletcher Brock-man's advice and expectations, Yale University's "Christian tone," and friendships with his Beta fraternity brothers. His wife once commented, "The driving force which has brought this movement through such dif-ficulties and heavy odds stems from Jim's deep conviction from the start that this work is not his, but God's." He had mystical prayer experiences during times of decisions, for example, when he first devoted his life to peasants, when he led workers to Dingxian, and when he started IIRR.[60]

Yan also paid special attention to self-cultivation. "To build his health, he kept a regular schedule and retired before eleven every night. To build his spirit, he prayed every morning and took time to think, to plan and do systematic research." He enjoyed singing hymns that focused on the cross and found guidance from reading devotional lit-erature, such as the writings of St. Catherine of Sienna. People joined him in his vision and stayed on because he combined technical teaching with the motivation of following the example of Jesus. "The call is for those with the Christ spirit, who like the Good Shepherd know and love their sheep and stand ready to lay down their lives for them."[61]

In 1985, during a time of reform, with warmer political winds blowing in China, Yan as a wizened 92-year-old was invited to come to Beijing by Zhou Gucheng, vice president of the National People's Congress. Besides formal visits with Zhou at the Great Hall of the People, he visited for four hours with former premier Zhou Enlai's widow, Deng Yingchao, in Zhongnanhai, the working residence of the top Chinese leaders, located next to the Forbidden City. During his three-day stay at Dingxian, he found that his house, where his life work had crystallized and where he and his wife had brought up their five children, had been converted into a museum with an exhibition of his work in China and around the world.

When he returned again to the capital two years later, he accepted an invitation to serve as honorary president of the Western Returned Students' Association. He told his audience that the most important thing for China was to open to the outside world. He encouraged intellectuals to "tap the pent-up intelligence, vitality and strength" of the people, the foundation of any society.[62] After stepping down from the chair of IIRR in 1988, he left the Philippines and settled in New York City. Two years later Yan died in Manhattan at the age of ninety-seven. He was buried next to his wife in the Philippines.

Lasting Legacy

Yan serves as a model of how one individual responded to the needs of the Chinese people. After intensively studying rural problems, he introduced adaptations from Western experience. For the first time in Chinese history, a large group of intellectuals voluntarily lived in villages.[63]

In the 1990s, the Central Educational Science Institute in Beijing established the James Yen Association, and more than ten volumes on Yan's thoughts and approaches to rural reconstruction and development were written and published in China. In 1994 the IIRR participated in the Ford Foundation's Yunnan Upland Management program and in

1995 it partnered with the Guangxi government to train two hundred county teachers, government officials, village leaders, and farmers in environmental education, solid waste management, and integrated pest management. The Communist Youth League of a school in Dingxian sponsors a "Dr. Yen Day" each year in July. In 2001, the China Central TV station broadcast a program nationwide on Yan in its series of outstanding Chinese leaders of the twentieth century.[64]

Yan also received much international acclaim for his contributions. As professor William Lyon Phelps presented Yan an honorary master's degree from Yale in 1928, he said, "Few graduates have accomplished more in ten years than this enterprising, able, and unselfish man." The citation commended his "extraordinary intelligence and ingenuity, combined with most unselfish and contagious enthusiasm for a great cause."[65] In 1943, Yan was honored at the celebration of the four-hundredth anniversary of the death of Copernicus, the Polish astronomer. Yan joined nine other "modern revolutionaries," including Albert Einstein, Orville Wright, Walt Disney, Henry Ford, and John Dewey, who attended the award ceremony at Carnegie Hall in New York. His citation read, "Illustrious inventor of a simple, easily mastered system of written Chinese whereby the book of knowledge has been opened to millions of previously illiterate minds, a leader of his great people in applying scientific methods to the enrichment of their soil and the increase of the fruits of their toil."[66]

Having chosen to exile himself for much of his life from the People's Republic of China, the Republic of China on the island of Taiwan, and the United States, Yan spread his dream of rural reconstruction as a worldwide indigenous people's movement that overcame the barriers of politics, race, and geography.[67]

TIME LINE

China

1839–42 China loses first Opium War with Britain and is forced to sign the Treaty of Nanjing.

1850–64 Taiping Rebellion and other ethnic and peasant rebellions.

1856–60 Second Opium War. After British and French troops occupy Beijing, China is forced to sign the Treaties of Tianjin.

1860s The Qing court adopts "self-strengthening" programs.

1868 China–U.S. Burlingame Treaty allows student exchanges.

1871 The Qing court approves the Chinese Educational Mission (CEM) to the United States.

Salt and Light

1828 Rong Hong born in Zhuhai, Guangdong.

1858 Tang Guo'an born in Zhuhai, Guangdong.

1866 Fan Zimei born in Suzhou, Jiangsu.

1872–75 Four detachments of CEM students arrive in the United States; Rong Hong is a co-commissioner and Tang Guo'an a student.

1873 Shi Meiyu born in Jiujiang, Jiangxi.

1881   The Qing court orders the CEM's closure.

1882   The U.S. Congress passes the Chinese Exclusion Act.

1875   Rong Hong appointed China's co-minister to the United States, Spain, and Peru.

1888   Wei Zhuomin born in Zhuhai, Guangdong.

1889   Mei Yiqi born in Tianjin.

1890   Ding Shujing born in Shandong.

1893   Wu Yifang born in Wuhan, Hubei. Yan Yangchu born in Sichuan.

1895   China suffers a shocking military defeat by Japan. The YMCA begins work among urban Chinese.

1890s   *Globe* magazine promotes reform ideas.

1898   The Empress Dowager crushes the "Hundred Days Reform" and rules China while the Emperor reigns in name only.

1900   Anti-foreign Boxer Uprising. After foreign troops occupy Beijing, China is forced to sign the Boxer Protocol, which includes paying indemnities.

1900   Tang Guo'an flees to Hong Kong due to conflict in North China; he serves as chairman of the first board for Hong Kong's YMCA. Shi Meiyu flees to Japan briefly. Upon return she establishes the Elizabeth Danforth Hospital in inland China.

1901   Lin Qiaozhi born in Xiamen, Fujian.

1902   Fan Zimei becomes editor of *Globe* magazine.

1904   The U.S. Congress renews the Chinese Exclusion Act.

1905   The traditional Confucian examination system is abolished; modern reforms in education and governance begin.

1906   U.S. educators and missionaries encourage President Roosevelt to use the excess

Boxer Indemnity funds to
educate Chinese students.

1908   The Guangxu Emperor and
the Empress Dowager die.
President Roosevelt signs an
executive order to establish a
preparatory school in China
and offers scholarships to
one hundred Chinese stu-
dents each year.

1909   First Boxer Indemnity examinations are held.

1909   Tang Guo'an speaks at first
International Opium Conference in Shanghai. Tang
Guo'an accompanies the first
forty-seven "Indemnity"
students to the United States.

1911   The 1911 Revolution and
founding of the Republic of
China. Sun Yat-sen becomes
Provisional President.
Tsinghua School opens.

1911   Fan Zimei becomes editor-
in-chief of the *Progress*.

1912   Yuan Shikai becomes
President of the Republic.

1912   Rong Hong dies in Hartford,
Connecticut. Tang Guo'an
becomes president of Tsinghua College.

1913   Tang Guo'an attends the
second International Opium
Conference at The Hague;
he later dies in Beijing.

1914–18   The First World War.

1916   President Yuan Shikai dies; .
China is ruled by regional
warlords.

1916   Ding Shujing joins the new
YWCA city association in
Beijing.

1918–19   Yan Yangchu teaches literacy to Chinese laborers in
France.

1919   The May Fourth Movement
protests the concessions of
Chinese territory to Japan
in the Treaty of Versailles,
which China refused to sign.

1920   Shi Meiyu opens the Bethel
Mission in Shanghai.

1922   First conference of the
Chinese National Christian
Council. Protest against the
World Students' Christian
Federation convention at
Tsinghua U. in Beijing.

1923   Yan Yangchu founds the
Mass Education Movement.

1924–28 Movement to restore Chinese control over education.

1925 The May 30 Movement protests deaths of Chinese workers killed by Western police in clash in Shanghai.

1926 The Northern Expedition under the first United Front between the Communist (CCP) and Nationalist (KMT) parties unites the country under the Republic of China.

1926 Yan Yangchu begins rural reform in Dingxian County. Ding Shujing becomes general secretary of the YWCA in China.

1927 The KMT kills Communist leaders and activists during the "white terror" in Shanghai.

1927–37 The Nanjing Decade, during which the KMT rules China.

1928 Wu Yifang becomes president of Jinling Women's College.

1929 Lin Qiaozhi is first woman hired as a resident physician by Peking Union Medical College (PUMC). Wei Zhuomin becomes president of Central China University.

1931 The Japanese occupy Manchuria (northeast China), set up a puppet regime for "Manchukuo," and attack Shanghai.

1931 Mei Yiqi becomes president of Tsinghua University.

1932 PUMC sends Lin Qiaozhi to England and Austria as a visiting scholar.

1934–35 The Communists' Long March to Yan'an.

1935 The December 9th Movement protests the Nationalists' weak resistance to Japan.

1935 Ding Shujing attends YWCA convention in Japan.

1936–37 The Japanese army attacks Beijing, and then invades and occupies coastal and central China.

1937 Ding Shujing dies in Shanghai. Wei Zhuomin helps plan World Council of Churches.

1938 Founding of the World Council of Churches.

1938–46 Mei Yiqi leads three northern universities to merge, forming "Xinan Lian Da,"

the National Southwest
Associated University, in
Kunming, Yunnan.

1939   Fan Zimei dies in Shanghai.
Lin Qiaozhi is first woman
appointed as director of
a hospital department of
obstetrics and gynecology.

1941   Japan attacks Pearl Harbor;
the United States enters the
war.

1945   World War II in Asia ends in
August. The United Nations
established at a conference
in San Francisco.

1945   Wu Yifang signs the United
Nations charter.

1945–49 Civil war in China between
the KMT and the CCP.

1946   Wei Zhuomin attends
World Council of Churches
conference in Cambridge,
England. He is one of three
vice chairmen.

1949   Founding of the People's
Republic of China (PRC).

1950–53 The Korean War. The "Resist
America, Aid Korea" Move-
ment. Political campaigns
begin against landlords, intellectuals, and Christians.

1952   Universities reorganized
following the Soviet model.

1954   Shi Meiyu dies in Pasadena,
California. Yale University
celebrates the hundredth
anniversary of Rong Hong's
graduation.

1956–57 The Hundred Flowers
Movement, in which the
government encourages in-
tellectuals to raise criticisms
of it, leads to launching of
the Anti-Rightist Campaign.

1958–61 The Great Leap Forward
creates rural communes,
leading to famine. All but a
few churches are closed.

1960   Yan Yangchu founds the
International Institute of
Rural Reconstruction.

1962   Mei Yiqi dies in Taipei,
Taiwan.

1966–76 The "Great Proletariat Cultural Revolution."

1972	Lin Qiaozhi leads first PRC medical delegation to North America.
1976	Mao Zedong dies.
1976	Wei Zhuomin dies in Wuhan, Hubei.
1978	Deng Xiaoping launches economic reforms and opening to the outside world.
1983	Lin Qiaozhi dies in Beijing.
1985	Wu Yifang dies in Nanjing.
1989	June Fourth tragedy in Tiananmen Square, as the military attacks civilian demonstrators.
1990	Yan Yangchu dies in New York City.

NOTES

Introduction

1. The half-joking phrase is attributed to Li Hongzhang as early as 1862 in Samuel C. Chu and Kwang-Ching Liu, eds., *Li Hung-Chang and China's Early Modernization* (Armonk, NY: Sharpe, 1994), 11.

2. Francis Fukuyama, *The Great Disruption: Human Nature and the Reconstitution of Social Order* (New York: Simon & Schuster, 1999), 14, 264, 268.

3. Fukuyama, *The Great Disruption*, 266–68, 270.

4. For background, see Richard Hofstadter, *The Age of Reform: From Bryan to F.D.R.* (New York: Random House, 1955); and James T. Kloppenberg, *Uncertain Victory: Social Democracy and Progressivism in European and American Thought, 1870–1920* (Oxford: Oxford University Press, 1986).

5. Edwin Woodrull Tait, "The Cleansing Wave," and William Kostlevy, "Saving Souls and Bodies," *Christian History and Biography* 82 (Spring 2004): 22–25, 28–31.

6. Murray Rubenstein, *The Origins of the Anglo-American Missionary Enterprise in China, 1807–1840* (Lanham, MD: Scarecrow, 1996), 359.

7. Andrew Porter, "Introduction," in Andrew Porter, ed., *The Imperial Horizons of British Protestant Missions, 1880–1914* (Grand Rapids: Eerdmans, 2003).

8. Ryan Dunch, "Locating China in the World: Space and Time in Late Qing Protestant Missionary Texts" (paper, Association for Asian Studies annual meeting, Boston, March 22–25, 2007), 10. Dunch cites Alexander Williamson, in a preface to *Jidu shilu* [Life of Christ] in the 1880s, as an example of this: "Here we have true Evolution or rather Progression—which word I greatly prefer—and, I may add, in the Church of Christ alone have we aids adequate to the highest development of man, and provision made for the noblest forms of human society."

9. Jessie Gregory Lutz, *China and the Christian Colleges* (Ithaca, NY: Cornell University Press, 1971), 5–6.

10. Kostlevy, "Saving Souls and Bodies," 29.

11. The 1927 and 1931 conferences are discussed in Thomas H. Reilly, "Preaching the Social Gospel: Protestants and Economic Modernization in Republican China" (paper, "The Meeting of East and West: Celebrating the 200th Anniversary of Rev. Robert Morrison's Arrival in China and the Fifth Conference on the Contemporary History of Christianity in China," conference held at Chung Chi College, The Chinese University of Hong Kong, April 26–27, 2007).

12. Jessie G. Lutz, "China and Protestantism: Historical Perspectives, 1807–1949," in Stephen Uhalley Jr. and Xiaoxin Wu, eds., *China and Christianity: Burdened Past, Hopeful Future* (Armonk, NY: Sharpe, 2001), 191.

13. Heidi A. Ross, "'Cradle of Female Talent': The McTyeire Home and School for Girls, 1892–1937," in Daniel H. Bays, ed., *Christianity in China from the Eighteenth Century to the Present* (Stanford: Stanford University Press, 1996), 211.

14. Fukuyama, *The Great Disruption*, 255–62.

Chapter 1

Acknowledgment

Adapted from Stacey Bieler, *"Patriots" or "Traitors"? A History of American-Educated Chinese Students* (Armonk, NY: Sharpe, 2004). Used by permission. Special thanks also to Edward Rhoads for alerting the author to the picture of Rong Hong and Joseph Twichell.

Notes

1. Yung Wing, *My Life in China and America* (New York: Holt, 1999), 37–38.

2. Edmund H. Worthy Jr., "Yung Wing in America," *Pacific Historical Review* 34 (August 1965): 274.

3. Thomas E. LaFargue, *China's First Hundred: Educational Mission Students in the United States, 1872–1881* (Pullman: Washington State University Press, 1987), 40.

4. The three phrases are from W. C. Flagg, John Worthington Hooker, and Robert E. Taylor to Yung Wing, in Yale College, *Class of* 1854 [class album belonging to Yung Wing] (Yb71 854y), Manuscripts and Archives, Yale University Library.

5. Ruthanne Lum McCunn, *Chinese American Portraits: Personal Histories 1929–1988* (San Francisco: Chronicle Books, 1988), 17; Bill Lann Lee, "Yung Wing and the Americanization of China," *Amerasia Journal* 1.1 (1971): 28.

6. Rev. Joseph H. Twichell, "An Address by the Rev. Joseph H. Twichell, Delivered before the Kent Club of the Yale Law School, April 10, 1878," in Yung Wing, *My Life*, 247–73.

7. Yung, *My Life*, 1, 2, 8, 10–12. The Morrison School in Macao was begun in November 1939 by Rev. Samuel Robbins Brown and his wife.

8. Ibid., 13–15.

9. Ibid., 252; James L. Bowen, "Yung Wing and His Work," *Scribner's Monthly* 10 (May 1875): 106; "1854," Yung Wing Papers (MS 602), Manuscripts and Archives, Yale University Library.

10. Yung, *My Life*, 35–36; Paul William Harris, "Missionaries, Martyrs, and Modernizers: Autobiography and Reform Thought in American Protestant Missions" (PhD diss., University of Michigan, 1986), 309.

11. LaFargue, *China's First Hundred*, 48–51; Worthy, "Yung Wing in America," 270, 274.

12. Y. C. Wang, *Chinese Intellectuals and the West*, 1872–1949 (Chapel Hill: University of North Carolina Press, 1966), 42.

13. Edwin Pak-wah Leung, "China's Decision to Send Students to the West: The Making of a 'Revolutionary' Policy," *Asian Profile* 16.4 (1988): 392, 399.

14. Twichell, "An Address," in Yung, *My Life*, 262–63.

15. Jonathan Porter, *Tseng Kuo-fan's Private Bureaucracy* (Berkeley: Center for Chinese Studies, University of California, Berkeley, 1972), 126–27; LaFargue, *China's First Hundred*, 26–28; Yung, *My Life*, 166–67; Valery M. Garrett, *Mandarin Squares: Mandarins and Their Insignia* (Hong Kong: Oxford University Press, 1990), 28–29, 40.

16. Frederick Wakeman Jr., *Fall of Imperial China* (New York: Free Press, 1975), 185–86.

17. Yung, *My Life*, 171–75; LaFargue, *China's First Hundred*, 30, 32–33; "Document 23: The Proposal of Tseng and Li in 1871," in Ssu-yu Teng and John Fairbank, *China's Response to the West: A Documentary Survey, 1839–1923* (Cambridge: Harvard University Press, 1954), 91–94.

18. Twichell, "An Address," in Yung, *My Life*, 270.

19. Edwin Pak-wah Leung, "The Making of the Chinese Yankees: School Life of the Chinese Education Mission Students in New England," *Asian Profile* 16.5 (1988): 402.

20. LaFargue, *China's First Hundred*, 34; B. G. Northrup, Commissioner of the Connecticut Board of Education, "Report on the Response of American Families from Mr. Low to Prince Kung," October 1, 1872, *Foreign Relations of the United States, 1873–74*, vol. 1 (Washington, DC: United States Government Printing Office, 1874), 141–42; Bowen, "Yung Wing," 106; B. G. Northrop, "To the 'Teachers of the Chinese Students,' October 9, 1871," *Foreign Relations, 1873–74*, 142.

21. Arthur G. Robinson, "The Senior Returned Students: A Brief Account of the Chinese Educational Commission (1872–1881) under Dr. Yung Wing," *P. and T. Times* (June 24, 1932; repr., Tianjin, China: Tientsin Press, 1932), 13–14; Yung Shang Him, "The Chinese Educational Mission and Its Influence," *T'ien Hsia* [All under heaven] *Monthly* 9 (October 1939): 231–32; LaFargue, *China's First Hundred*, 40.

22. Yan Phou Lee, *When I Was a Boy in China* (Boston: Lothrop, 1887), 109, 111; LaFargue, *China's First Hundred*, 35, 40, 90–91; Sao-ke Alfred Sze, "Address of Dr. Sao-ke Alfred Sze, the Chinese Minister, at a Banquet Held in Hartford, Conn., on October 13, 1925," MS 81877, Chinese Educational Mission Records, 1870–1998, box 1, p. 4, The Connecticut Historical Society, Hartford, Connecticut.

23. Yung, *My Life*, 192.

24. Ibid., 195.

25. Ibid., 191–96; Charles Desnoyers, "'The Thin Edge of the Wedge': The Chinese Educational Mission and Diplomatic Representation in the Americas, 1872–1875," *Pacific Historical Review* 61 (May 1992): 253–56.

26. Twichell, "An Address," in Yung, *My Life*, 252, 254; LaFargue, *China's First Hundred*, 42.

27. LaFargue, *China's First Hundred*, 40.

28. Wakeman, *Fall of Imperial China*, 71–82; LaFargue, *China's First Hundred*, 39–40, 45–46; Robinson, "Senior Returned Students," 14–15.

29. LaFargue, *China's First Hundred*, 45–46, 140.

30. "Yale College" and "Colleges Attended by Chinese Educational Students, Other Than Yale," MS81877, Chinese Educational Mission Records, 1870–1998, box 2, folder A, The Connecticut Historical Society, Hartford, Connecticut.

31. Yung, *My Life*, 181–82, 201–303.

32. Rev. Joseph H. Sawyer, "The Chinese Christian Home Mission," *The Independent* (July 1894): 13–14.

33. Yung Shang Him, "Chinese Educational Mission," 225; Worthy, "Yung Wing in America," 280–81; Edwin Pak-wah Leung, "Education of the Early Chinese Students in America," in Genny Lim, ed., *The Chinese American Experience* (San Francisco, CA: Chinese Historical Society of America: Chinese Culture Foundation of San Francisco, 1984), 205–6; Yung, *My Life*, 201.

34. Shu Xincheng, *Jindai zhongguo liuxue shi* [The history of overseas study in modern China] (Shanghai: Zhonghua Publishers, 1927; reprinted as *Minguo cong shu* [Republic of China book series], series 1, vol. 49, Shanghai: Shanghai shudian [Shanghai bookstore], 1989), 13, footnote 1; Yung, *My Life*, 205–7; Teng and Fairbank, *China's Response*, 94; Rev. Joseph H. Sawyer, "The Chinese Christian Home Mission," *The Independent* (July 5, 1854): 13–14.

35. Ron Takaki, *Strangers from a Different Shore: A History of Asian Americans* (New York: Penguin, 1989), 101; Leung, "Education of the Early Chinese Students," 206; Worthy, "Yung Wing in America," 278–80; Thomas E. LaFargue, "Chinese Educational Commission to the United States," *Far Eastern Quarterly* 1 (November 1942): 66–69.

36. LaFargue, *China's First Hundred*, 47–48.

37. Ibid., 47–48; Yung, *My Life*, 207–9; James McCabe, *A Tour around the World by General Grant* (Philadelphia: National, 1879), 688–89, 702–3; J. F. Packard, *Grant's Tour around the World* (Philadelphia: Flint, 1880), 713.

38. LaFargue, *China's First Hundred*, 41, 48–49.

39. Yung, *My Life*, 211, 214; "Young, John Russell," *Dictionary of American Biographies*, vol. 8 (New York: Charles Scribner's Sons, 1937), 631; LaFargue, *China's First Hundred*, 50; Albert Bigelow Paine, ed., *Mark Twain's Autobiography*, vol. 1 (New York: Harper & Brothers, 1924), 21–24.

40. LaFargue, *China's First Hundred*, 49.

41. Ibid., 54, 140–44.

42. Wong Kai Koh [Huang Kaijia] to Mrs. Bartlett, January 28, 1882, Papers of Thomas LaFargue, Cage 255, Washington State University, Pullman, Washington.

43. Robinson, "Senior Returned Students," 13, 16; out of a total of 120 students sent, 70 percent were from the region around Guangzhou. LaFargue, *China's First Hundred*, 33–34, 38–39, 65; Laurence A. Schneider, *A Madman of Ch'u: The Chinese Myth of Loyalty and Dissent* (Berkeley: University of California Press, 1980), 13, 95, 108, 206; "Doc. 24: Letters of Li Hung-chang [Li Hongzhang] Concerning the End of the Mission, 1880–1881," in Teng and Fairbank, *China's Response*, 94.

44. Wong to Bartlett; Jerome Ch'en, "The Uprooted," *Etudes Chinoise* [Chinese studies] 4.2 (1985): 75.

45. Yung, *My Life*, 217–18.

46. LaFargue, *China's First Hundred*, 58–60.

47. Ibid., 65, 77–78, 107–8.

48. Robinson, "Senior Returned Students," 20; Yung Shang Him, "Chinese Educational Mission," 225; LaFargue, *China's First Hundred*, 13, 15.

49. Yung, *My Life*, 220.

50. Ibid., 222–23.

51. Ibid., 227–28.

52. Ibid., 228–38, passim.

53. J. Y. Wong, "Three Visionaries in Exile: Yung Wing, K'ang Yu-wei and Sun Yat-sen, 1894–1911," *Journal of Asian History* 20.1 (1986): 1–32.

54. The Empress Dowager exiled the emperor on an island in the Summer Palace and beheaded several reformers. Wakeman, *Fall of Imperial China*, 212–15.

55. LaFargue, *China's First Hundred*, 4; Dana B. Young of www.CEMConnections. org, personal communication with author.

56. Worthy, "Yung Wing in America," 286.

57. P. W. Kuo, "The Academy, and the Future of China," *The Chinese Students' Monthly* (December 1910): 181–82.

58. "Honorable Yung Wing, A.B., L.L.D. (Yale)," *The Chinese Students' Monthly* (June 1912): 644; C. T. Kwei, "The First Chinese Graduate of Yale," *The Chinese Students' Monthly* (February 1916): 258.

Chapter 2

Acknowledgments

I owe thanks to Stacey Bieler for ideas and materials on Tang Guo'an, Prof. Tang Shaoming for advice based on his research on the Tang family, Dana B. Young and Edward Rhoads for information from their research on the CEM, C. W. (Zhiwei) Cheung in Hong Kong for Chinese language material on Tang and the YMCA, and Shi Tianjun for research assistance and technical support. Several archivists were very helpful in finding rare material: Martha Lund Smalley at the Day Library of the Yale Divinity School, Rebecca Hatcher, Kevin Glick, and Tao Yang at the Yale University Archives and Manuscripts, Cheryl Adams at the Library of Congress, and Edouard Des Rochers at Phillips Exeter Academy.

Notes

1. C. L. Boynton, "The Club's History in Outline," in *American University Men in China* (Shanghai: Comacrib, 1936), 20.

2. Shirley S. Garrett, *Social Reformers in Urban China: The Chinese Y.M.C.A., 1895–1926* (Cambridge: Harvard University Press, 1970), 85, 113.

3. William W. Lockwood, "The Chinese Students in America," *The Independent* 71 (September 28, 1911): 680.

4. D. Y. Lin, "The Late Mr. Tong Kai-Chen," *The Chinese Students' Monthly* (November 1913): 34–35; see Stacey Bieler, *"Patriots" or "Traitors"? A History of American-Educated Chinese Students* (Armonk, NY: Sharpe, 2004), 96–97.

5. Biographical information on Tang Guo'an's family and career, unless otherwise

noted, is from Tang Shaoming, personal communication with author, Summer 2007, or Tang Shaoming, trans. Peng Hongbing, "The First President of Tsinghua College," Tsinghua University, http://www.tsinghua.edu.cn/docse/ghdxjk/xxyg.html. At Prof. Tang's recommendation, I have used Tang's name Guo'an (Kwoh-on) from his youth, by which he is best known in China since his death, rather than the name Jiechen (Kai-son), which he used as a professional in Shanghai and Beijing. Tang Guo'an came from Jishan Village in Tangjiawan (Tang Family Bay) township, Xiangshan County (after 1911, renamed Zhongshan County to honor native son President Sun Yat-sen, or Zhongshan). The entire area later became part of Zhuhai City and today's Zhuhai Special Economic Zone, bordering the Macau Special Administrative Region

6. Tang Shaoming, researching the Tang clan archives in Zhuhai, has corrected some errors in earlier studies that mention Tang Guo'an, such as Thomas E. LaFargue, *China's First Hundred: Educational Mission Students in the United States,* 1872–1881 (Pullman: Washington State University Press, 1987). These corrections include an earlier birth date (1858) and a different father (Tong Daofu, a poor farmer, not K. S. Tang (Tang Jingxing), famous and wealthy entrepreneur and clan head), who with his two brothers knew Rong Hong through study at the Morrison School.

7. Leonard M. Daggett, ed., *A History of the Class of [18]84, Yale College* (1880–1914), 419–21, Records of Alumni from the Classes of 1701–1978, maintained by the Alumni Records Office, Yale University (RU 830), box 52, Manuscripts and Archives, Yale University Library. Used with permission. Tang's biography in this source notes that he was a Christian from boyhood and studied English in Shanghai for one year before coming to the United States. Mary Delight Twichell was his first host and teacher in Plantsville, Connecticut. In 1875, Tang moved to the Northampton, Massachusetts, home of Martha Ely Matthews and lived there while he attended public high school. According to Prof. Edward Rhoads, in personal communication with the author (December 2007), Miss Matthews (later Mrs. McClean) hosted a number of students over the years with whom she corresponded once they returned to China. For information on Tang and other CEM students, see http://www.cemconnections.org/studentbios/TongKwoOn.html.

8. Lu Yin, "Tang Jiechen [Tang Guo'an] xiansheng shilüe" [Biographical sketch of Mr. Tang Jiechen], *Qingnian* [China's young men] 17, no. 9 (October 1914), 199–204. Early issues of *Qingnian* cited here can be found in the Shanghai municipal archives. Lu Yin cited an autobiographical article Tang had written in English about his experience in the United States. *History of the Class of* 1884 states that Tang's article, "History and Outcome of the CEM," was published in *The Missionary Review of the World.* There is some confusion about the exact name of the association founded by the CEM students. Rev. Joseph N. Sawyer, "The Chinese Christian Home Mission," *The Independent* 861 (July 5, 1894), 13, provides its history. A biographical note for an article from Tong Kai-son, "Difficulties of the Chinese Clergymen," *Chinese Recorder* (February 1905): 70, written in 1905 by Tang just mentions a "Christian union" in noting his service as secretary of the organization.

9. Daggett, *History of the Class of [18]84.* The Delta Kappa Epsilon home page (http://www.dke.org/H2.html/) points out that these criteria have remained unchanged since the chapter's founding at Yale in 1844. Another "Deke" and friend of Tang was Liang Dunyan, who later served as China's foreign minister.

10. David G. Hinners, *Tong Shao-Yi and His Family: A Saga of Two Countries and Three Generations* (New York: University Press of America, 1999), 9, cites letters written in 1883 by Liang Ruhao, a member of the third CEM group, to his host family.

Liang expresses disgust at the corruption pervading the imperial bureaucracy, in which he was serving as a lowly clerk.

11. Daggett, *History of the Class of* [18]84 lists Tang's early employers.

12. Ibid. Tang Taofu died in 1879, Liang Ah Chun in 1885. Guo'an's wife, Kwan Yueh-Kwai, was the daughter of Kwan Yung-Fa.

13. LaFargue, *China's First Hundred*, 96, 126, and Daggett, *History of the Class of* [18]84, state that in 1882 Tang was in Tianjin, the latter source identifying him as a medical student in the viceroy's hospital. Other CEM returnees were already there as students in a new school for assaying and mining. They became China's first mining engineers. The biographical note included in Tong, "Difficulties of the Chinese Clergymen," 70, says that Tang "returned to China in 1882, and at once entered the Government service. But finding this distasteful to him, he soon relinquished it and took up a commercial career."

14. For background on Kaiping, see Ellsworth C. Carlson, *The Kaiping Mines, 1877–1912*, 2nd ed. (Cambridge: East Asian Research Center, Harvard University, 1971); on K. S. Tang, see Samuel C. Chu and Kwang-Ching Liu, *Li Hung-chang and China's Early Modernization* (Armonk, NY: Sharpe, 1994), 220–35.

15. Hinners, *Tong Shao-Yi*, 5, 26, states that Tang Shaoyi's father, Tang Yongda, was "head of the main branch of the Tang clan," and that in 1907–09, Shaoyi's household included nearly two hundred relatives and retainers.

16. W. W. Yen [Yan Huiqing], *East-West Kaleidoscope 1877–1944: An Autobiography* (New York: Center of Asian Studies Modern World Series, No. 14, St. John's University Press, 1974), 39, 257.

17. George S. Eddy, *Pathfinders of the World Missionary Crusade* (New York: Abingdon-Cokesbury, 1945), 208.

18. Information on Tang's employment from Rhoads, personal communication.

19. Lu Yin, "Tang Jiechen." The quotation is from D. Y. Lin, "The Late Mr. Tong Kai-Chen."

20. W. W. Yen, *East-West Kaleidoscope*, 34–37. Tang Rongjun (Tong Wing Chun, also known as Tong Kidson) succeeded his father, the elder brother of K. S. Tang (Tang Jingxing), as general manager of Jardine, Matheson & Company. Tang Shaoming explains that the Chinese characters for "Kidson" and "Kai-son" (Guo'an) are different but are pronounced the same in Mandarin, causing the two CEM students to often be confused with each other. For a biographical sketch of Rev. Yan, see "Yan, Yongjing," Biographical Dictionary of Chinese Christianity, http://www.bdcconline.net/bdc_stories/china/shanghai/yan_yjing.html.

21. "Li, Denghui," Biographical Dictionary of Chinese Christianity, http://www.bdcconline.net/bdc_stories/china/shanghai/li_denghui.html.

22. Tang Jiechen [Tang Guo'an], "Love the Enemy," *Shanghai Qingnian huibao* [Shanghai YMCA Newsletter] 1.9 (November 20, 1903): 2.

23. W. W. Yen, *East-West Kaleidoscope*, 35; "Zhongxi hebian" [Inter-association debate], *Shanghai qingnian huibao* [Shanghai YMCA Newsletter] 1.10 (November 27, 1903): 2. Other reports in this paper suggest that Tang helped start up the debate and literature forum shortly after arriving in Shanghai from Hong Kong, giving a talk at its first session in September 1903.

24. Lu Yin, "Tang Jiechen."

25. W. W. Yen, *East-West Kaleidoscope*, 35–36.

26. Lu Yin, "Tang Jiechen."

27. Tong Kai-son [Tang Guo'an], "An Appeal to China's Foreign-Educated Men,"

China's Young Men (date unknown), quoted in *Baptist Missionary Magazine* (October 1905): 394, and included in Marshall Broomhall, *Present-Day Conditions in China: Notes Designed to Show the Moral & Spiritual Claims of the Chinese Empire* (New York: Revell, 1908), 27–28.

28. Tong Kai-son, "Difficulties of Chinese Clergymen," 70–75.

29. Tong Kwoh Onn [Guo'an], "Obstacles to Christian Missions in China," *The Missionary Review of the World* 18, nos. 8–12 (August–December 1905): 561–68 (no. 8), 686–89 (no. 9), 761–69 (no. 10), 845–48 (no. 11), 918–24 (no. 12).

30. Stephen Uhalley Jr., "The Wai-wu Pu: The Chinese Foreign Office from 1901–1911," *Journal of the China Society* 5 (Taipei, 1967), 9–27.

31 Stephen G. Craft, *V. K. Wellington Koo and the Emergence of Modern China* (Lexington: University Press of Kentucky, 2004), 32–33.

32. Hinners, *Tong Shao-Yi*, 15–20, posits that there was a significant shift in late Qing foreign policy under this "young China group," following the thesis of Louis T. Sigel, "T'ang Shao-yi (1860–1938): The Diplomacy of Chinese Nationalism" (PhD diss., Harvard University, 1972).

33. Tang's work for the Yuan family is mentioned in Lu Yin, "Tang Jiechen," the financial strain by W. W. Yen, *East-West Kaleidoscope*, 54–55.

34. Thomas F. Millard, "'Japan Has No Moral Superiority over Us or Right to Direct our Future'—Yuan," *New York Times*, June 14, 1908, in ProQuest Historical Newspapers: *The New York Times* (1851–2003), SM1.

35. Ibid.

36. Hinners, *Tong Shao-Yi*, 17–19, shows how Tang Shaoyi had been laying the groundwork on both fronts in the previous two years. Rong Hong wrote up a plan for suppressing the opium trade in China and for extinguishing poppy growing in China and India as early as 1882. But court officials dismissed the idea due to staff shortages.

37. Kathleen L. Lodwick, *Crusaders against Opium: Protestant Missionaries in China, 1874–1917* (Lexington: University Press of Kentucky, 1996), 137–47 nn. 57–58.

38. Tang's speech in Lodwick, *Crusaders*, 140–41 n. 51.

39. Lodwick, *Crusaders*, 58–59 n. 51.

40. D. Y. Lin, "The Late Mr. Tong Kai-Chen," 44–45.

41. A. J. Broomhall, *The Shaping of Modern China: Hudson Taylor's Life and Legacy*, vol. 2 (1868–1990), (Pasadena, CA: William Carey Library and Overseas Missionary Fellowship, 2005), 503–8, 570–73, 752.

42. Bieler, *"Patriots" or "Traitors"?* 42–44.

43. Information on Tang's visits to early friends is from Rhoads, personal communication.

44. Daggett, *History of the Class of [18]84*, 88, 419–21.

45. W. W. Yen, *East-West Kaleidoscope*, 56–57.

46. Ibid. The students selected in 1909–11 through strict examination returned to China to serve at the top of their professional fields, including as presidents of the best universities.

47. W. W. Yen, *East-West Kaleidoscope*, 60, 86–87.

48. John Israel, "Draft History of Qinghua University," *Chinese Education* 15.3–4 (Fall–Winter 1982–83), 23, 42–49.

49. Jessie Gregory Lutz, *China and the Christian Colleges 1850–1950* (Ithaca, NY: Cornell University Press, 1971), 72–73. *The Chinese Students' Monthly* (January 1913) reported on the sixth national YMCA convention in Beijing, December 12–15, 1912.

On the history of the Asian games, see Sadec.com, "Asian Games History,"
http://www.sadec.com/Asiad98/asiad2.html.

50. Quotation from Chen Heqin, *My Half Lifetime,* referenced in Tang Shaoming,
"The First President of Tsinghua."

51. D. Y. Lin, "The Late Mr. Tong Kai-Chen."

52. Thus there were actually five generations, including Guo'an.

53. Kuang Fuzhuo, "Tang Jun Jiechen mo ci" [Obituary for Mr. Tang Jiechen],
Shanghai qingnian huibao [Shanghai YMCA Newsletter] 12.31 (September 26, 1913), 5.

Chapter 3

1. More on Shi's childhood can be found in the various articles in the Mary Stone
File, Missionary Biographical Files, United Methodist Archives, Drew University,
Madison, NJ (hereafter cited as UMA) and in Margaret Burton, *Notable Women of
Modern China* (Chicago: Fleming H. Revell Company, 1912). For a fuller account of
Shi's childhood, including the importance of the mutual influence between her father
and Gertrude Howe, see Connie Shemo, "An Army of Women: The Medical Ministries
of Kang Cheng and Shi Meiyu, 1873–1937" (PhD diss., SUNY-Binghamton, 2002),
chapter 1.

2. For more on missionary attitudes toward turning control over to Chinese, see
Daniel Bays, "Rise of an Indigenous Christianity," in Daniel Bays, ed., *Christianity in
China: From the Eighteenth Century to the Present* (Stanford: Stanford University Press,
1996), 265–68.

3. Mary Stone, "Miss Gertrude Howe," Mary Stone File, Missionary Biographical
Files, UMA.

4. For more on Xu Jinhong's family, see Ryan Dunch, *Fuzhou Protestants and the
Making of a Modern China, 1857–1927* (New Haven: Yale University Press, 2001),
45-47.

5. The fact that they wore Chinese dress was especially important to Liang Qichao
in his praise of Kang's early medical work. Liang Qichao, "Zhi Jiangxi Kang nüshi" [An
essay on Miss Kang of Jiangxi], *Yinbingshi heji* [Collected works from the ice drinker's
studio] 1, no. 1 (1936; repr., Shanghai: Zhonghua shuchu [Zhonghua book company],
1989), 119–20.

6. Untitled, undated article in Ida Kahn File, 1467-2-1:01, UMA. For more detail,
see Shemo, *Army of Women,* chapter 2.

7. Burton, *Notable Women,* 169–82.

8. Liang, "Zhi Jiangxi Kang nüshi," 119–20.

9. For more details, see Burton, *Notable Women,* 233–54.

10. Burton, *Notable Women,* 212–13. As Burton does not cite her sources, it is un-
clear exactly where she found this reply. It seems likely that she interviewed Danforth
and perhaps was shown the letter by him.

11. The best description of this living arrangement can be found in Jennie Hughes's
letters to her sister, found in the Eliza Anne Hughes Davis Papers, Department of
Special Collections, University of Oregon Library System.

12. For the most detailed descriptions of Shi's relationships with these children and

her household with Hughes, see Edward Perkins, *A Glimpse of the Heart of China* (New York: Revell, 1911).

13. Wesley K. C. Mei, "Bethel Mission of China: An Address to the 11th World Vision Conference, Calvary Baptist Church; New York, March 14, 1947," ACC 69, box 1, folder 11, Special Collections and Archives on Women and Medicine, Medical College of Pennsylvania, Drexel University College of Medicine Archives & Special Collections on Women in Medicine and Homeopathy (hereafter cited as SCAWM).

14. Mary Stone, "What I Consider the Most Pressing Need of Central China's Medical Work Among Women," Central Conference Minutes (1913), 65, UMA.

15. Central Conference Minutes (1909), 43, UMA.

16. Mary Stone, "What I Consider the Most Pressing Need."

17. Mary Brown Bullock makes this argument in *An American Transplant: Peking Union Medical College and the Rockefeller Foundation* (Berkeley: University of California Press, 1980).

18. This is discussed in more detail in Shemo, *Army of Women*, chapter 6.

19. See the Jennie Hughes File, UMA.

20. The different reasons offered for the founding of Bethel are discussed at length in Shemo, *Army of Women*.

21. The woman's name was Tseo Pang-yuen. For more detail, see the Danforth Memorial Hospital File, UMA.

22. The information on Bethel for this section comes from the official Bethel publication, "Bethel Heart Throbs," ACC 69, box 1, folders 1–13, SCAWM.

23. See "Bethel Heart Throbs" for data from these years. The controversy over registration is treated in more detail in Shemo, *Army of Women*, chapter 8.

24. An August 5, 1938, Bethel newsletter included a statement from Madame Chiang Kai-shek (Soong Mei-ling) praising Shi Meiyu, "whom I know well." ACC 69, box 1, folder 13, SCAWM.

Chapter 4

1. Editor, "Jinian Fan Zimei Xiansheng" [In memory of Fan Zimei], *Tong gong* [Colleague] 183–84 (November 1939): 33.

2. Biographical information is from Fan Bihui [Fan Zimei], "Wushiqi nian dushu zishu" [Self-account of reading in the past fifty-seven years], *Qingnian jinbu* [Association progress] 102 (April 1927): 64–67 (hereafter cited as QNJB).

3. See Wang Shuhuai, *Wairen yu wushu bianfa* [Foreigners and the Wushu Reform Movement] (Taipei: Institute of Modern History, Academia Sinica, 1965), 26–29, 48–62; Luke S. K. Kwong, *A Mosaic of the Hundred Days: Personalities, Politics, and Ideas of 1898* (Cambridge: Council on East Asian Studies, Harvard University, 1984), 96–98, 209.

4. Adrian A. Bennett, *Missionary Journalist in China: Young J. Allen and His Magazines, 1860–1883* (Athens: University of Georgia Press, 1983), 149–225.

5. Fan Zimei, "*Wanguo gongbao* de erbai ce zhi zhuci" [The two-hundredth number of the Globe magazine], *Wanguo gongbao* [Globe magazine], n.s., 200 (September 1905; repr., Taipei: Huawen chubanshe [Huawen publishing house], 1968), 38:23611

(hereafter cited as *WGGB*).

6. Fan Yi [Fan Zimei], "Quandi wudazhou nüsu tongkao shuhou" [A postscript to women in all lands], *WGGB*, n.s., 176 (September 1903), 35:22040.

7. Chang Hao, *Chinese Intellectuals in Crisis: Search for Order and Meaning (1890–1911)* (Berkeley: University of California Press, 1987), 8.

8. Fan Yi [Fan Zimei], "Zhen Jiaohua wei jiu Zhongguo zhi benshui" [The Christian true civilization the only hope of China], *WGGB*, n.s., 163 (August 1902), 34:21168.

9. Ibid., 21170.

10. Fan Zimei, "Lun rujiao yu Jidujiao zhifen" [Differences between Confucianism and Christianity], *WGGB*, n.s., 182 (March 1904), 36:22417–18.

11. Fan, "*Wanguo gongbao* de erbai ce zhi zhuci," 23613.

12. Li Xiaoti, *Qing mo de xiaceng shehui qimeng yundong, 1901–1911* [Lower-class enlightenment in the late Qing period, 1901–1911] (Taipei: Institute of Modern History, Academia Sinica, 1992), 12.

13. Fan Zimei, "Lun wenyi zhi yuan" [Plagues and epidemics], *WGGB*, n.s., 165 (October 1902), 34:21280–83.

14. Fan, "*Wanguo gongbao* de erbai ce zhi zhuci," 23611.

15. Fan Zimei, "*Tongxue bao xu*" [Preface to General knowledge news], *WGGB*, n.s., 205 (February 1906), 39:24035.

16. Fan Zimei, "Xi guan yu qingnian" [Habits and the youth], *QNJB* 37 (November 1920): 1–2.

17. Heidi A. Ross, "'Cradle of Female Talent': The McTyeire Home and School for Girls, 1892–1937," in Daniel H. Bays, ed., *Christianity in China: From the Eighteenth Century to the Present* (Stanford: Stanford University Press, 1996), 209–42.

18. Fan Zimei, "Zhongxi nüshu zhangcheng xu" [Account of McTyeire School for Girls and its work], *WGGB*, n.s., 199 (August 1905), 38:23545–47.

19. Fan Zimei, "Lun Zhongguo baidai funu zhi zhidu" [How women were treated in ancient China], *WGGB*, n.s., 194 (March 1905), 37:23238.

20. Fan Zimei, "Shehui zaizao wenti zhi shangque" [Another discussion of social regeneration issues], *QNJB* 29 (January 1920): 8.

21. Fan Zimei, "De mo ke la xi zhi fanmian" [The opposite of democracy], *QNJB* 29 (January 1920): 11–13.

22. Fan Zimei, "Guomin chengdu yu sanjiaoxing" [Triangular form of citizen standards], *QNJB* 38 (December 1920): 1–3.

23. Fan Zimei, "*Qingnian jinbu* fakan ci" [Preface to the first edition of Association progress], *QNJB* 1 (March 1917): 1.

24. Fan Zimei, "Qingnian zhi rensheng guan" [Youth's view of life], *QNJB* 39 (January 1921): 5.

25. Fan Zimei, "Ben zazhi shinian lai zhi huigu" [A ten-year retrospect], *QNJB* 100 (February 1927): 254.

26. Ibid., 256; see also Fan Zimei, "Wuyi jie de Zhongguo yiyi" [The meaning of Labor Day for China], *QNJB* 133 (May 1930): 3–4.

27. Fan, "Ben zazhi shinian lai zhi huigu," 255–56; see also Fan Zimei, "Heping xingzhi de Zhongguo wenhua yu Jidujiao zai xiandai shijie zhi hezuo" [Cooperation between peaceful Chinese civilization and Christianity in the contemporary world], *QNJB* 73 (May 1925): 35–36.

28. Cited in David W. Lyon, "Will Confucianism Be a Force to Be Reckoned With in the Coming Days in China?" *Chinese Recorder* 59, no. 2 (February 1928): 80.

29. Fan Zimei, "Wu zhi guocui baocun guan" [My views on rejuvenating the national essence], *QNJB* 26 (October 1919): 11–12.

30. Ibid., 11.

31. Fan Zimei, "Why So Few Literary Lights among the Chinese Christians?" *Chinese Recorder* 51, no. 9 (September 1920): 648–49.

32. Fan, "Ben zazhi shinian lai zhi huigu," 254.

33. Xing Jun, *Baptized in the Fire of Revolution: The American Social Gospel and the YMCA in China, 1919–1937* (London: Associated University Press, 1996), 70.

34. Fan Zimei, *Wode xin Yesu guan* [My new concept of Jesus] (Shanghai: Association Press, 1929), 23.

35. Lyon, "Will Confucianism Be a Force?" 87.

36. Fan, "Wushiqi nian dushu zishu," 68.

Chapter 5

Abbreviations for Endnotes

USA – The National Archives of YWCA of the USA, subject files up to and including 1950 (on microfilm), Sophia Smith Collection, Neilson Library, Smith College, Northampton, MA. (The collection's index indicates that microfilm reels 51 and 52, in which some of the cited records appear, have been lost.)

World – World YWCA Archives, Country: China (People's Republic of), Geneva, Switzerland. The World YWCA has reorganized their China materials since the author's research was completed, and thus some citations may no longer accord with their catalog.

YDSL, CRP, MPP – Yale Divinity School Library, China Records Project, Miscellaneous Personal Papers.

1. "Secretary" was the title given all YWCA professional staff.

2. Ding Shujing to Mrs. Waldegrave, July 2, 1923, box 399, folder 2, World, China; "Address given by Rosalee Venable," March 19, 1924, Microfilm 50.2, Correspondence with National General Secretaries, Rosalee Venable, USA, China (hereafter cited as Venable Correspondence).

3. Biographical information on Ding Shujing is from "Miss Ting Shu Ching," *Chinese Recorder* (December 1936): 578–79; Various authors, "Some Appreciations of Ting Shu-Ching, Late General Secretary of the Young Women's Christian Association of China 1926–1936," Group 8: MPP, Ruth White Carr, File: YWCA, Who's Who 1917, 1936, CRP, YDSL (hereafter cited as "Some Appreciations"); *Nü qingnian bao* [China's young women], December 1922, Microfilm collection, YDSL, 16; "Ding Shujing nüshi shengping jianlüe" [A summary of the life of Miss Ding Shujing] in *Ding Shujing nüshi jinian ce* [Memorial of Miss Ding Shujing], National Committee of the YWCA of China, 1936, box 410: 1934/1935/1936 Correspondence and Reports, File: 1936

Reports, World, China; *Who's Who in China: Biographies of Chinese Leaders* (Shanghai: The China Weekly Review, 1917–1950; repr., Hong Kong: China Materials Center, 1982, 3 volumes); "In Memory of Miss Ting Shu Ching 1890–1936: A Memorial Fund of $100,000," October 1936, Venable Correspondence (hereafter "Ting Memorial").

4. Margaret MacKinlay, "Some Appreciations," 3.

5. "Message to the China Group from Ting Shu Ching [Ding Shujing], under appointment of general secretary of the China National Committee," n.d., Microfilm 50.2, Correspondence with National General Secretaries, Ting Shu Ching, USA, China (hereafter cited as Ting Correspondence).

6. Dr. Sun Yat-sen Global Huaren [Chinese] Foundation, http://www.huaren.org/ Home/home/Home; the quotation in Chinese is "*Da Dao zhi xing ye, tian xia wei gong, xuan xian yu neng, jiang xin xiu mu.*"

7. "Give-and-Take: China YWCA, 1926," Microfilm 50, USA, China.

8. "Copy of extract of a personal letter from Miss Ting to Miss Lyon, November 1, 1927," Ting Correspondence.

9. In 1910 there were 1,402 male missionaries, 957 missionary wives, and 829 single women in China. Two years later, there were 1,908 men, 1,322 wives, and 1,500 single women. Kenneth Scott Latourette, *A History of Christian Missions in China* (London: Society for the Promotion of Christian Knowledge, 1929), 406; Alison R. Drucker, "The Role of the YWCA in the Development of the Chinese Women's Movement, 1890–1927," *Social Service Review* (September 1979): 425.

10. Sarah Goodrich to Miss Miner, May 28, 1916, Group 8: MPP, S. Goodrich, box 89, file 118, CRP, YDSL.

11. One account mentions her coming to work part-time but others simply state that she joined the staff. Grace Coppock to Miss Ella D. MacLaurin, October 23, 1920, Microfilm 50.2, Correspondence with National General Secretaries, Grace Coppock, USA, China.

12. There is no extant history of the Chinese YWCA. The most complete accounts are An Zhenrong, *Zhonghua Jidujiao nüqingnianhui yanjiu 1916–1937* [Studies of China's YWCA 1916–1937] (MA thesis, National Taiwan Normal University Graduate Program in History, 2001) and Elizabeth A. Littell-Lamb, "Going Public: The YWCA, 'New' Women and Social Feminism in Republican China" (PhD diss., Carnegie Mellon University, 2002).

13. Spencer reports, Hong Kong, 1907, box 396: 1899–1921 Correspondence, folder: File Reports 1907–1909, World, China.

14. "Address," Venable Correspondence.

15. Quarterly Report, Theresa Severin, Peking, April 1920, box 397, untitled folder, World, China; "The Young Women's Christian Association in China 1922," box 398, folder: Minutes and Reports 1922 (Shanghai: National Committee of the YWCA, 1922), World, China.

16. Coppock to MacLaurin, October 23, 1920.

17. Lina Willis to Miss Charlotte Niven, World YWCA, London, March 24, 1922, World, China, box 399, folder: 1922 Correspondence, World, China.

18. Rosalee Venable to Mrs. Waldegrave, July 2, 1923, box 399, folder 2, World, China (hereafter cited as "Waldegrave Letter").

19. Rosalee Venable to Miss Harriet Taylor, Foreign Division, National Board, YWCA of the USA, April 6, 1923, Venable Correspondence; "Waldegrave Letter;" "Address," Venable Correspondence; "First National Convention, Hangchow, October 19–25,

1923," Microfilm 50.1, Background History, Convention Reports, USA, China, xi.

20. Venable to Taylor; "Waldegrave Letter;" "Address," Venable Correspondence.

21. Minutes of the National Committee of China, October 1, 1923, box 399, folder 2, World, China; "Miss Ting: Scholarship," May 8, 1924, Ting Correspondence.

22. Minutes of the National Committee of China, February 9, 1925, box 403, folder 1, World, China.

23. Rosalee Venable to Miss Sarah Lyon (YWCA of the USA), March 13, 1925, Venable Correspondence.

24. Rosalee Venable to "Fellow Workers," February 28, 1925, Venable Correspondence; "Message to the China Group," Ting Correspondence.

25. The May 30 Incident followed months of labor unrest in Shanghai's International Settlement, especially at Japanese-owned factories. A dozen or more Chinese protesters were killed or wounded by Settlement police. Massive protests broke out in cities across China, resulting in more violence and death.

26. "Message to the China Group," Ting Correspondence.

27. "Annual Report of National Committee, December 1, 1925," box 403, folder: China Reports 1925–1926, World, China, 4.

28. Lily Haass to Mary Dingman, November 7, 1927, box 405, folder: Correspondence, Mary Dingman, et. al., World, China (hereafter Dingman Correspondence).

29. "Ting Shu Ching," October 1936, Venable Correspondence.

30. "For the World Service Council Meeting, May 19, 1925," Ting Correspondence.

31. "Message to the China Group," Ting Correspondence.

32. The United Front was an alliance between the Nationalist and Communist parties brokered by Sun Yat-sen and Soviet advisors to the Chinese Communist parties in 1923. It collapsed when Chiang Kai-shek unleashed attacks on the leaders of Shanghai's labor movement and other perceived radical elements in the dawn hours of April 12, 1927.

33. Eleanor Hinder to Mary Dingman, April 10, 1927, Dingman Correspondence, 3.

34. "Copy of Newspaper Notification being sent by a Chinese Secretary of the Shanghai YWCA to the Foreign Press, April 8, 1927," box 404, folder: 1927 Report, World, China.

35. Hinder to Dingman, April 10, 1927.

36. "Ting Memorial;" *Who's Who in China*, 1936, 229.

37. "Reports of the Conference of Industrial Secretaries of the YWCA, September 1 and 2, 1927," box 404, folder: 1927 Industrial Miscellaneous Reports, World, China.

38. Kyong Bae-tsung [Gong Peizhen], "Education of Industrial Women and Girls," *The "Green" Year Supplement* (November 1928): 15–17; Emily Honig, *Sisters and Strangers: Workers in Shanghai Cotton Mills, 1910–1949* (Stanford: Stanford University Press, 1986), 218–23.

39. Ting Shu Ching, "Profession Ideals and Standards," in "Report of the Second Conference of Industrial Secretaries of the YWCA held at Shanghai, February 20–24, 1930," box 408, untitled folder, subfile: Social and Industrial, World, China (underlining is in the original).

40. "National Committee Minutes," September 19, 1930; Cora Deng to Mary Dingman, October 16, 1930; "China: News from Cora Deng, National Industrial Secretary in China" in a letter dated October 16, 1930, box 408, untitled folder, World, China.

41. "Report of Work of Industrial Department, Shanghai YWCA, September to October, 1930," box 408, untitled folder, subfile: Social and Industrial 1930, World, China; "A Few Facts about the Industrial Department and its Work," box 407, subfile: Social and Industrial, World, China.

42. "Address," Venable Correspondence.

43. Ding Shujing to National Committee Members and Staff in China, March 26, 1929, Ting Correspondence.

44. Ding Shujing to Mrs. John Finlay (YMCA USA National Headquarters), January 23, 1931, Ting Correspondence.

45. Ding Shujing to Sarah Lyon, March 29, 1934, Ting Correspondence.

46. Tabitha A. Gerlach, "Glimpses of Ting Shu Ching," in "Some Appreciations."

47. "Miss Ting Shu Ching," *Chinese Recorder* (September 1936): 578–79.

48. Rosalee Venable, "Ting Shu Ching [Ding Shujing]," October 1936, Ting Correspondence.

49. Ruth Woodsmall to Lily Haass, January 28, 1936, box 410: 1934/1935/1936 Correspondence and Reports, folder: 1936 Reports, World, China.

50. Venable, "Ting Shu Ching," Ting Correspondence.

51. The quotations from memorial messages are from "Ting Memorial."

52. Gerlach, "Glimpses," in "Some Appreciations."

53. Sarah S. Lyon, "A Talk at Memorial Service for Miss Ting," in "Some Appreciations."

Chapter 6

Acknowledgments

Adapted from Stacey Bieler, *"Patriots" or "Traitors"? A History of American-Educated Chinese Students* (Armonk, NY: Sharpe, 2004). Used by permission. Some biographical material comes from "Mei Yi-Ch'i," in Howard L. Boorman, ed., *Biographical Dictionary of Republican China*, vol. 3 (New York: Columbia University Press, 1967), 29–31; Huang Yanfu, "Mei Yiqi," in *Tsinghua renwuzhi* [Tsinghua personages], vol. 3 (Beijing: Tsinghua University Press, 1994), 1–28.

Notes

1. Ernest O. Hauser, "Poverty Campus," *Saturday Evening Post* (November 6, 1943): 94.

2. Hauser, "Poverty Campus," 19, 92; Gilbert Baker, *The Changing Scene in China* (London: SCM, 1946), 51.

3. Han Yonghua, "Tonggan gongku sishinian: ju wo suo liaojie de Mei Yiqi" [The joys and sorrows of forty years: Mei Yiqi whom I understand], *Wenshi ziliao xuan bian* [Selected cultural and historical data] 18 (1983): 3, http://www.luobinghui.com/myq/hy/200509/5834.html.

4. John Israel, *Lianda: A Chinese University in War and Revolution* (Stanford:

Stanford University Press, 1998), 129, 303; Zheng Tianting, "Mr. Mei Yiqi and Southwest Associated University," *Chinese Education* 21.2 (1988), 23.

5. Zheng, "Mr. Mei Yiqi," 23.

6. Mei Zuyan, "In Remembrance of My Late Father, President Mei Yi-chi," email to author, November 26, 1999.

7. Zheng, "Mr. Mei Yiqi," 25.

8. John Israel, "Southwest Associated University: Preservation as an Ultimate Value," in Paul K. T. Sih, ed., *Nationalist China during the Sino-Japanese War, 1937–1945* (Hicksville, NY: Exposition, 1977), 142–43; John King Fairbank, *Chinabound: A Fifty-Year Memoir* (New York: Harper & Row, 1982), 194.

9. Han, "Tonggang gongku," 1.

10. *The Aftermath*, 1914, WPI Archives & Special Collections, George C. Gordon Library, Worcester Polytechnic Institute, Worcester, MA, 109.

11. Chih Meng, *Chinese American Understanding: A Sixty-Year Search* (New York: China Institute in America, 1981), 168.

12. Han, "Tonggang gongku," 2.

13. Meng, *Chinese American Understanding*, 168-89; Han Yonghua, "Wo yu Mei Yiqi" [Mei Yiqi and I], in *Wenhua shiliao* [Cultural history] 4 (January 1983): 1, http://www.luobinghui.com/myq/hy/200510/7001.html; Han, "Tonggang gongku," 2.

14. Han, "Tonggang gongku," 2.

15. Meng, *Chinese American Understanding*, 65, 82.

16. S. Z. Yang, "Dr. Yi-chi Mei in Worcester 'Tech.,'" *Qinghua xiaoyou tongxun* [Tsinghua alumni communications], no. 2 (Taipei: Tsinghua Alumni News Agency, 1962), 98; Buwei Yang Chao, *An Autobiography of a Chinese Woman*, trans. Yuenren Chao (New York: John Day, 1947), 253.

17. Han, "Tonggang gongku," 2.

18. Meng, *Chinese American Understanding*, 139, 141, 145–46.

19. Mei Zu-yan, "In Remembrance."

20. John Israel, ed., "Draft History of Qinghua University," *Chinese Education* 15:3-4, 76–79, 84–85, 87–89; "Accomplishments of an Alumnus of W.P.I. in China," Correspondence of Ralph Earle, WPI president, 1925–1939, WPI Archives & Special Collections, George C. Gordon Library, Worcester Polytechnic Institute, Worcester, MA.

21. C. H. Liu, "Dr. Mei Yi-Chi and Tsing Hua University," *Qinghua xiaoyou tongxun* [Tsinghua alumni communications], no. 2 (Taipei: Tsinghua Alumni News Agency, 1962), 87–88.

22. Chih Meng, "Recollections of Chinese-American Cultural Persons: A Sampling," *Chinese Studies in History* 11.2 (1977–78): 22–23.

23. Liu Ziqiang, email to author, December 27, 2007.

24. John Israel, *Student Nationalism in China 1927-1937* (Stanford: Stanford University Press, 1966), 48, 55, 98–99, 100–101, 114.

25. Israel, *Student Nationalism*, 114, 120–27.

26. Ibid., 114–17, 141, 143–47, passim; Israel, "Draft History," 111, 113.

27. Israel, *Lianda*, 19.

28. Wilma Fairbank, *Liang and Lin: Partners in Exploring China's Architectural Past* (Philadelphia: University of Pennsylvania Press, 1994), 89.

29. Chao, *An Autobiography*, 273.

30. Israel, *Lianda*, 80–81, 90–91; Robert Payne, *Eyewitness: A Personal Account of a Tumultuous Decade, 1937-1946* (Garden City, NY: Doubleday, 1972), 247, 250–51.

31. Lincoln Li, *Student Nationalism in China*, 1924–1949 (Albany: State University of New York Press, 1994), 84, 87. See also Israel, "Draft History," 179, ftn. 188; Israel, *Lianda*, 20, 132, 135.

32. "Mei Yi-pao," in Boorman, *Biographical Dictionary*, vol. 3, 32.

33. "70th Commencement," *Journal of the Worcester Polytechnic Institute* 43.6 (1940): 5, in Mei Yi Chi file, WPI Archives & Special Collections, George C. Gordon Library, Worcester Polytechnic Institute, Worcester, MA.

34. Israel, "Draft History," 77; Mei Zu-yan, "In Remembrance."

35. Zheng, "Mr. Mei Yiqi," 24.

36. Mei Zu-yan, "In Remembrance."

37. Israel, "Draft History," 137–40; Israel, *Lianda*, 135.

38. Israel, *Lianda*, 134, 209–10, 272, 335.

39. Tang Pei-sung, "Aspirations, Reality, and Circumstances: The Devious Trail of a Roaming Plant Pathologist," *Annual Review of Plant Physiology* 34 (1983): 3, 11–12.

40. Israel, *Lianda*, 166.

41. Israel, "Draft History," 32.

42. Cheng Li, *China's Leaders: The New Generation* (New York: Rowman & Littlefield, 2001), 91.

43. Vera Schwarcz, *The Chinese Enlightenment: Intellectuals and the Legacy of the May Fourth Movement of 1919* (Berkeley: University of California Press, 1986), 45–47.

44. Israel, "Southwest Associated University," 136.

45. Fairbank, *Chinabound*, 223; Israel, "Draft History," 129–31, 133; Israel, *Lianda*, 100–102.

46. Fairbank, *Chinabound*, 192, 197–98; Fairbank, quoted in Israel, *Lianda*, 304.

47. Han, "Mei Yiqi and I," 2.

48. Zheng, "Mr. Mei Yiqi," 21–23.

49. Israel, *Lianda*, 334, 354.

50. Ibid., 373; Payne, *Eyewitness*, 270–74.

51. Israel, *Lianda*, 371–72, 385.

52. Ibid., 378–80.

53. Suzanne Pepper, *Civil War in China: The Political Struggle, 1945–1949* (Berkeley: University of California Press, 1978), 142–45; Wong Young-tsu, "The Fate of Liberalism in Revolutionary China: Chu Anping and His Circle, 1946–1950," *Modern China* 19.4 (1993): 482.

54. Wong, "Fate of Liberalism," 477–79.

55. Lim Boon Keng, *The Li Sao: An Elegy on Encountering Sorrows*, trans. Chu Yuan (Shanghai: Commercial Press, 1929), 160.

56. Israel, "Draft History," 159–62; Liu, "Dr. Mei Yi-Chi," 90.

57. Israel, "Draft History," 163.

58. Wilma Fairbank, *Chinese Students in the United States, 1948–55: A Study in Government Policy* (New York: Committee on Education Interchange Policy), 141; Hongshan Li, *U.S.-China Educational Exchange: State, Society, and Intercultural Relations, 1905–1950* (New Brunswick, NJ: Rutgers University Press, 2008),167–68.

59. Mei Zu-yan, "In Remembrance;" Wilma Fairbank, *Chinese Students*, 4.

60. Huang Chi-lu, quoted in Liu, "Dr. Mei Yi-Chi," 89–90.

61. Liu, "Dr. Mei Yi-Chi," 87–90; Wilma Fairbank, *America's Cultural Experiment in China, 1942–1949* (Washington, DC: Department of State, 1976), 141.

62. Han, "Mei Yiqi and I," 3.

63. Yang Shuren, "A Bundle of Letters from Hu Shi," *Chinese Studies in History* 30.2 (2006–2007): 78, 81, 88; Mei Zu-yan, "In Remembrance."

64. "2005 Memorabilia of TUEF," Tsinghua University Education Foundation, http://210.73.71.6/vhost/bj/www.tuef.org.cn/admin/infofiles/view_news.php?id=51;

Jiang Xuequin, "China's Top 2 Universities Try for 'World Class' Status," *Chronicle of Higher Education* 48.17 (December 21, 2002), A33–34; quote from Mei Zu-yan, "In Remembrance."

Chapter 7

1. Biographical information, unless otherwise noted, is from Zhang Qinping, *Lin Qiaozhi* (2005; repr., Beijing: Baihua wenyi chubanshe [Baihua literature and art publishing house], 2006).

2. Li Yading, managing director of the *Biographical Dictionary of Chinese Christianity* (www.BDCConline.net), personal communication with author, June 2007.

3. One source claims she died of cervical cancer, but others believe such a specific diagnosis was unlikely at that time. See All-China Women's Federation, "Lin Qiaozhi: Guardian Angel of Mothers, Babies," *Women of China* (December 6, 2007); Wu Chongqi, *Lin Qiaozhi*, 3rd rev. ed. (Fuzhou: Fujian kexue jishu chubanshe [Fujian science and technology publishing house], 1997), 23.

4. Bill Brown, Professor of Management, Xiamen University MBA Center, graciously provided information on Lin's childhood and memorial. Personal communication with author, December 2007 and March 2008.

5. Carmelite nun St. Thérèse of Lisieux (1873–1897) was also known as the "Little Flower of Jesus;" her *Story of a Soul* was translated into English in 1901. Edith Donovan, "St. Thérèse of Lisieux," *The Catholic Encyclopedia*, vol. 17, supp. 1 (New York: Encyclopedia Press, 1922), http://www.newadvent.org/cathen/17721a.html.

6. Translation from "Prayer of Saint Francis," http://en.wikipedia.org/wiki/Prayer _of_Saint_Francis.

7. Zhang, *Lin Qiaozhi*, 28.

8. Ibid., 28.

9. PUMC was founded in 1906 by the imperial government with the support of a group ("union") of six Anglo-American mission agencies. Beginning in 1915, it was run by the China Medical Board (established and supported by the Rockefeller Foundation). PUMC is now affiliated with the Chinese Academy of Medical Sciences, with an independent graduate school and undergraduate premed programs formerly in the biology department of Peking University and now in Tsinghua University (since 2006).

10. All-China Women's Federation, "Lin Qiaozhi."

11. Zhang, *Lin Qiaozhi*, 291.

12. All-China Women's Federation, "Lin Qiaozhi."

13. Zhang, *Lin Qiaozhi*, 161.

14. Ibid., 174.

15. From a photograph of the stone tablet, courtesy of Dr. Bill Brown, December 2007.

16. Wu Chongqi, *Lin Qiaozhi*; AmoyMagic, "Madame Dr. Lin Qiaozhi: Pioneer Obstetrician and Gynecologist," http://www.amoymagic.com/discovergulangyu6med.htm#linqiaozhi.

17. All-China Women's Federation, "Lin Qiaozhi."

18. Zhang, *Lin Qiaozhi*, 250.

19. AmoyMagic, "Madame Dr. Lin."

20. Zhang, *Lin Qiaozhi*, 296.

21. Yan Jiaqi and Gao Gao, *Turbulent Decade: A History of the Cultural Revolution*, trans. and ed. D. W. Y. Kwok (Honolulu: University of Hawaii Press, 1996), 67.

22. Zhang, *Lin Qiaozhi*, 334.

23. "Barefoot doctors" were rural youth trained to practice simple medical services. A wealthy village could afford a one-room clinic for the doctor; poorer villages could only provide a medical chest.

24. Zhang, *Lin Qiaozhi*, 372.

25. Ibid., 390.

26. From photographs of the stone markers, courtesy of Dr. Bill Brown, December 2007.

27. People's Daily Online, "China Marks 100th Birthday of Chinese Gynecological Pioneer," http://English.people.cn/200112/22/print20011222_87258.html.

Chapter 8

Acknowledgment

Thanks to the Research Grant Committee of Hong Kong, which supported my Competitive Earmarked Grant Research Project (HKIEd.4549/06H) on "Glocalization and Localization: Comparative Research on Christianity in Chinese Societies," from which the basic concept and thesis of this paper emerged.

Notes

1. Francis C. M. Wei, *The Spirit of Chinese Culture* (New York: Charles Scribner's Sons, 1947), vii, viii. Latourette went on to say, "If we are to know the Chinese we must become aware of the systems of thought and the religions which have had so large a share in making them what they are. This insight into the Chinese is of peculiar importance for Americans."

2. The saying was popular in the *chung hua shenggonghui* (Chinese Anglican/ Episcopalian Church). See Peter Tze Ming Ng, "Lecture III: On T. C. Chao," in *Wo suo huainian de si wei Shenggong zong shenxuejia* [The four Anglican theologians I respect most] (Kowloon, Hong Kong: All Saints' Church, 2006), 28–39.

3. Zhongshan, named for Sun Yat-sen, who also was born there, is now in the Zhuhai Special Economic Zone. Wei was married to Dai Huixiong, who bore a son named Bao E and a daughter named An Na. Bao E was a scientist working for the Wuhan branch of the Chinese Academy of Sciences.

4. For a brief history of the university, see John L. Coe, *Huachung [Huazhong]*

University (New York: United Board for Christian Higher Education in Asia, 1962) and E. D. Burton, *Christian Education in China: A Study Made by the Educational Commission Representing the Mission Boards and Societies Conducting Work in China* (New York: The Education Commission, 1922), 129–32.

5. Peter Tze Ming Ng, *Quanqiu diyuhua shijiaoxia de Zhongguo Jidujiao daxue* [Christian higher education in China: As seen from the perspective of glocalization] (Taiwan: Cosmic Light, 2006), 139–64; Lei Fazhang, ed., Wan Xianfa, trans., *Wei Zhuomin boshi jiaoyu wenhua zongjiao lunwenji* [Dr. Wei Zhuomin's writings on education, culture, and religion] (Taibei: Huazhong Daxue Wei Zhuomin Ji Nian Guan [Central China University Wei Zhuomin Memorial Hall], 1980).

6. Miner S. Bates was a professor of history at the University of Nanking from 1920 to 1950. Various versions of his "A List of Prominent Chinese Christians" can be found in the Bates Papers in the Special Collections of the Yale Divinity School Library. A Chinese translation of the list is in Zhang Kaiyuan, ed., *Christian Colleges and Social Transformation in China* (Hankou: Hubei Educational Press, 1998), 369–486.

7. For a brief biography listing such activities, see Howard L. Boorman, ed., *Biographical Dictionary of Republican China*, vol. 3 (New York: Columbia University Press), 403–5.

8. Coe, *Huachung University*, 56.

9. Ibid., 129.

10. At the Cambridge Conference of 1946, John Foster Dulles (United States) was appointed as chair, and Marc Boegner (France), Sir Kenneth Grubb (United Kingdom) and Wei Zhuomin (China) were appointed as vice chairs. See John Nurser, *For All People and All Nations* (Geneva: WCC Publications, 2005), 133.

11. Winifred E. Hubert, "Dr. Wei: Builder of the Kingdom in China," *The Spirit of Missions* 99 (1935): 19–23.

12. Ma Min, ed., *Wei Zhuomin Jidujiao wenji* [Wei Zhuomin's writings on Christianity] (Hong Kong: Institute of Sino-Christian Studies, 2000), 188.

13. Wei Zhuomin, *Jidujiao de jiben xinyang* [Basic elements of the Christian faith] (Hong Kong: The Council on Christian Literature for Overseas Chinese, 1965), 1.

14. Francis C. M. Wei, "Synthesis of Cultures of East and West," *China Today through Chinese Eyes*, 2nd series (London: SCM, 1926), 74–85.

15. Wei, "Synthesis of Cultures," 77.

16. Ibid., 75.

17. Indeed, Wei suggested that the best way to encounter foreign cultures was not to reject nor to accept all of them, but to seek a higher level, or the global elements of foreign cultures. See also discussions in Lei, *Wei Zhuomin boshi*, 53–62. Also see Ma, *Wei Zhuomin*, xxv.

18. Francis C. M. Wei, "Religious Beliefs of the Ancient Chinese and Their Influence on the National Character of the Chinese People," translated as "Gudai Zhongguo ren zhi zongjiao xinyang jiqi dui Zhongguo minzu xing de yingxiang" in Lei, *Wei Zhuomin boshi*, 1–25.

19. The thesis was first published in *The Boone Review* and immediately appeared in two parts in *Chinese Recorder* 42.6 (Wilmington, DE: Scholarly Resources, 1911): 319–28, and 42.7 (1911), 403–15. Kathleen Lodwick has compiled *The Chinese Recorder Index: A Guide to Christian Missions in Asia, 1867–1941*, vols. 1 and 2 (Wilmington, DE: Scholarly Resources, 1986).

20. Hubert, "Dr. Wei: Builder," 19–23.

21. According to Coe, *Huachung University*, 45, Wei's doctoral dissertation was "On Confucian Ethics" and his degree was from the School of Economics, University of London. However, according to a photocopy of the dissertation's title page provided by the Senate House Library of the University of London, the exact title was, "A Study of the Chinese Moral Tradition and Its Social Values."

22. Wei presented the lectures at Andover-Newton Theological School, Newton Centre, and the Episcopal Theological School (Cambridge, MA), as well as Union Theological Seminary, New York.

23. Chen Yuan, "A Brief History of Christianity in China," *Zhenli yuekan* [Truth magazine weekly] 2.18 (July 1924). Chen Yuan was the president of Fu Jen Catholic University in Beijing in 1929. Earlier, as a lecturer at Yanjing University in 1924, Chen was the first to expound on the history of Christianity in China in terms of four distinctive periods.

24. The Chinese Rites Controversy was a dispute between the Chinese government and the Roman Catholic Church from 1630 to the early eighteenth century concerning whether the Chinese ancestral rites and offerings to the emperor constituted idolatry. Pope Clement XI favored the Dominican view and proclaimed Chinese rites as incompatible with Catholicism, whereupon the Chinese emperor Kangxi banned all Christian missions from China in 1692. The Jesuits had taken a more open view regarding the rites issue. For more details, see D. E. Mungello, ed., *The Chinese Rites Controversy: Its History and Meaning* (San Francisco: The Ricci Institute for Chinese-Western Cultural History, 1994).

25. Wei, *The Spirit of Chinese Culture*, 17.

26. The terms "expanding Christendom" and "colonization" were seen as identical perhaps even earlier. See Dana L. Robert, "Christianity in the Wider World," in Howard Clark Kee, ed., *Christianity: A Social and Cultural History*, 2nd ed. (Upper Saddle River, NJ: Prentice-Hall, 1998), 525–80.

27. *Records of the General Conference of the Protestant Missionaries of China Held at Shanghai, May* 10-12, 1877 (Shanghai: American Presbyterian Missionary Press, 1878).

28. Andrew F. Walls, "The Old Age of the Missionary Movement," *International Review of Mission* 77 (January 1987): 26–32.

29. Milton T. Stauffer, ed., *The Christian Occupation of China* (Shanghai: China Continuation Committee, 1922).

30. Francis Wei, "Viewpoints on the Present Situation: Some Aspects of the Relations of the People's Revolution to the Christian Movement," *Chinese Recorder* (March 1927): 219–20.

31. 31 Jiang Meng Lin, *Xi chao* [Tidings from the West] (Taiwan: China Daily Press, 1957), 3-4.

32. Wei's speech was later published with the same title, "Projecting the Future of Mission Policy in China," *The Spirit of Missions* 93 (1929) 141–44.

33. Wei's points echoed the views of Zhao Zichen (T. C. Chao), who made an opening address to the National Christian Council in 1922, entitled "On the Strengths and Weaknesses of the Chinese Church," in which he said firmly that there would not be any future for the Chinese church unless it could do away with the image of "foreign religion" and discard Western denominationalism. See Zhao Zichen, "On the Strengths and Weaknesses of the Chinese Church," *Sheng ming yuekan* [Life monthly] 3.5 (1923), 1–8.

34. The address was translated by Prof. Ma Min into Chinese and collected in Ma, *Wei Zhuomin*, 97–107.

35. Wei, *The Spirit of Chinese Culture*, 159–60.

36. See further discussion in Peter Tze Ming Ng, "Wei Zhuomin boshi yan zhong de Jidujiao jiqi yu Zhongguo wenhua zhi guanxi" [Christianity and Chinese culture as seen from the eyes of Wei Zhuomin], in Ma Min, ed., *Kuayue zhongxi wenhua de juren* [A giant bridging the gap between the Chinese and Western cultures] (Wuhan: Huazhong Normal University Press, March 1995), 83–98.

37. Lei, *Wei Zhuomin boshi*, 115–38.

38. Wei, *The Spirit of Chinese Culture*, 22.

39. Lei, *Wei Zhuomin boshi*, 115–38.

40. Wei, *The Spirit of Chinese Culture*, 27.

41. See, e.g., Wei, "Projecting the Future," 144. See also Wei, *The Spirit of Chinese Culture*, 158–60.

42. Wei, *The Spirit of Chinese Culture*, 158.

43. Ibid., 155.

44. Francis Wei, "As China Regards Christianity," in Anderson Wu, ed., *The Christian World Mission* (Nashville: Parthenon, 1946). The Chinese translation can be found in Ma, *Wei Zhuomin*, 109–14.

45. Wei, *The Spirit of Chinese Culture*, 158. See also Wei, "Synthesis of Cultures," 74–85.

46. Note that the journal published in the earlier years of WCC (1935–48) was named *Christendom* but in 1948 the journal entered a new phase and was renamed *Ecumenical Review*. See, e.g., Jurjen A. Zeilstra, *European Unity in Ecumenical Thinking 1937–1948* (Zoetermeer: Uitgeverij Boekencentrum, 1995), as reported in John Nurser, *For All People and All Nations* (Geneva: WCC Publications, 2005), 12.

47. Zhao Zichen (T. C. Chao) was the Chinese delegate at the WCC who helped draft a proposal for the United Nations to consider in creating its Universal Declaration of Human Rights. See John Nurser, *For All People*, 132–34.

48. Lei, *Wei Zhuomin boshi*, 132.

49. Wei, *The Spirit of Chinese Culture*, 32.

50. Francis C. M. Wei, *Jidujiao de jiben xinyang* [Basic elements of the Christian faith] (Hong Kong: The Council on Christian Literature for Overseas Chinese, 1965), 4–7.

51. Ibid.; see also the discussion in Ng, *Quanqiu diyuhua*, 181–84.

52. Wei, "Synthesis of Cultures of East and West," 75.

53. "The Post-War Re-Development Plan of Huazhong University, 1944," UBCHEA Archives, series 4, box 170, folder 3145, Yale Divinity School Library Special Collections.

54. Francis Wei, "Making Christianity Live in China," *Chinese Recorder* 57 (February 1926): 118–21. The speech also appeared in Chinese as "Yaoshi Jidujiao zai Zhongguo you huode shengming li" in *Jiaoyu jikan* [Education quarterly] 2.1 (Shanghai: Zhongguo Jidujiao xiehui [National Christian Council], 1926): 27–31.

55. Wei, "Making Christianity Live in China."

56. Ibid.; see also the discussion by Jessie G. Lutz, "Dr. Francis Wei: A Christian, a Scholar and a Patriot," in Ma, *Kuayue zhongxi*, 78–82.

57. "The Post-War Re-Development Plan." See also Francis Wei, "The Proper Attitude of Young People in Changing Chinese Cultures," *Nanjing Theological Review* 14 (1932): 13–17.

58. Francis Wei, "What Makes a College Christian," *The Christian Recorder* (March 1941): 115–24.

59. Wei, "Synthesis of Cultures of East and West," 79.

60. For the conference proceedings, see Ma, *Kuayue Zhongxi*, 289.

61. Zhang Kaiyuan, "Preface," in Ma, *Kuayue Zhongxi*, 1–6.

62. Jessie G. Lutz, "Dr. Francis Wei," 78–82.

63. Zhang, "Preface," 3. See the discussion in Chan Kwong Pui, "Francis Wei, the President of Huazhong University," in Peter Tze Ming Ng, ed., *Jidujiao daxue huaren xiaozhang yanjiu* [Chinese presidents of Christian colleges in China] (Fuzhou: Fujian Educational Press, May 2001), 85.

Chapter 9

1. Wu Yifang, "Jiuzhi zhici" [Inaugural address], reprinted in *Jinling nüzi daxue xiaokan* [Jinling College magazine] (March 1929).

2. Dzo Ging-ru, "As President: The Thirties," *Ginling Alumnae Association Newsletter* no. 10, April 1956, pp. 12–14, RG 11, series 4, box 154, folder 2957, Archives of the United Board for Christian Higher Education in Asia (hereafter cited as UBCHEA), Special Collections, Yale Divinity School (hereafter cited as YDS).

3. Huang Xuechao, "Muxiao yu wo, wo ai muxiao" [My alma mater educated me, I love my alma mater], in *Jinling nüer* [Daughter of Jinling], vol. 2 (Nanjing: Jinling College, Nanjing Normal University, 2000), 23.

4. "Reminiscences of Dr. Wu: Pre-Ginling Biography; Citation (Mrs. Lawrence E. Thurston)," from biographical notes dictated to Helen Loomis (Wu's secretary) in 1936, *Ginling Alumnae Association Newsletter* no. 10, April 1956, pp. 9–11, RG 11, series 4, box 154, folder 2947, UBCHEA, YDS.

5. Zhu Xuepo, *Wu Yifang* (Nanjing: Jiangsusheng zhengxie wenshi ziliao weiyuanhui [Jiangsu CPPCC cultural and historical materials committee, 1993), 4–9.

6. Wu Yifang, "Bashi shengchen ganyan" [A speech on my eightieth birthday], in Sun Yue et al., eds., *Wu Yifang jinian ji* [In memory of Wu Yifang] (Nanjing: Jiangsu jiaoyu chubanshe [Jiangsu education publishing house], 1987), 81.

7. Zhu, *Wu Yifang*, 13–33.

8. Wu Yifang, "A Memorial for My Close Friend Mrs. Yuh-Tsung Zee New," June 3, 1981, *Ginling Alumnae Association Newsletter: Biennial Meeting Issue*, June 1981, RG 8, box 268, folder 23, Emily Case Mills Papers, China Records Project Miscellaneous Personal Papers Collection, YDS.

9. "Reminiscences of Dr. Wu."

10. See, for example, Wu, "Bashi shengchen ganyan," 81.

11. "Reminiscences of Dr. Wu."

12. Liu Gein-chiu [Liu Jianqiu] et al., *The Pioneer* (Shanghai: Presbyterian Mission Press, 1919), 38.

13. Zhu, *Wu Yifang*, 8–9.

14. Georgia G. Chester, "Mrs. Chester Writes of Chinese 'Strike,'" *Caldwell Progress*, RG 11, series 4, box 135, folder 2720, UBCHEA, YDS. Liu et al., *The Pioneer*, 33–35; "A Pioneer Commencement," n.d., RG 8, box 140, folder 49, China Records Project

Miscellaneous Personal Papers Collection, Frederica Mead Papers, YDS; Wu Yifang, "Jinnüda sishi nian" [Forty years of Jinling College], reprinted in Sun et al., *Wu Yifang*, 112–14.

15. Y. F. Wu, "A Message from the President," *The Chinese Christian Student* (November 1925): 1.

16. Zhu, *Wu Yifang*, 203–5; Huang Jin and Yan Guoning, "Genshen maiyuan hua zheng mao: Nanshida Jinling nüzi xueyuan chengli shisan nian jishi" [The roots are deep, the lifeline is long, and the flowers are flourishing: A record of thirteen years of Jinling College, Nanjing Normal University], in *Jinling nüer*, vol. 2, 3.

17. Matilda Thurston and Ruth M. Chester, *Ginling College* (New York: United Board for Christian Colleges in China, 1955), 20.

18. Wu, "Jinnüda sishi nian," 111.

19. Eva Spicer, "Ginling's Wartime Odyssey," Summer 1949, RG 11, series 4, box 158, folder 2998, UBCHEA, YDS; Wu Yifang, "Report to Board of Directors of Ginling College," November 9, 1946, RG 11, series 6, box 127, folder 2620, UBCHEA, YDS.

20. Wu Yifang to Dr. Fenn, January 14, 1950, RG 11, series 2, box 76, folder 2075, UBCHEA, YDS.

21. Hu Xiuying, *Jinling yu wo* [What Jinling gave me], quoted in Zhu Feng, *Jidujiao yu jindai Zhongguo nüzi gaodeng jiaoyu: Jinling nüda yu Huanan nüda bijiao yanjiu* [Christianity and modern Chinese women's higher education: A comparison of Jinling Women's College and Huanan Women's College] (Fujian: Fujian jiaoyu chubanshe [Fujian education publishing house], 2002), 389–90.

22. Wu Yifang to Mereb Mossman, January 25, 1939, RG 11, series 4, box 144, folder 2866, UBCHEA, YDS.

23. Wu Yifang to Li Mei-yun, July 9, 1943, RG 11, series 4, box 138, folder 2929, UBCHEA, YDS.

24. "Quotations from Student Diaries, Summer Service 1939," RG 11, series 4, box 159, folder 3008, UBCHEA, YDS.

25. "Statement from Dr. Wu," annual meeting, Ginling Board of Founders, May 7, 1943, RG 11, series 4, box 158, folder 2999, UBCHEA, YDS.

26. Bao Huisun, "Laoshao jiaoliu, qing sheng yiqie" [Exchange between the young and the old, with deep sincere feeling], in *Jinling nüer*, vol. 2, 392.

27. Zhu, *Wu Yifang*, 184.

28. Mrs. Hsien Wu [Yan Caiyun], "Contemporary and Friend," *Ginling Alumnae Association Newsletter* no. 10, April 1956, p. 12, RG 11, series 4, box 154, folder 2957, UBCHEA, YDS.

29. Wu Yifang to Board of Founders, October 16, 1937, RG 11, series 4, box 148, folder 2911, UBCHEA, YDS; Wu Yifang to Miss Griest, May 20, 1940, RG 11, series 4, box 148, folder 2915, UBCHEA, YDS.

30. Zeng Xinghua, "Wu xiaozhang zai wode xinzhong" [President Wu is in my heart], in *Jinling nüer*, vol. 2, 131–32.

31. Zhu, *Wu Yifang*, 43.

32. Mrs. Hsien Wu, "Contemporary and Friend."

33. Bingxin, "Yidai de chonggao nüxing: jinian Wu Yifang xiansheng" [A great woman of her generation: In commemoration of Wu Yifang], in Sun et al., *Wu Yifang*, 140.

34. Minnie Vautrin, diary entry, October 28, 1937, box 9, folder 7, MRL 6: Matilda Calder Thurston Papers, The Burke Library Archives (Columbia University Libraries) at Union Theological Seminary, New York (hereafter cited as UTS).

35. Wu Yifang to Miss Griest, July 31, 1937, RG 11, series 4, box 143, folder 2848, UBCHEA, YDS.

36. Minnie Vautrin, diary entry, August 29, 1937, box 9, folder 5, MRL 6: Matilda Calder Thurston Papers, UTS; Minnie Vautrin to friends, November 24, 1937, RG 11, series 4, box 145, folder 2875, UBCHEA, YDS.

37. Helen Plaum, *Ginling College Newsletter,* n.d. ("received July 1947" written on top), RG 11, series 4, box 140, folder 2801, UBCHEA, YDS.

38. Zhu, *Wu Yifang,* 68.

39. Wu Yifang to Mrs. MacMillan and Miss Griest, December 9, 1939, RG 11, series 4, box 148, folder 2914, UBCHEA, YDS.

40. "Dr. Wu's Talk at the Annual Dinner," May 1943, RG 11, series 4, box 148, folder 2922, UBCHEA, YDS.

41. "Dr. Lobenstine's Departure for China," in "Minutes of Meeting of the Board of Founders of Ginling College," September 27, 1939, RG 11, series 4, box 125, folder 2600, UBCHEA, YDS.

42. Xianyu Mingyi, "Muxiao he lao xiaozhang, yinxiang liuzai woxin shang yingxiang liuzai wo shen shang" [My alma mater and my president; their impression remains in my heart, their influence remains in me], in *Yongjiu de sinian* [Memory forever], (Nanjing: Jinling Alumnae Association, 1993), 32; Wu Bingheng, "Jinling de zhongzi, zai Tainan shenggen, chengzhang" [A Jinling seed that took root and grew to maturity in Tainan], in *Jinling nüer* [Daughter of Jinling], vol. 1 (Nanjing: Jiangsusheng jiaoyu chubanshe [Jiangsusheng education publishing house], 1995), 244; Zhu, *Wu Yifang,* 84.

43. Wu Yifang to friends, December 30, 1944, RG 11, series 4, box 142, folder 2829, UBCHEA, YDS; Wu Yifang to Mrs. New, December 1 and 6, 1944, RG 11, series 4, box 149, folder 2925, UBCHEA, YDS; Wu Yifang to Mrs. Mills, November 27, 1944, RG 11, series 4, box 158, folder 3000, UBCHEA, YDS.

44. Hong Fan, "Gaoji jianzhushi, Xiao Lin" [Xiao Lin, a senior architect], in *Jinling nüer,* vol. 1, 300.

45. Zhu, *Wu Yifang,* 111; see also Zhang Xiaojing, "Chunyu rutu cui miao zhang" [The spring rain on the soil speeds the growth of the sprout], in *Jinling nüer,* vol. 1, 247; Suo Fengguang, "Zoushangle wenxue zhilu" [I took the path of literature], in *Jinling nüer,* vol. 1, 339.

46. Zhu Enjen, "Bi muqin hai qin" [Closer than a mother], in *Yongjiu de sinian,* 47.

47 Zhu, *Wu Yifang,* 106–8.

48. *Ginling Alumnae Association Newsletter,* Spring 1973, p. 22, RG 8, box 268, folder 22, Emily Case Mills Papers, China Records Projects Miscellaneous Personal Papers Collection, YDS. See also Zhu, *Wu Yifang,* 171–73.

49. For Wu's Cultural Revolution experiences, see Zhu, *Wu Yifang,* chapter 10.

50. "Ginling College Primer," n.d., RG 11, series 4, box 156, folder 2973, UBCHEA, YDS.

51. Dai Aiyun and Shen Yunfen, "Cuoduo suiyue nairenwei" [Thought-provoking days of the past], in *Jinling nüer,* vol. 1, 391.

52. Lei Anmei, "Xiaoyuan shenghuo jishi" [A record of campus life], in *Jinling nüer,* vol. 2, 88.

53. *Ginling College Newsletter,* February 1934, box 9, folder 29, MRL 6: Matilda Calder Thurston Papers, UTS.

54. "Report to the Board of Founders of Ginling College," April 23, 1945, RG 11, series 4, box 149, folder 2926, UBCHEA, YDS; Wu Yifang to Mr. Earle H. Ballou, December 4, 1944, RG 11, series 4, box 149, folder 2925, UBCHEA, YDS.

55. Wu, "Jinnüda sishinian," 108.

56. Wu Yifang to Miss Tyler, March 14, 1936, RG 11, series 4, box 147, folder 2907, UBCHEA, YDS.

57. Wu Yifang to Miss Griest, July 31, 1937, RG 11, series 4, box 143, folder 2848, UBCHEA, YDS; Wu Yifang to Mrs. MacMillan, September 29, 1939, RG 11, series 4, box 148, folder 2914, UBCHEA, YDS.

58. Sun et al., *Wu Yifang*, 129.

59. Mrs. Mills to friends, June 9, 1943, RG 11, series 4, box 148, folder 2922, UBCHEA, YDS; "Statement from Dr. Wu," May 7, 1943, RG 11, series 4, box 158, folder 2999, UBCHEA, YDS. The group consisted of Wu Yifang, Yan Yangchu, Gui Zhiyan, Chen Yuan, Wu Jingchao, and Li Zhuomin.

60. Wu Yifang to Jane [Thomas], December 13, 1943, RG 11, series 4, box 135, folder 2711, UBCHEA, YDS.

61. Zhu, *Wu Yifang*, 99–100, 116–17.

62. "Excerpts from Letters from President Wu Yi-fang," June 25, 1938, box 9, folder 9, MRL 6: Matilda Calder Thurston Papers, UTS.

63. Wu Yifang to Mrs. Mills, November 17, 1942, RG 11, series 4, box 148, folder 2921, UBCHEA, YDS.

64. Shi Ximin, "Daonian Wu Yifang nüshi" [Mourning Ms. Wu Yifang], in Sun et al., *Wu Yifang*, 141.

65. Bingxin, "Yidaide chonggao nüxing," 140.

66. Wu Yifang to Dju Djuoh-fang [Zhu Jiaofang], August 5, 1941, RG 668, folder 89, Second National Historical Archives, Nanjing, China.

67. Wu Yifang to Matilda Thurston, March 30, 1930, box 5, folder 3, MRL 6: Matilda Calder Thurston Papers, UTS.

68. Wu Yifang to Matilda Thurston, November 15, 1948, box 5, folder 7, MRL 6: Matilda Calder Thurston Papers, UTS; Wu Yifang to Dr. McMullen, December 29, 1948, RG 11, series 2, box 76, folder 2073, UBCHEA, YDS.

69. Wu, "Jinnüda sishinian," 106.

70. Zhu, *Wu Yifang*, 119; Wu Yifang, "Huiyi yu zhuhe: xiezai jianguo sanshiwu zhounian qianxi" [Recollections and congratulations: On the eve of the thirty-fifth anniversary of the founding of the PRC], September 27, 1984, in Sun et al., *Wu Yifang*, 119.

71. Wu Yifang to Dr. McMullen, June 6, 1949, RG 11, series 2, box 76, folder 2074, UBCHEA, YDS.

72. See, for example, Wu, "Huiyi yu zhuhe," 119.

73. She served, for example, as a member of the standing committee of the CPPCC, delegate to the NPC, vice chairman of the Women's Federation, vice chairman of the APD, and vice chairman of Jiangsu Province. Zhu, *Wu Yifang*, 174.

74. Ibid., 174; also quoted in Sun et al., *Wu Yifang*, 135.

75. Gan Kechao, "Qidai liangan xiaoyou jiaoliu hunjimengrao Jinlingnüda: ji Wu xiaozhang bingzhong qijiande zhufu" [Looking forward to cross-Strait alumnae exchange, with Jinling College always in mind: An account of President Wu's entreaties when she was very ill], in *Yongjiude sinian*, 69–70.

76. Huang and Yan, "Genshen maiyuan," 3.

77. Hu, *Jinling yu wo*, quoted in Zhu, *Jidujiao yu jindai Zhongguo nüzi gaodeng jiaoyu*, 393.

Chapter 10

Acknowledgments

Adapted from Stacey Bieler, *"Patriots" or "Traitors"? A History of American-Educated Chinese Students* (Armonk, NY: Sharpe, 2004). Used by permission. Special thanks to Liu Hong for translating materials.

Notes

1. Yu Chuen James Yen [Yan Yangchu], "Mass Education in China," *The Chinese Students' Monthly* (February 1929): 171–77.

2. For biographical background, unless otherwise noted, see "Yen Yang-ch'u," in Howard L. Boorman, *Biographical Dictionary of Republican China*, vol. 4 (New York: Columbia University Press, 1967), 32–34.

3. Charles W. Hayford, *To the People: James Yen and Village China* (New York: Columbia University Press, 1990), 45.

4. Her husband, Xiong Xiling (Hsiung Hsi-ling), had served as finance minister in Tang Shaoyi's cabinet. He became premier in late summer of 1913. Yen, "Mass Education," 173–74; Hayford, *To the People*, 50–51.

5. The board included Tao; Zhang Boling, founder of the Nankai Middle School; Jiang Menglin, president of Peking University; Admiral Cai Tinggan, the former Chinese Education Mission student who advised President Yuan Shikai; Zhou Yichun, former president of Tsinghua University; and several bankers. Hayford, *To the People*, 49–53.

6. For a longer list of Yen's contacts, see Hayford, *To the People*, 78–80.

7. Ibid., 73.

8. Ibid., 14.

9. Ibid., 15–16; Wu Hsiang-Hsiang, *Yan Yangchu zhuan: wei quanqiu xiangcun gaizao fendou liushi nian* [James Yen and his sixty years of struggle with rural reconstruction for the peasant people of the world] (Taiwan, 1981; repr., Changsha, Hunan: Yuelu chubanshe [Yuelu publishing house], 2001), 8.

10. Hayford, *To the People*, 17.

11. Ibid., xii, 15–19; Kenneth Scott Latourette, *World Service: A History of the Foreign Work and World Service of the Young Men's Christian Associations of the United States and Canada* (New York: Association Press, 1957), 63–64.

12. Hayford, *To the People*, 20–21; James Yen, "A Challenge to My Beta Brothers," Oxford Cup Acceptance Speech, 148th Convention of Beta Theta Pi, August 20, 1987, box 93, IIRR Collection, Rare Book and Manuscript Library, Columbia University (hereafter cited as IIRR Collection); P. T. Chen, "Chinese Fraternities in America," in American University Club of Shanghai, ed., *American University Men in China* (Shanghai: Comacrib Press, 1936), 160–61.

13. Hayford, *To the People*, 27.

14. Ibid., 27–29.

15. *The Chinese Labor Weekly* 11 (April 30, 1919), cited in Wu, *Yan Yangchu zhuan*, 24.

16. *The Chinese Labor Weekly* 12 (May 7, 1919), cited in Wu, *Yan Yangchu zhuan*, 25.

17. *The Chinese Labor Weekly* 13 (May 14, 1919), cited in Wu, *Yan Yangchu zhuan*, 25.

18. Hayford, *To the People*, 23; *The Chinese Labor Weekly* 14 (May 21, 1919), cited in Wu, *Yan Yangchu zhuan*, 25.

19. "Chinese Labor Battalions in France," *The Chinese Students' Monthly* (April 1918): 326–27; I. H. Si, "With the Chinese Laborers 'Somewhere in France,'" *The Chinese Students' Monthly* (June 1918): 447–52; "James Yen's Speech on His 90th Birthday," October 26, 1983, box 93, IIRR Collection; J. P. McEvoy, *Jimmy Yen and the People's Crusade* (Pleasantville, NY: Reader's Digest Association, 1955), 7.

20. Hayford, *To the People*, 31.

21. Wu, *Yan Yangchu zhuan*, 29; James Yen to Brockman, August 13, 1920 and September 9, 1920, box 6, IIRR Collection.

22. Hayford, *To the People*, 40.

23. Yen to Brockman, September 9, 1920.

24. Chang Fu-liang, *When East Met West: A Personal Story of Rural Reconstruction in China* (New Haven, CT: Yale-in-China Association, 1972), 24; for more about the Huie family, see Bieler, *"Patriots" or "Traitors"?* 152–56.

25. Wu, *Yan Yangchu zhuan*, 128.

26. Ibid., 58, 67–69.

27. "Who's Who of the Chinese National Association of the Mass Education Movement," attachment to E. C. Carter's letter to John D. Rockefeller, November 10, 1928, box 6, IIRR Collection; McEvoy, *Jimmy Yen*, 6.

28. Pearl S. Buck, *Tell the People: Mass Education in China* (New York: Institute of Pacific Relations, 1945), 60–62.

29. Sidney D. Gamble to friends, February 25, 1932, p. 4, box 5, IIRR Collection; "Reshaping a Chinese Community," *The Chinese Students' Monthly* (June 1928): 20–21.

30. Sidney D. Gamble, *Ting Hsien: A North China Rural Community* (Stanford: Stanford University Press, 1954), vi, xvii–xviii.

31. Hayford, *To the People*, 52, 146.

32. Wu, *Yan Yangchu zhuan*, 160.

33. Ibid., 150–51; Gamble, *Ting Hsien*, 186.

34. Hayford, *To the People*, 132–40.

35. Ibid., 232.

36. Wu, *Yan Yangchu zhuan*, 219.

37. Hayford, *To the People*, 105–6, 179, 185.

38. Hayford, *To the People*, 74–77.

39. Ibid., 120.

40. Chang, *When East Met West*, 34.

41. Wu, *Yan Yangchu zhuan*, 657–58.

42. Hayford, *To the People*, 146–47.

43. Ibid., 103–4.

44. Ibid., 143–44; [Chen] Heng-zhe, "Dingxian nongcun chongjian daode pingmin hui shiye [The enterprise of Commoner Education Association in Ding County] *Duli pinglun* [The independent critic] 51 (May 28, 1933): 19–25.

45. Gamble to friends, February 25, 1932.

46. Hayford, *To the People*, 167.

47. Ibid., 164–79.

48. Ibid., 187–88.

49. T. H. Sun, "The Church in China's Rural Reconstruction," *Chinese Recorder* (August 1940): 494; Y. C. James Yen, "New Life for the Rural Masses," *Chinese Recorder* (June 1940): 365–68.

50. Hayford, *To the People*, 193–94; Wu, *Yan Yangchu zhuan*, 659.

51. Yen, "Graduation speech," 1945, box 3, IIRR Collection.

52. T. V. Soong telegram to James Yen, received January 4, 1945, James Yen cablegram to [T. V.] Soong, January 15, 1948, and James Yen letter to T. V. Soong, January 18, 1948, box C, IIRR Collection.

53. Hayford, *To the People*, 207.

54. Yen Yangchu, Liang Yaotsu, Sun Tsejang, and Chu Shiying (Chu Chunung), handwritten oath, March 20, 1947, box 120, IIRR Collection.

55. Hayford, *To the People*, 209–14, 225.

56. James Yen, talk with acting president Li [Zongren], July 13, 1949, pp. 3–5, box 93, IIRR Collection; Hayford, *To the People*, 225–28.

57. Ibid., 215, 227–28, 231.

58. Ibid., 225–28; McEvoy, *Jimmy Yen*, 11; Wu, *Yan Yangchu zhuan*, 512–24.

59. "James Yen's Speech on His 90th Birthday."

60. Gardner M. Tewkesbury, "My Friend Jimmy Yen," March 18, 1968, pp. 4, 5, box 32, IIRR Collection; Wei Chengtung, "Creative Transformation and Self-Realization in Yen Yangchu's Thinking and Personality," in *Y. C. James Yen's Thought on Mass Education and Rural Reconstruction: China and Beyond* (New York: IIRR, 1993), 53.

61. Wei, "Creative Transformation," 53; Tewkesbury, "My Friend Jimmy Yen," 3–6.

62. Pingsheng Yen Chin, "IIRR Founder Returns to China to Survey Rural Progress," *IIRR Report* (Winter 1986): 1–4; Dong Yuguo, "Returned Students' Association: A Home Back Home," *Beijing Review* (November 10–December 6, 1987): 32; Hayford, *To the People*, 233.

63. "Reshaping a Chinese Community," 19–21; Yen, "New Life for the Rural Masses," 366.

64. Pingsheng Yen Chin letters to author, October 24, 1999, October 29, 1999, and May 29, 2002; "Philippines Group Switches Focus to Guizhou," *Chinabrief* 3, no. 2 (Summer 2000): 6.

65. Yale University, *History of the Class of* 1918, vol. 2, p. 380, Manuscripts and Archives, Yale University Library.

66. James R. Angell, chairman, to Dr. James Y.C. Yen, May 11, 1943, "Poland Is Saluted at Copernicus Fete," pp. 25–66, and "A Copernican Citation Presented to Y.C. James Yen," box 121, IIRR Collection.

67. Chang, *When East Met West*, 34.

CONTRIBUTORS

Stacey Bieler is the author of *"Patriots" or "Traitors"? A History of American-Educated Chinese Students*. She received her MA in history in 1994 from Michigan State University (MSU). An independent scholar, she has coauthored *China At Your Doorstep* and *Chinese Intellectuals and the Gospel*. Ms. Bieler has served as the president of Community Volunteers for International Programs at MSU.

Carol Lee Hamrin is a research professor at George Mason University and senior associate with the Global China Center, both in Virginia. Dr. Hamrin holds a PhD in Chinese and comparative world history from the University of Wisconsin and served twenty-five years as a research specialist at the Department of State. Hamrin received the Center for Public Justice Leadership Award for outstanding public service in 2003, has taught in graduate schools in the Washington, D.C., area since 1980, and has published widely. Her books include *God and Caesar in China: Policy Implications of Church-State Tensions*, *Decision Making in Deng's China*, and *China and the Challenge of the Future*.

Elizabeth A. Littell-Lamb is an assistant professor in the Department of Government and World Affairs, History and Sociology at the University of Tampa. She received a PhD in Chinese and comparative women's history from Carnegie Mellon University. Dr. Littell-Lamb has taught at St.

Vincent College (Latrobe, PA), Ball State University (Muncie, IN), and St. Bonaventure University (Olean, NY). She is a frequent presenter at academic conferences and the author of a chapter in Melissa Huang, ed., *Gender, Culture, and Power: Chinese and Western Women Interact in Late Imperial and Early Modern China* (forthcoming).

Peter Tze Ming Ng is a professor in the Department of Educational Policy and Administration and Director of the Centre for Religious and Spirituality Education, at the Hong Kong Institute of Education. He serves as Chair of the North East Asia Council for the Study of the History of Christianity (NEACSHC). From 1986 to 2006, he was professor in the Department of Cultural and Religious Studies at the Chinese University of Hong Kong (CUHK), and he served from 2000 to 2007 as Director of the Centre for the Study of Religion and Chinese Society, Chung Chi College at CUHK. Professor Ng has been a research or teaching affiliate at Yale University Divinity School; Church Divinity School of the Pacific, Berkeley; the Ricci Institute, University of San Francisco; and Wolfson College, Cambridge University, where he was Henry Martyn Lecturer of 2007. His recent work includes coediting *Christian Responses to Asian Challenges: A Globalization View on Christian Higher Education in East Asia* (2007).

Connie Shemo is an assistant professor at Plattsburgh State University. She received her doctorate from State University of New York–Binghamton and spent three years as Lecturer in History at Princeton University. Dr. Shemo is currently working on a book, *An Army of Women: The Medical Ministries of Kang Cheng and Shi Meiyu, 1873–1937*. She is coeditor of a forthcoming volume on the work of American women missionaries in a variety of cultural contexts, *Competing Kingdoms: Women, Mission, Nation and Empire, 1812–1960*, and has contributed a chapter to a forthcoming volume on Chinese Christian women edited by Jessie Lutz.

Mary Jo Waelchli received her PhD in Chinese history from The Ohio State University in 2002. Her dissertation was entitled "Abundant Life: Matilda Thurston, Wu Yifang and Ginling College, 1915–1951."

Guowei Wright is a graduate of the Beijing Broadcasting Institute (now China Communication University), where she majored in International Journalism. She worked as an editor at New World Publishing House in Beijing for five years and since then has worked as a translator.

Fuk-tsang Ying is Associate Professor at the Divinity School of Chung Chi College, Chinese University of Hong Kong (CUHK), where he is Associate Director of both the Centre for Christian Studies and the Centre for the Study of Religion and Chinese Society. He is also Secretary of the Society for the Study of the History of Christianity in China. Recent publications include "'Christian Manifesto' and the Making of a Patriotic Protestant Church in the People's Republic of China," *Bulletin of the Institute of Modern History, Academia Sinica* 56 (June 2007), and "The Regional Development of Protestant Christianity in China: 1918, 1949 and 2004," *Sino-Christian Studies: An International Journal of Bible, Theology & Philosophy* 3 (June 2007).

SOURCES OF ILLUSTRATIONS

1-1 Hopkins Twichell Papers, Yale Collection of American Literature, Beinecke Rare Book and Manuscript Library, Yale University.

1-2 The Connecticut Historical Society, Hartford, Connecticut.

2-1 *The Chinese Students' Monthly* (December 1909). Courtesy of Center for Research Libraries, Chicago, Illinois. [cropped]

2-2 *The Missionary Review of the World* 18, no. 8 (August 1905). Courtesy of the Library of Congress.

3-1 Margaret E. Burton, *Notable Women of Modern China* (New York: Fleming H. Revell, 1912).

3-2 Courtesy of the General Commission on Archives and History of the United Methodist Church.

4-1 *Zhonghua Jidujiao qingnian hui wushi zhounian jinian ce* [China YMCA fiftieth anniversary album] (Shanghai: Zhonghua Jidujiao qingnian hui [YMCA], 1935). [cropped]

5-1 Maud Russell Papers, Manuscripts and Archives Division, The New York Public Library, Astor, Lenox, and Tilden Foundations. [cropped]

5-2 "Women in Changing China," China YWCA, 1928, Country: China (People's Republic of) 17 1926–1933 Printed Material, World YWCA Archives, Geneva, Switzerland.

6-1 *"Zhui dao Mei xiao zhang zhuan kan* [President Mei memorial special edition]," *Qinghua xiaoyou tongxun* [Tsinghua alumni communications], no. 2 (Taipei: Tsinghua Alumni News Agency, 1962).

6-2 *"Zhui dao Mei xiao zhang zhuan kan* [President Mei memorial special edition]," *Qinghua xiaoyou tongxun* [Tsinghua alumni communications], no. 2 (Taipei: Tsinghua Alumni News Agency, 1962).

7-1 Courtesy of the Gulangyu (Xiamen) Lin Qiaozhi Memorial.

7-2 Courtesy of the Gulangyu (Xiamen) Lin Qiaozhi Memorial.

8-1 Central China Normal University Archives, Wuhan.

8-2 Central China Normal University Archives, Wuhan.

9-1 Special Collections, Yale Divinity School Library.

9-2 UN/DPI Photo. [cropped]

10-1 Courtesy of Alice Yen Hing.

10-2 Courtesy of Alice Yen Hing.

INDEX OF NAMES AND SUBJECTS

Commercial Press, 157

Confucian Examination System,
17, 37

Confucian Statecraft School. *See*
Statecraft School

Confucianism, 41, 67–70, 72–73,
76, 78, 172

Confucius, 34, 46, 82–83, 175

Coppock, Grace, 86

Cornell University, 107, 175, 181, 182

Cultural Revolution, 131, 152, 165,
171

Danforth Hospital, 56–57, 62

Danforth, I. N., 56, 57

December Ninth Movement (1935),
106

Delta Kappa Epsilon Society, 34

Democratic League, 111, 112

Deng Yingchao, 130, 191

Ding Shujing (Ting Shu Ching), 11,
13, 81–99

Dingxian (Ting Hsien), 173, 174–
75, 181–86, 188, 190, 191, 192

Dong Biwu, 169

Dongting Lake, 132

Eastern Olympics, 50

Eddy, Sherwood, 103

Education, Ministry of, 48, 167, 187

1898 Reform. *See* Hundred Days
Reform

Empress Dowager. See Cixi

Fan Zimei (T. M. Fan, Fan Yi), 67–80

First Opium War, 117, 193

Foreign (Affairs), Ministry of, 48,
49, 106; *See also* Foreign Office

Foreign Office, 33, 43; *See also*
Foreign (Affairs), Ministry of

Fu Baozhen (Paul Fugh), 181

Fudan College/University, 38, 109

Gamble, Sidney, 103

General Knowledge News, 68, 71,
134

Gerlach, Talitha, 98

Globe magazine, 68–69, 71, 73

Golden Rule, 46

Grant, Ulysses S., 24, 25

Great Hall of the People, 134, 191

Guang Xu (Emperor), 29

Han Yonghua (Mrs. Mei Yiqi), 101,
103, 110–11, 114

Hangzhou Girls School, 156

Harvard Medical School, 183

Harvard University, 23, 28, 107,
109, 136, 138, 181

Health, Ministry of, 131

Hinder, Eleanor, 92

Hobson, Benjamin, 17

Hong Kong University, 177

Howe, Gertrude, 52–54, 55–56, 57

Hua Luogeng, 110

Hubbard, Hugh, 181

Hughes, Jennie, 58, 59, 61–62, 63, 64

Huie, Alice, 180; *See also* Yan, Alice

Huie Kin, 180

Hundred Days Reform (1898), 8,
29, 30, 34, 55, 68

Imperial Court, 34, 35, 68, 142; *See
also* Qing Court

Imperial Railway Administration,
35, 36

Imperial Tsinghua Academy,
9, 48–50; *See also* Tsinghua
School/College

Institute of Pacific Relations (IPR),
175, 189

International Institute of Rural
Reconstruction (IIRR), 190

International Missionary
Conference, 137, 167